Digital Business and Sustainable Development

The Internet has ushered in a new era in the economies of networking. With the increasing need for optimization based on these network economies, the IT-based e-business has become a platform for study as well as daily practice. In a similar vein, global warming has raised many issues which come into conflict with traditional research and policies. The Internet revolution has also shifted our society from a government- and company-led economy to a 'netizen'- and consumer-led business world.

This book enlightens us on why a harmonized participation of traditional network members or interested groups is necessary and how we can create values from diverse fields of interests and objectives, including the corporate social responsibility (CSR) and eco-friendly productivity.

Digital Business and Sustainable Development integrates the platforms from these two fields of study based on the comparative analysis of Asian and other developing countries.

Yongrok Choi is Inha Fellow Professor (IFP) in the Department of International Trade at Inha University, South Korea. He served as president of Global e-Business Association in 2009 and has organized and operated the Sustainable Asia Conference since 2009 as the president of Asia Business Forum.

Routledge Frontiers of Business Management

For a full list of titles in this series, please visit www.routledge.com/series/rfbm

1 **Managing Innovation and Cultural Management in the Digital Era**
The case of the National Palace Museum
Edited by Rua-Huan Tsaih and Tzu-Shian Han

2 **Managing Convergence in Innovation**
The new paradigm of technological innovation
Edited by Kong-rae Lee

3 **Corporate Sustainability Assessments**
Sustainability practices of multinational enterprises in Thailand
Edited by Jerome D. Donovan, Cheree Topple, Eryadi K. Masli and Teerin Vanichseni

4 **Knowledge Spillover-based Strategic Entrepreneurship**
Edited by João J. Ferreira, Leo-Paul Dana and Vanessa Ratten

5 **Japanese Management**
International perspectives
Hitoshi Iwashita

6 **Strategic Human Resource Management in China**
A multiple perspective
Min Min, Mary Bambacas and Ying Zhu

7 **Fostering Local Entrepreneurship in a Multinational Enterprise**
Joe J. Amberg and Sara L. McGaughey

8 **Digital Business and Sustainable Development**
Asian Perspectives
Yongrok Choi

Digital Business and Sustainable Development

Asian Perspectives

Yongrok Choi

Routledge
Taylor & Francis Group
LONDON AND NEW YORK

First published 2017 by Routledge

2 Park Square, Milton Park, Abingdon, Oxfordshire OX14 4RN
52 Vanderbilt Avenue, New York, NY 10017

Routledge is an imprint of the Taylor & Francis Group, an informa business

First issued in paperback 2019

British Library Cataloguing-in-Publication Data
A catalogue record for this book is available from the British Library

Library of Congress Cataloging-in-Publication Data
A catalog record for this book has been requested

ISBN: 978-1-138-18954-6 (hbk)
ISBN: 978-0-367-35047-5 (pbk)

Typeset in Galliard
by Apex CoVantage, LLC

Contents

Illustrations

Figures

Tables

Preface

Since the global economic crisis in 2008, the global world has been experiencing the new normal era, implying that the deep stagnation with low economic growth and increasing unemployment worldwide was over. The companies are just accumulating its internal reserve revenues without any impetus of the new investment due to the intrinsic oversupply dilemma. The role of the government has been decreasing as a result of ever-complicated and complex issues among the diverse interest groups. It is difficult to find the optimal path control for the government as well as the leading companies for the future challenges, because all these challenges are interrelated. Thus, they need to be harmonized to bring in the win-win results for all. That is the background of the new norm of innovation and creative economy. Instead of production process reengineering, we need to change everything from quantitative-oriented input-based economic growth to the qualitative-oriented innovation-oriented economic revolution.

In the middle of this turmoil, it is noteworthy to understand the underpinning of this new normal in terms of two important platforms: sustainable development and smart IT revolution. These two platforms have been transforming all the traditional policies and business practices into networking-oriented harmonized solution for all the future challenges. They have the common paradigm of the *value creation based on the network management*. The most important goal of this book is to understand this new paradigm and apply it to the government policies, as well as the business activities. Unfortunately, most Asian countries have a totally different approach toward this challenge due to their cultural background and history. In most of Asian countries, the governments want to lead this new normal with strong regulation but weak promotion policies, while the governments of Western counties have been listening to the market voices and tried to catch the market-oriented de facto standard for the future challenges. Unfortunately, these two extremes do not seem optimal to handle the challenges under new normal due to the huge risks and uncertainties. Therefore, we definitely need to harmonize not only the conflicting issues, but the economic entities to handle these issues as well. To harmonize these two extremes of government-led economies and market-oriented approach, this book suggests a collaborative way to form partnerships for the future. If we do not compete with each other, certainly we can "make larger pizzas". Even if we do know this solution, however, it is not easy to accept and practice this partnership under the traditional competitive solution-oriented paradigm.

Therefore, we need to implement a new norm of green IT for sustainable development as well as the smart revolution. This book challenges this sustainable, green IT in terms of three pillar perspectives. In Part I, the book analyzes the historical trend and background of sustainable development to convince the readers it is not a new burden but great opportunities on the future horizon. In Part II, the book begins to explain the conceptual characteristics of e-business and then the future trend of smart revolution in terms of green IT. In Part III, the book is ready for the readers to apply all the basic knowledge about the green IT to our everyday businesses and social activities with diverse case studies about the web application of smart revolution toward a greener way. Throughout the book, it is very important to practice harmonized network management, saying that once a friend, forever a friend! Under the traditional paradigm toward the competitive solution, it is easy and clear for the economic entity to maximize its own profit or efficiency. However, this competitive approach lead to persistent oversupply problems, and thus we cannot find the exit from this global economic depression era by using a competitive approach. Therefore, it is the right time to change our paradigm toward the harmonized value creation. This book will help the readers to understand and utilize this paradigm shift.

It would not have been possible to publish this book without numerous partners, and it is not possible to list them all. However, I have to mention few partner researchers: Dr. Chen Shi-Chi for the precious field trip to Taiwan, and Dr. Zhang Ning and Dr. Liu Yu for the unforgettable field trip to China. Without these field trips, I would not have been able to organize the Asian way to show the harmonized optimal path for the green IT. Special thanks go to my wife and children for their love and encouragement. Without their help, I would not have been able to finalize this book. In addition, during these three years of research, I was fortunate to make new friends like you, a new reader of this book. I should say again, therefore, once a friend, forever a friend.

September, 2016

Acknowledgments

This work was supported by the National Research Foundation of Korea Grant funded by the Korean Government (NRF- 2014S1A5B1011422).

Part I

Sustainable governance

Overview

The most outstanding challenges in the twenty-first century may come from the strong effect of global warming and Internet revolution. It is quite striking that the former may bring a very complicated and complex, yet unsustainable, disaster to humankind, while the latter proposes the new frontier to solve these disasters with a cooperative network. As we know, environment has always been changing, and this environmental change brings the opportunities and threats simultaneously as history has shown. It is noteworthy that the optimistic, proactive leaders have changed the history, and this is the right time for the leaders like you, the readers of this book, to understand and overcome these challenges for the sustainable development.

The first part of the book will give an overview of the historical background of sustainable development and propose the most important governance factor of governance-oriented intermediaries. We live in the interdependent society, and thus each one of us belongs to these interdependent networks, such as human network, information network, cooperative social network, business network, etc. Unfortunately, some networks are not working properly due to the missing links among the activities of partners. To promote sustainable performance of all these networks, therefore, we desperately need to find out the governance factors for the interoperable mechanism among the participants. This performance-oriented governance is the *paradigm* of the digital business or web business as "the value creation based on the harmonized networking management". The traditional studies have always focused on the competitive efficiency, while the two extreme challenges of global warming and the Internet revolution require harmonized procedural approaches to create the relation, maintain the relation, and finally to share the created values based on the collaborative relationship. Therefore, the role of network manager is the key concept for this book to analyze all the governance factors and to promote their role for the successful performance.

This part of the book will give an overview of the historical background of sustainable development and propose the most important governance factor for governance-oriented intermediaries. It shows how the relatively new paradigm of sustainable development has evolved through international consensus and how the relatively new paradigm of public–private partnerships, or the harmonized third sector, could be the optimal solution from the perspective of intermediation. Most of all, this study emphasizes governance, resulting in the following proposition of the intermediary role of public–private partnerships in a strength–weakness–opportunity–threat matrix: facilitator, collaborator, network manager, and service provider.

1 Overview of sustainable development

1. Background of the green wave advent

The most outstanding challenges in the twenty-first century may come from the strong effect of global warming and Internet revolution. It is quite striking that the former may bring a very complicated and complex, yet unsustainable, disaster to humankind, while the latter proposes the new frontier to solve these disasters with a cooperative network. As we know, environment has always been changing, and this environmental change brings the opportunities and threats simultaneously as history has shown. It is noteworthy that the optimistic, proactive leaders have changed the history, and this is the right time for the leaders like you, the readers of this book, to understand and overcome these challenges for the sustainable development.

Environmental issues are one of the most challenging cases of traditional market failures, because a decision unit can use up all environmental resources, with resulting deterioration for other decision units. If any economic entity, such as manufacturing companies or household consumers, disposes its waste, dirty water, and greenhouse gases (GHGs) during the production and/or consumption process, it does not need to pay for these undesirable outputs of its action unless the resulting environmental deterioration affects this economic entity directly. Unfortunately, most of the company's undesirable outputs such as GHGs affect other companies and the public, even in other countries, as there are no time and space limits. Environmental harm can occur in a specific area during a specific time, but can have global effects for a much longer period. Therefore, it is extremely difficult to deal with this kind of traditional market failure.

Nonetheless, such a company and/or its country may be blamed around the world, and its reputation may suffer. Thus, companies and governments should give greater consideration to these environmental issues, because if they fail to do so, there is no guarantee of the sustainable performance or sustainable management. Therefore, all economic entities should harmonize the short-term objectives of profit maximization and long-term sustainable performance. Thus, this harmonization is crucial in overcoming the ever-increasing, complex challenges of our environment and society.

How can we establish this harmonized value in our daily lives? Fortunately, we have the strong impulse of the Internet, which gives us new hope to analyze, monitor, measure, and compensate for undesirable outputs of all our daily life. For example, a person can buy a coke and drink it, after which, he or she should dispose of the empty can smartly enough to receive his or her environmental protection deposit back. Following the same logic, if a company produces more dirty water by increased production and/or deteriorating technologies, it should pay more to compensate for its waste (or consumption) of precious environmental resources, such as clean water and clean air, resulting in higher loyalties from potential customers in the long term. All these decisions and activities require fair and precise evaluation of the market failure of the individual or company. Moreover, there should be substantial cooperative networking to enhance better technologies and eco-friendly productivity, and to create the values based on a value-sharing system. The Internet revolution could bring these green information technology (IT) solutions.

Since the two issues are the most outstanding challenges of the contemporary global economy, it is important to understand the foundations of their connection and their role in establishing an optimal control path for the new frontier of sustainable development or green growth.

From this perspective, Korea, China, and Japan, the northeast Asian countries, are in a unique position, since the region is the most economically dynamic in the world, especially in terms of its IT success. Moreover, Korea hosts the Green Climate Fund, so-called second International Monetary Fund in the field of green growth, and China has experienced serious environmental problems of particulate matter (PM) resulting from its rapidly growing economy. Beijing has PM smog for more than one-third of the year, directly and indirectly resulting in deaths of thousands of people. This industrial disaster is transferred to the Korean peninsula and Japan, and thus, international cooperation is not an option in the region, but a necessary survival tool to overcome environmental problems in Northeast Asia. This study deals with this region as the most outstanding dynamic area in the world with many insightful field-oriented case studies. In the following chapters, we first deal with the historical background of sustainable development, then, with the conceptual characteristics of sustainable development, and finally, with the paradigm shift from traditional business and economics toward green business and green economics.

2. The green wave in Northeast Asia

Since the turn of the twenty-first century, humankind has been experiencing rapidly changing environmental conditions, resulting in turmoil and a paradigm shift. Global warming and a worldwide environmental crisis are the phenomena behind the fourth revolution of the green wave [1]. For example, China faces huge environmental challenges and costs, especially to clean up air pollution, which it is trying to do on its own. China estimates that pollution cost is roughly 3.5 per cent of gross domestic product (GDP) in 2010, while life expectancy in the northern provinces of China has decreased by about 5.5 years due to air pollution [2]. Almost 75 per cent of Chinese biggest cities failed to meet the country's environmental protection standards, and only 19 out of 74 larger cities met the standards. It is very common for air pollution in most parts of China to breach levels considered by some experts to be hazardous. This has drawn much public rage and became a worry for the government, which fears any discontent that might challenge stability. Therefore, China declared "war against pollution" at the opening of the annual meeting of parliament in March 2014. The government unveiled detailed measures to tackle what has become a pressing social issue. Curbing pollution has become a key part of efforts to upgrade the economy, shift the focus away from heavy industry, and tackle the perennial problem of overcapacity, with smog described as "nature's red-light warning against inefficient and blind development" [3]. China should turn its back on being the so-called global factory, and instead, take a new step toward qualitative policies to curb its growth potential. China will cut outdated steel production capacity by a total of 27 million ton in 2015, reduce cement production by 42 million ton, and shut down 50,000 small coal-fired furnaces across the country. This could constrain its growth potential significantly, but at the same time, it will provide new approaches to playing a leading role in the green growth of global economy.

Korea and Japan have experienced similar challenging issues of environmental disasters, and thus, have strongly promoted eco-friendly sustainable economic development policies, or so-called green growth. It seems that green growth is not simply an optional alternative, but the means to survive the global environmental crisis. Here, green growth means fostering eco-friendly economic growth and development, while ensuring that natural assets continue to provide the resources and environmental services on which our well-being relies. To do this, it must catalyze investment and innovation, which will underpin sustainable growth and give rise to new economic opportunities. Sustainable development provides an important context for green growth. In general, sustainable development is defined as development that meets the needs of the present without compromising the ability of future generations to meet their own needs [4]. Green growth is not an alternative to sustainable development, but rather, should be considered a subset of it, entailing an operational policy agenda that can help to achieve concrete, measurable progress at the interface between economic needs and the environment [5]. Northeast Asia is the most dynamically growing region in the world, and thus the northeast Asian countries do fear more for the global warming than any other country in the world as well. Therefore, it is really noteworthy to examine the feasibility of the green growth policies in Northeast Asian countries.

Green growth is based on the theory of green economics ("greenomics" in short), and it represents the fourth wave after the agricultural, industrial, and IT industrial (or Internet-oriented) revolutions in world history. Greenomics is based on not only traditional economics and simple interdisciplinary study, but also innovative and creative multidisciplinary studies. This is because greenomics, as a core part of sustainable development, resulted from revolutionary technological innovation, like the other three preceding revolutions. Economic growth and environmental protection cannot be integrated easily (coupling), and thus, sustainable development should be multi-dimensional and interdisciplinary at its core. However, the technical revolution has filled this missing link between economic demands and environmental protection, resulting in the feasibility of decoupling; there is great potential for both higher economic development and a better quality of life [6].

That is the reason we call the historical fourth revolution of green wave, because it is not easy to integrate the economic demand and the environmental protection by the innovative decoupling way. Green wave should be innovative because it requires the new way of thinking, new approach of our daily life, new business and industries resulting from the innovative green technologies. The reduction of GHGs may result in increased cost and/or productivity loss in traditional measures, while creating new frontiers for renewable energy industries, green financing, and so on. Moreover, green growth policies even increase the performance of traditional "brick" industries by the creation of value as the invisible long-term sustainable values earned from the loyalty of diverse interest groups. The global warming and environmental crisis should become not threat but challenging opportunity for all countries, regardless of their economic level and/or cultural differences [7, p.7]. Thus, we can refer to this phenomenon of the new green wave, consisting of green growth policies and strategies, as the fourth revolutionary paradigm shift in human history.

Green growth is a much more practical concept in its detail, compared with the more abstract terms and conditions of sustainable development, because green growth is based on field- and performance-oriented measures, as well as feasible policies of governments and strategies of the private sector [8]. This provides the background for the first part of the book, which overviews most of the revolutionary factors of green growth by comparing different policies and business strategies, and examines their feasibility using theoretical modeling of the strengths–weaknesses–opportunities–costs (SWOT) analysis. Based on the SWOT Matrix, the following chapter proposes feasible roles and functions of public–private partnerships (PPPs) as the best alternative intermediary to fill the missing link in the paradigm shift of green growth [1].

2 Conceptual structure of sustainable development

1. Paradigm shifts toward the green growth

1.1 Historical background

The interrelationship between technology, productivity, and growth has long been discussed in the history of human civilization. The importance of technological innovation cannot be overestimated in relation to paradigm shift over time. It is the central determinant of long-term success or failure of human history [9]. Based on this technological innovation in history, the first agricultural revolution in the prehistoric era was a great stepping-stone for humankind to begin the civilization of the next 3,000 years. This is called the "classical economy" based on the *self-sufficiency* paradigm, represented by the famous Say's law, saying that supply creates its own demand. Everything produced is consumed in this classical or agricultural economy, and thus there is no oversupply and/or shortage of the product by the invisible hand of market price. Due to this permanent equilibrium of all the markets, there is no unemployed labor, and the full employment is guaranteed. These three axioms of invisible hand for market equilibrium, full employment, and the Say's law made the unique characteristics of agriculture-based classical economy for 3,000 years of history.

The second shift of the industrial revolution, as the first wave in the history, symbolized by steam and railroads in Britain during 1780–1860, expanded around the world in the next 300 years, and brought mass production, mass media, and mass consumption by the new paradigm of *economies of scale*; that is, the more you produce, the higher productivity it gives to you. This mass-oriented second wave of industrialization changed whole society and economic structure, from agricultural society to the company-led urbanization and modernization of the investment of the capital for technological innovation. Unfortunately, the supplier-led industrialization brought the oversupply issues as a permanent problem of the government, and thus they had to search for new market, or new colony, resulting in the big depression worldwide in the 1930s and the World Wars I and II.

After World Wars I and II, the innovative introduction of computers and information and communication technology enhancement successfully transformed the society with the new paradigm of *economies of networking*, serving as a new economic engine and introducing better life quality for 30 years with the second wave of *informatization*. This new paradigm of *economies of networking* changed mass-quantity-based economies into quality-oriented economies of the smart revolution; the more they share information and experiences, the better they "create" values by group intelligence. In particular, since 2000, the Internet has accelerated the new era of "knowledge as the quality-oriented information." By the flood of information on the Internet, the popular slogan in the industrial revolution era, "information is power and money," has changed to "knowledge helps make smart decisions and activities." Here, the new concept of "knowledge" is defined as the information to "*activate*" the best alternative decision and/or activities [10].

The quality-oriented paradigm shift caused a diverse innovative way of our daily life, and also the third green wave revolution. The industrial revolution caused energy-intensive industries to dominate all economic development processes in every country. It caused a plethora of environmental problems, such as deforestation, GHG emissions, and water pollution, resulting in frequent, unforeseeable disasters, such as floods, drought, earthquakes, toxic air and water, and melting glaciers. Each and every country faces the challenges of these unforeseeable disasters, and so, sustainable development at last has become the core of qualitatively enhanced economic policies [1].

To understand the historical background of the green wave, we first need to understand sustainable development trend systematically. Sustainable development, a concept that emerged in the context of growing awareness of an imminent ecological crisis, has been treated more seriously since the 1980s. From the perspective of field-oriented government policy perspective, the United Nations Conference on the Human Environment (UNCHE), held in Stockholm, Sweden, in 1972, should be recorded as the first cornerstone meeting toward the green wave, because it was the first major international gathering focused on human activities in relationship to the environment. The conference acknowledged that the goal of reducing human impact on the environment would require extensive international cooperation, as many of the problems affecting the environment are global in nature, that is, caused by one country locally, while affecting other countries. In this UNCHE summit, the participating countries concluded with a future challenging direction based on the 3Ps – people, planet, and profit – representing social, ecological, and economic perspectives, respectively.

To promote the spirit of this cornerstone meeting, the UN established World Environment Day on June 5. Every year, June 5 is the World Environment Day (WED) intended to raise global awareness to take positive environmental action to protect nature and the planet Earth. The United Nations General Assembly established WED in 1972 to celebrate the first meeting of the UNCHE, because after the meeting, sustainability became the key word for the human future. Since then, there have been diverse national, regional, and global movements toward achieving an eco-friendly, sustainable society, especially with the strong, enhanced support of IT applications.

In 1982, the UN World Charter for Nature (UNWCN) established five principles of conservation by which human conduct affecting nature is to be guided and judged, as follows.

1 Nature should be respected and its essential processes should not be impaired.
2 The genetic viability on the Earth should not be compromised, and the population levels of all life forms, wild and domesticated, must be at least sufficient for their survival; to this end, necessary habitats should be safeguarded.
3 All areas of the Earth, both land and sea, should be subject to these principles of conservation; special protection should be given to unique areas, representative samples of all the different types of ecosystems, and the habitats of rare or endangered species.
4 Ecosystems, organisms, and the land, marine, and atmospheric resources that are utilized by humans, should be managed to achieve and maintain optimum sustainable productivity, but not in such a way as to endanger the integrity of other ecosystems or species with which they coexist.
5 Nature should be secured against degradation caused by warfare or other hostile activities.

After the conference, the United Nations Environmental Program (UNEP) was launched to encourage UN agencies to incorporate environmental measures into their programs. Thereafter, the UN commissioned a group of 22 people from developed and developing countries to identify long-term environmental strategies for the international community. This World Commission on Environment and Development (WCED), better known as the Brundtland Commission, submitted its report, titled *Our Common Future*, to the UN in 1987 (WCED 1987). The Brundtland Report is well known for its definition of sustainable development as,

> Sustainable development is development that meets the needs of the present without compromising the ability of future generations to meet their own needs.
>
> It consists of two key concepts:
>
> - the concept of "needs" implies the essential needs of the world poorest, to which overriding priority should be given; and
> - the idea of limitations imposed by the contemporary state of technology and social organization on the environment's ability to meet present and future needs [4].

The Brundtland Report focused primarily on the needs and interests of humans and was concerned with securing global equity for future generations by redistributing resources towards poorer nations to encourage their eco-friendly economic growth in order to enable all human beings to achieve their basic needs (see Figure 2.1). The paradigm of the Brundtland Report became the platform for all subsequent international action plans. Based on the Brundtland

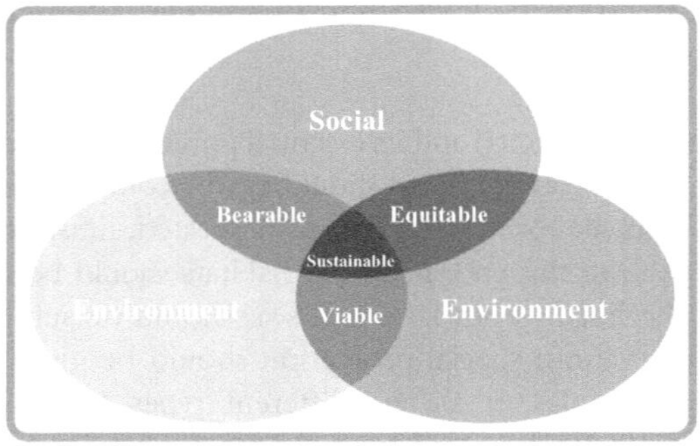

Figure 2.1 Paradigms of the sustainable development (Tree Polar Layer, TPL)

Source: Wikipedia (https://en.wikipedia.org/wiki/Sustainable_development). Accessed on Aug. 15, 2016.

Report, the UN Conference on Environment and Development (UNCED), also known as the Rio Summit or Earth Summit, was held to promote a more systematic action plan to initiate sustainable development worldwide in Rio de Janeiro in 1992. At the Rio summit, the green growth paradigm is represented by the triple bottom line as an accounting framework with the three parts of social, environmental (or ecological), and economic sustainability as shown in the Figure 2.1. Sustainable development policies should, simultaneously, be socially equitable, economically viable, and environmentally bearable. Unfortunately, it is not easy to find the best solution to satisfy all these three categories, but at the same time, it is not impossible to establish optimal path controls using all three criteria. The Earth Charter made it clearer to do so with 16 main principles and 61 supporting principles. They are summarized in the four pillars of *respect and care for the community of life; ecological integrity; social and economic justice; and democracy, non-violence, and peace.*

The Rio Summit published the *Agenda 21* action plan as well as key building blocks to help countries achieve development that recognizes these interdependent pillars. *Agenda 21* is a non-binding, but voluntarily implemented action plan for all the member countries of the UN with regard to sustainable development. *Agenda 21* consists of 40 chapters under four sections as follows.

Section I: Social and economic dimensions. This section is focused on solving poverty, especially in developing countries, changing consumption patterns, promoting health, achieving a more sustainable population, and sustainable settlement in decision making. All the measures in this dimension should be bearable for social equity, as shown in Figure 2.1.

Section II: Conservation and management of resources for development. This section covers atmospheric protection, solving deforestation, protecting fragile environments, conservation of biological diversity (biodiversity), pollution control, and the management of biotechnology and radioactive waste. Thus, development policies should be viable between economic needs and environmental limits.

Section III: Strengthening the role of major groups. This section includes the roles of children and youth, women, NGOs, local authorities, business and industry, and workers, and strengthens the role of indigenous people, their communities, and farmers. Government policies and the strategies of its implementing agencies and intermediaries should be equitable.

Section IV: Means of implementation. This section includes science, technology transfer, education, international institutions, and financial mechanisms. It involves diverse, complicated, yet transparent accountable measures.

1.2 UNFCC and Kyoto Protocol regime

One of the most important achievements of the Rio Summit was the UN Framework Convention on Climate Change (UNFCCC), which later led to the Kyoto Protocol. The UNFCCC is an international environmental treaty, and currently, the only international climate policy venue with broad legitimacy, due in part to its virtually universal membership negotiated at the UNCED. The objective of the treaty is to manage GHG concentrations in the atmosphere "at a level that would prevent dangerous anthropogenic interference with the climate system" [11]. The treaty is considered legally non-binding, but provides a framework for negotiating specific international treaties (called "protocols") that may set binding limits on GHGs. The UNFCCC was adopted in 1992, and it entered into force in 1994; as of December, 2015, it had 197 member parties, almost all countries in the world. The parties to the convention have met since 1995 at annual Conferences of the Parties (COPs) to assess progress in dealing with climate change, and met every year after this first COP meeting, as the most influencing talk to combat the global warming.

In December 1997, in the third COP summit at Kyoto of Japan, the Kyoto Protocol is signed to control the emissions of greenhouse gases by 38 countries and the European Union. It established legally binding obligations, first in history, for the participating developed countries to reduce their emission levels of six GHGs, namely, CO_2, CH_4, N_2O, HFC_S, PFC_S, and SF_6, under the principle of "*common but differentiated responsibilities*". The detailed rules for the implementation of the Kyoto Protocol were adopted at COP7 in Marrakesh, Morocco, in 2001 and are referred to as the "Marrakesh Accords". Its first commitment period started in 2008 and ended in 2012. A second commitment period was agreed to in 2012 and is known as the Doha Amendment. The UNFCCC has contributed great steps forward with the creation of flexible, yet market-oriented mechanisms for the successful governance of performance. One of the first tasks set by the UNFCCC was for signatory nations to establish national inventories of GHG emissions and reductions, which were used to create the 1990 benchmark levels for accession of Annex I countries to the Kyoto Protocol and for the commitment of those countries to GHG reductions. Updated inventories must be submitted regularly by Annex I countries, and other countries may do so voluntarily.

The Kyoto Protocol has been ratified by all Annex I Parties that participated in the first Kyoto commitment period, excluding the United States, and successfully completed its first round of carbon emission abatement projects till 2012. With regard to the second Kyoto round, 37 Annex I countries as well as the EU have agreed to targets. Unfortunately, the United States has not ratified the Kyoto Protocol, and thus, it caused a significant bottleneck for the other parties not to move toward a post-Kyoto Protocol regime. There is another inherent bottleneck: the non-participation of the largest CO_2 emitters, including China, India, and Brazil. Due to the moral hazard known as "not-in-my-backyard" (NIMBY), Japan, New Zealand, Canada, and Russia participated in the first Kyoto round but have not taken on new targets in the second commitment period. As of July 2015, 36 states have accepted the Doha Amendment, while its entering into force requires the acceptances of 144 states. Unfortunately, due to the global economic crisis, there has been wide concern about the unforeseeable future of post-Kyoto commitments.

To facilitate the Kyoto protocol, Annex I Parties are allowed to use a range of sophisticated flexibility mechanisms to meet their reduction targets of CO_2 and other GHGs. The protocol defines three such *flexibility mechanisms*, that is, Joint Implementation (JI), the Clean Development Mechanism (CDM), and the Emission Trading System (ETS). The economic basis for providing this flexibility is that the marginal cost of reducing (or abating) emissions differs among countries, and thus, allows for the transfer of the externality of the local economy to the global markets.

The most important tool for the Kyoto Protocol is the Emissions Trading System, better known as the (carbon) emission trading system (ETS), which allows Annex I Parties to *trade* their emissions. The ETS is a so-called cap-and-trade scheme, where *cap* means a legal limit on the quantity of a certain type of GHG that an economic entity can emit each year. Lower than the cap, it can sell its decreased amount of carbon emission abatement rights, while over its cap, a company should buy to fit the cap. The ETS is a market-based approach used to control pollution by providing economic incentives for achieving reductions in the emissions of pollutants [12]. Various countries, groups of companies, and local governments have adopted ETSs as a strategy to mitigate climate change by addressing international GHG emissions. Each government sets a limit or cap on the amount of GHG pollutants that an entity is allowed to emit. The limit or cap is allocated and/or sold by the government to firms in the form of emissions permits, which represent the right to emit or discharge a specific volume of the specified pollutant. Permits can then be traded on secondary markets [13]. For example, the EU ETS trades primarily in European Union Allowances, the New Zealand scheme in New Zealand Units, the Australian scheme in Australian Units, and the Korean scheme in Korea Allowance Units (KAUs). Companies are required to hold a number of permits (allowances or carbon credits, known as KCUs in Korea) equivalent to their emissions. The total number of permits cannot exceed the cap, limiting total emissions to that level. Companies that need to increase their volume of emissions must buy permits from those that require fewer permits. By this trading system, those firms that can reduce emissions most cheaply could sell reduced amounts of GHGs, resulting in pollution reduction at the lowest cost in the society.

This can be illustrated graphically as in Figure 2.2. If firm A requires additional costs to mitigate 1 million tons of CO_2 at a unit cost US$ 30 per ton, the cap target introduced by the regulatory policies for the firm will cost US$ 30 million. Similarly, firm B incurs new additional mitigation costs of US$ 10 million to fulfill decreasing targets with a unit cost US$ 10 per ton of CO_2 emissions. If no trading of emission rights exists, then the total mitigation cost for the society is US$ 40 million. However, the introduction of the ETS makes firm B more competitive by its greater investment in green technology, and thus, provides incentives to mitigate more CO_2 and to sell an additional 1 million tons of emission rights to firm A. Since firm A is less efficient in eco-friendly technology than firm B, firm A incurs more costs to mitigate the same amount of CO_2 compared with firm B. Then, firm A could be better off when it purchases the emissions trading rights (in Korea, KAUs) from firm B. The trading price for one KAU could be between US$ 30 per ton, the maximum cost of firm A, and US$ 10, the minimum cost of firm B. By introducing an ETS, the economy could give firms incentives to invest more in green technology, and more efficient firms in green technology would lead the economy, while follower firms would have to catch up (the learning effect by ETS).

The CDM of the flexibility mechanisms defined in the Kyoto Protocol provides for emissions reduction projects that generate Certified Emission Reduction (CER) units, resulting in tradable rights in ETSs. The CDM is intended to meet two objectives. First, it is to assist parties, especially developing countries, not included in the Annex I list, to achieve sustainable development by advanced green technologies and know-how of the Annex I members (developed countries). Second mission is to assist parties included as Annex I countries to achieve compliance with their quantified emission limits and reduction commitments of

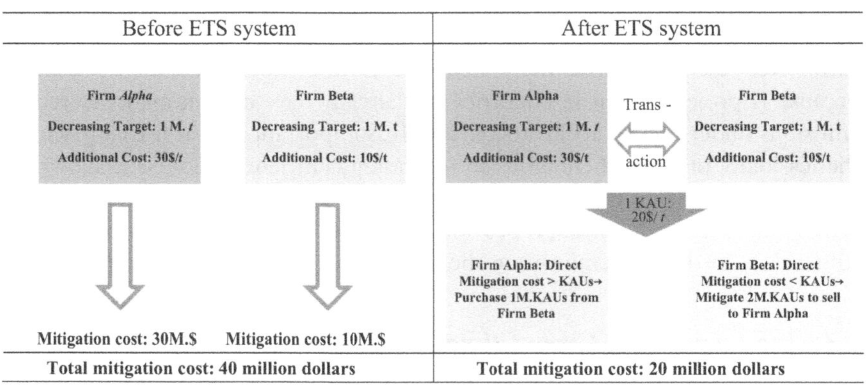

Figure 2.2 Mechanism of emission trading system (ETS)

GHG emission caps by participating more efficiently in mitigation projects in other (developing) countries. The CDM allows advanced countries to buy CERs and to invest in emissions reduction where it is cheapest globally [14]. This enhances not only effective technological transfer by international cooperation in a field of highly advanced environmental industries, but also the globally efficient internalization of GHG emissions around the world.

The CDM is important in that it widens feasibility of firms promoting CO_2 mitigation in a more eco-friendly and efficient ways, encourages greater investment in greener technology, and allows firms that should purchase allowance units from mitigation to catch up quickly with leading firms from global perspectives. Moreover, the CDM can result in technological transfer from the advanced Annex 1 countries to developing countries more effectively, because the mechanism allows firms in advanced countries to invest in the environmental projects of developing countries, and this participation promotes green technology transfer more easily and effectively over time. At the same time, firms in developing countries begin to recognize the economic importance of CO_2 mitigation, and thus, attempt to utilize the CDM opportunities. However, the CDM may result in a kind of moral hazard with free lunch, in which recipient firms in developing countries do not make enough efforts to focus more on green technology or local governments failure to provide appropriate local measures to match the funds from developed countries.

Joint implementation (JI), one of the three flexibility mechanisms in the Kyoto Protocol, is a project-based mechanism to help Annex I countries with binding GHG emissions targets to fulfill their obligations *in any other Annex I country* as an alternative to reducing emissions. By utilizing JI, a firm in an Annex I country can lower the costs of complying with its GHG targets by investing in projects in other Annex I member countries. JI project could reduce GHG emissions more efficiently in other Annex I countries where reducing emissions may be cheaper, and then, using the resulting Emission Reduction Units (ERUs) towards its commitment goal within the group of Annex I countries. Instead of a different industry, the target could be a different country. A JI project might involve *economies in transition*. For example, a coal-fired power plant may replace its facilities with a more efficient combined heat-and-power plant, resulting in extra ERU credits. Unlike the CDM, the JI does not have much popularity because JI projects occur in countries that already have commitments to reduce emissions under the Kyoto Protocol. The JI is important in that it clearly widens the feasibility of strengthening green technology efficiency, because it allows the sale and purchase of the amount of emissions mitigated across countries and across industries. In addition, it provides incentives for cooperative efforts among Annex I countries to demonstrate the significance of their mitigation efforts.

1.3 Inauguration of Green Climate Fund (GCF)

Following the Kyoto Protocol, the COP agreed to further commitments under the Bali Action Plan (2007), Copenhagen Accord (2009), Cancún agreements (2010), and Durban Platform for Enhanced Action (2012). The 2010 Cancún agreements state that future global warming should be limited to below 2°C (3.6 °F) relative to pre-industrial levels. The 2009 Copenhagen Accord by COP15 signaled the establishment of the Green Climate Fund (GCF) and via the 2010 Cancún agreements, the GCF's governing instrument was adopted at the 2012 COP17 in Durban.

The GCF is a fund within the UNFCCC framework founded as a mechanism to redistribute funds from the developed to the developing world, in order to assist developing countries in adaptation and mitigation projects to counter climate change. Here, adaptation to the climate change implies agile response to global warming that seeks to reduce the vulnerability of social and economic ecosystems to the rapidly changing climate change and thus offset the negative effects of global warming. Mitigation to the climate change implies efforts or actions to limit the magnitude or rate of long-term climate change, and to reduce the risks associated with human-induced undesirable outcomes toward the global warming.

The mission of GCF is to advance the goal of keeping the temperature increase on our home planet below 2°C based on the year 1990 level. For this purpose, GCF was established by 194 governments as a unique global initiative to respond to climate change by investing into low-emission and climate-resilient economic development. Given the urgency and seriousness of the climate challenge, the GCF is mandated to make an ambitious mission to unite global response against climate change. GCF is accountable to the United Nations. Under the principles and provisions of the UNFCCC, GCF is governed by a Board of 24 members, comprising an equal number of members from developing and developed countries.

The GCF is located in the Songdo district of Incheon, Korea, as a symbol of harmonization between developing and developed countries. The GCF is designed to support projects, programs, policies, and other activities in developing country members using thematic funding windows [15]. It is intended to be the centerpiece of efforts to raise climate finance of US$100 billion a year by 2020. This is not an official figure for the size of the fund itself, however. In addition, disputes remain as to whether funding will be based on public sources or whether leveraged private finance will be counted toward the total amount.

1.4 Historic summary before the Paris Agreement

Since its first meeting in 1992, parties to the UNFCCC have met at conferences ("Conferences of the Parties" or COPs) to discuss how to achieve the treaty's aims. At the first COP meeting, all the parties decided that the aim of Annex I parties stabilizing their emissions at 1990 levels by the year 2000 was appropriate but not enough. Thus, further discussions at later conferences led to the Kyoto Protocol. The Kyoto Protocol sets emissions targets for developed countries that are binding under international law. The Kyoto Protocol has had two commitment periods. The first period lasted from 2008 to 2012 and the second should run from 2012 to 2020, based on the Doha Amendment to the Protocol. However, the United States has not ratified the Kyoto Protocol, while Canada denounced it in 2012; still, the Kyoto Protocol has been ratified by all the other Annex I parties.

All Annex I parties, excluding the United States, participated in the first Kyoto commitment period that ran until 2012. Thirty-seven Annex I countries and the EU agreed to second-round Kyoto targets, which began in 2013. These countries include Australia, all members of the European Union, Belarus, Croatia, Iceland, Kazakhstan, Norway, Switzerland, and Ukraine. Belarus, Kazakhstan, and Ukraine have stated that they may withdraw from the Protocol or not put the Amendment into legal force with second-round targets. Japan, New Zealand, and Russia participated in the first round of the Kyoto Protocol, but these countries have not taken on new targets in the second commitment period. The United States has never made a commitment. Worse still, Canada withdrew from the Protocol in 2012.

In 2011, parties adopted the *Durban Platform for Enhanced Action.* At Durban, parties noted great concern that current efforts to hold global warming to below 2 or 1.5°C relative to pre-industrial levels appeared inadequate. Thus, all 196 parties to the convention came together for the UN Climate Change Conference in Paris in 2015 and adopted the Paris Agreement by consensus on December 12, which aimed at limiting global warming to below 2°C. If the Paris Agreement is to be ratified by 55 countries representing over 55 per cent of greenhouse gas emissions from 2016, then it will enter into force. Some people have said that this ambitious and balanced plan could be a historic turning point in the goal of reducing global warming [16].

The most important mission of the Paris Agreement is described in Article 2, which enhances the implementation of the UNFCCC more fully.

1 Temperature: Holding the increase in the global average temperature to well below 2°C above pre-industrial levels and pursuing efforts to limit the temperature increase to 1.5°C above pre-industrial levels, recognizing that this would significantly reduce the risks and impacts of climate change;
2 Approach: Increasing the ability to adapt to the adverse impacts of climate change and foster climate resilience and low greenhouse gas emissions development, in a manner that does not threaten food production;
3 Finance: Making finance flows consistent with a pathway toward low greenhouse gas emissions and climate-resilient development.

In the Agreement, the members promised to reduce their carbon output *as soon as possible,* and to do their best to keep global warming *to well below 2°C (or 3.6°F).* Countries furthermore aim to reach global peaks of greenhouse gas emissions as soon as possible. Even if the more aggressive commitment up to a 1.5°C decrease is much enhanced, and ambitious compared with the COP20 at Copenhagen, unfortunately, there is no forceful measure imposed on violators, and thus, it is much weaker than the Kyoto Protocol. The parties agreed that from the year 2050, a net zero carbon emission should be secured. Compared with the Kyoto Protocol, which bound only 37 Annex I countries, all 195 parties to the Paris COP21 meeting, more than its 187 members, agreed to participate in managing climate change. The contributions that each individual country should make to achieve the worldwide goal are determined by countries individually, and are referred to as *nationally determined contributions* (NDCs). The agreement requires them to be ambitious and to maintain the view of achieving the purpose of this Agreement. The contributions should be reported every 5 years and are to be registered by the UNFCCC Secretariat. Each further contribution should be more ambitious than the previous one. Countries can cooperate and pool their NDCs. The Intended NDCs pledged during the 2015 Climate Change Conference serve – unless provided otherwise – as the initial platform.

The level of NDCs set by each country will be binding targets for the country, as is the case in the Kyoto Protocol. Even if there is no mechanism to force a country to set a target in their NDC by a specific date and no enforcement by the financing mechanism or national loyalties when the set target in an NDC is not met, we should expect NDCs are the only invisible obligations as to providing the workable governance.

To support these implicit obligations more effectively, the agreement indicates a *non-binding* plan to provide $100 billion per year in aid to developing countries for implementing new procedures to minimize climate change until 2020 with additional amounts to be provided in subsequent years. This Green Climate Fund (GCF) will increase in the second stage in 2025. Most the funds will go to projects of adaptation and mitigation of the climate's changes. Based on these efforts, green IT shall contribute to the results of this ambitious mission for the future of humankind.

2. Paradigm of the green growth

2.1 Green growth as the new paradigm

Over time, sustainable development has transformed into green growth, with the latter placing more emphasis on the fact that it is essential to *decouple* economic growth from unsustainable environmental pressures, such as those leading to global climate change. Decoupling of economic development from the pressure of environmental protection provides significant opportunities for governments and companies to create values by innovative way of technological development, and it is a significant stepping-stone to expanding the green wave [17]. For example, from the perspective of sustainable development, it has been said that shifting the energy mix toward cleaner sources of energy and cleaning up polluting energy sources, such as CO_2 with carbon capture and sequestration (CCS), would tend to raise energy costs, at least for a period of time. By contrast, from the green growth perspective, investments in "new" energy-efficient technology for industries can be cost effective, with benefits cumulating over time. Unfortunately, there is no automatic link between cleaner energy and better market performance, but these goals could and should be made complementary.

The basic paradigm of green growth is better life quality, a healthier economy, and a more equitable society due to the innovative way of decoupling. However, the green wave as the third revolution may have flexible and diverse ways of complementary promotion, depending on the surrounding circumstances and cultural background of the countries. Each country should choose its own differentiated policies for green growth. There is no universally agreed political paradigm. Nonetheless, the most important goal currently is to set up a global standard for this green wave. This is because new technology, new products, and new green business affect not only the green growth economy, but also the whole society, as the Internet revolution has made a great impact on the daily life of all economic entities as well as the society itself. Unfortunately, the global standard for the world to embark on the next generation of the green wave remains uncertain. An entire new global standard should be defined with new technology as the basic engine, new financing to boost this new innovative phenomenon, and a changing way of thinking to maintain and expand the new phenomena. All these three facets are related to the global standard, and thus, competition to set a global standard is fierce, even if it is invisible. All governments and global companies are attempting to set this global standard to lead the global wave with their individual strategies or policy paradigms. Therefore, based on the historical sustainable development trend, it would be better to clarify the detailed concepts and definitions of the terms and conditions for sustainable development before finding a way to handle the policy paradigm.

2.2 Measurement issues of sustainable development

The concept of sustainable development is derived mainly from the 1987 Brundtland Report as a process toward qualitative human development goals, while maintaining the ability of natural systems to continue to provide the natural resources and ecosystem services for the needs of humankind without any time and space limits for a healthier life on Earth [4]. The concept stemmed from the environmental protection perspectives of the 1980s and transformed its focus from the environment toward social equity and healthier economic growth in 1990s. As shown before in Figure 2.1, sustainable development is based on the three pillars of economic, environmental, and social issues. However, sometimes, a fourth pillar of governance (or culture, institutions) could be separated from the economic and social dimensions. Under these three or four dimensions, sustainable development has managed diverse issues of ecological systems and services, energy and environment, transportation and logistics (green supply chain management); economics and business (especially, corporate social responsibility, CSR); and culture and education. Nowadays, the term "sustainable" has become the platform for much research and studies. Accordingly, the traditional paradigm, such as economies (or efficiency) in economics and profit maximization in business, should change to a new platform of multilateral harmonization of diverse, yet conflicting issues. There is a need to establish how to create values for all participants of interest groups without conflict in sustainable development from macro-economic perspectives, as well as sustainable management from micro-business perspectives. Therefore, the most important issue for the concept of sustainability is "harmonization on the cooperative network". We live in a world of networking. There is no one single entity to maximize satisfaction or happiness without the support of others. All firms should be supported by loyal workers, proactively participating customers, and an eco-friendly local society without any deterioration of the environment. This requires that we live in an interdependent economic structure of networking. In this society, it is very important to enlarge the shares of all partners, instead of maximizing the portions of single network members. Therefore, harmonized networking is crucial for "sustainable" performance. At the same time, we need economic growth, which is the green growth-decoupling paradigm by innovation. Thus, the creation of values by the proactive participation of all partners in cooperative networking is the crucial mission on the interdependent society.

Unfortunately, sustainable development is a very complicated process to create, not visible, short-term profit, but *invisible values* for more dependable ecosystems, healthier and higher-quality life enhancement, and still further economic growth. Even if diverse discussions and efforts for all these goals and objectives have moved toward sustainable development, none of the resulting systems tells us clearly how much the resulting outcome is sustainable. In particular, "sustainable" is an abstract term to realize its goals in practice, because its output of value is invisible in most cases and takes too much time to evaluate appropriately. It is an extremely difficult task to measure and monitor the performance of sustainable development. Many researchers with diverse academic backgrounds have attempted to establish a set of well-defined and harmonized indicators to make sustainability tangible. Sustainability measurement used a quantitative basis for the informed management of sustainability, but with qualitative characters. Thus, the metrics used for the measurement of sustainability, involving the sustainability of environmental, social, and economic domains, both individually and in various combinations, are still evolving. These measures include indicators, benchmarks, audits, indexes, and accounting, as well as assessment, appraisal, and other reporting systems.

However, sustainable development issues have inherent difficulties with measuring and monitoring, because the sustainable development process is quite complex across time and space, and it is extremely difficult to capture all outcomes from policies precisely and appropriately. For example, because of the yellow sand storm from the Mongolian deserts, Korea has experienced seasonal yellow sand storm disasters every spring and, thus, has attempted to plant as many trees as possible in Mongolia. However, it is very difficult to measure how much and how long the yellow sand storm could be abated from these activities. In addition, it is easy for a firm to contribute funding to the poorest people in society as CSR, but it is much more difficult for the company to monitor how much these funds improve the life quality of the recipient and how much they enhance the image of the company. Nonetheless, efforts to measure and monitor the sustainable performance tell us that the world is heading in the right direction, or that our current activities are sustainable. Moreover, most indicators incorporate some ecological, economic, and social elements, and thus, at least, we can be sure of which direction to proceed forward. Of all the indicators examined in the experimental research, one of the most outstanding may be the Sustainable Society Index (SSI), International Organization for Standardization (ISO) 26000, and Global Reporting Initiative (GRI) indicators.

The SSI was developed by the Sustainable Society Foundation to provide the public with a transparent and easy tool to measure how sustainable a society is from a whole macro-perspective indicator. The SSI is based on the Brundtland definition and is comprised of 24 indicators, which show at a glance the level of sustainability of 151 countries [18]. These can be aggregated into eight categories, three well-being dimensions, and finally, one overall index, as shown in Figure 2.3.

Sustainable Society	Human Well-being	Basic Needs	1. Sufficient Food 2. Sufficient Drinking Water 3. Safe Sanitation
		Personal Needs	4. Healthy Life 5. Education Opportunities 6. Gender Equality
		Well-Balanced Society	7. Good Governance 8. Income Distribution 9. Population Growth
	Environmental Well-being	Healthy Environment	10. Air Quality (Humans) 11. Air Quality (Nature) 12. Surface Water Quality
		Climate & Energy	13. Renewable Energy 14. Emission GHGs 15. Energy Consumption
		Natural Resources	16. Renewable Water Resource 17. Forest Area 18. Biodiversity
	Economic Well-being	Preparation for the Future	19. Material Consumption 20. Organic Farming 21. Genuine Savings
		Economy	22. GDP 23. Employment 24. Public Debt

Figure 2.3 Composition of Sustainable Society Index

Source: "Framework SSI2010" by Geurt.vandekerk. (https://commons.wikimedia.org/wiki/File:Framework_SSI2010.gif#/media/File:Framework_SSI2010.gif). Accessed on Aug. 15, 2016.

In the macro perspectives using SSI as shown in Figure 2.4, China has relatively sound genuine savings due to its large land scale, while Korea has relatively sound sanitation and a healthy system compared to China. Both countries are in stronger positions in the social dimensions of human well-being but are in weaker positions in the environmental well-being dimension, especially, the energy subsector.

The SSI measures only the macro version of evaluation from country perspectives, while the GRI measures sustainability on a micro-organization level. Founded in 1997, the GRI is an international independent standards organization that helps businesses, governments, and other organizations to understand and communicate their impacts on such issues as climate change, human rights, and social soundness. The GRI produces one of the world most widely used standards for sustainability reporting. Also known as ecological footprint reporting, this abbreviation measures environmental, social, and governance reporting, triple bottom line reporting, and CSR reporting. As of 2015, 7,500 organizations used GRI guidelines for their sustainability reports. The GRI framework aims to enable third parties to assess the environmental impact of the activities of a specific company and its supply chain, as shown in Figure 2.5 [19].

Founded in 1947, the ISO is an international standard-setting body composed of representatives from various national standards organizations. To measure environmental sustainability, the ISO established a series of ISO 14000 and 26000 standards. The ISO 14000 series measures how an organization (a) minimizes its operations (processes, etc.) that negatively affect the environment (i.e., cause adverse changes to air, water, or land); (b) complies with applicable laws, regulations, and other environmentally oriented requirements; and (c) continually improves on the above-mentioned points. The ISO 14000 family includes, most notably, the ISO 14001 standard, which represents the core set of standards used by organizations for designing and implementing an effective environmental management system (EMS). It does not specify requirements for environmental performance, but maps out a framework that a company or organization can follow to set up an effective EMS. The ISO 14001 standard can be used by any organization that wants to improve resource efficiency, reduce waste, and enhance eco-friendly efficiency.

For the CSR, the ISO established a new global standard, ISO 26000, which contributes to global sustainable development by encouraging business and other organizations to practice social responsibility to improve their impacts on their workers, natural environment, and communities. ISO 26000 offers guidance on socially responsible behavior and possible actions. This standard is designed for companies to meet particular requirements for activities such as manufacturing, managing, accounting, and reporting. ISO 26000 is the designation of the future international standard giving guidance on social responsibility. It is intended for use by organizations of all types, in both public and private sectors, in developed and developing countries. ISO 26000 contains guidance, not requirements, unlike ISO 9001:2000 and ISO 14001:2004. Nonetheless, since most global trading partners require ISO 26000 as a strong reference for their business transactions,

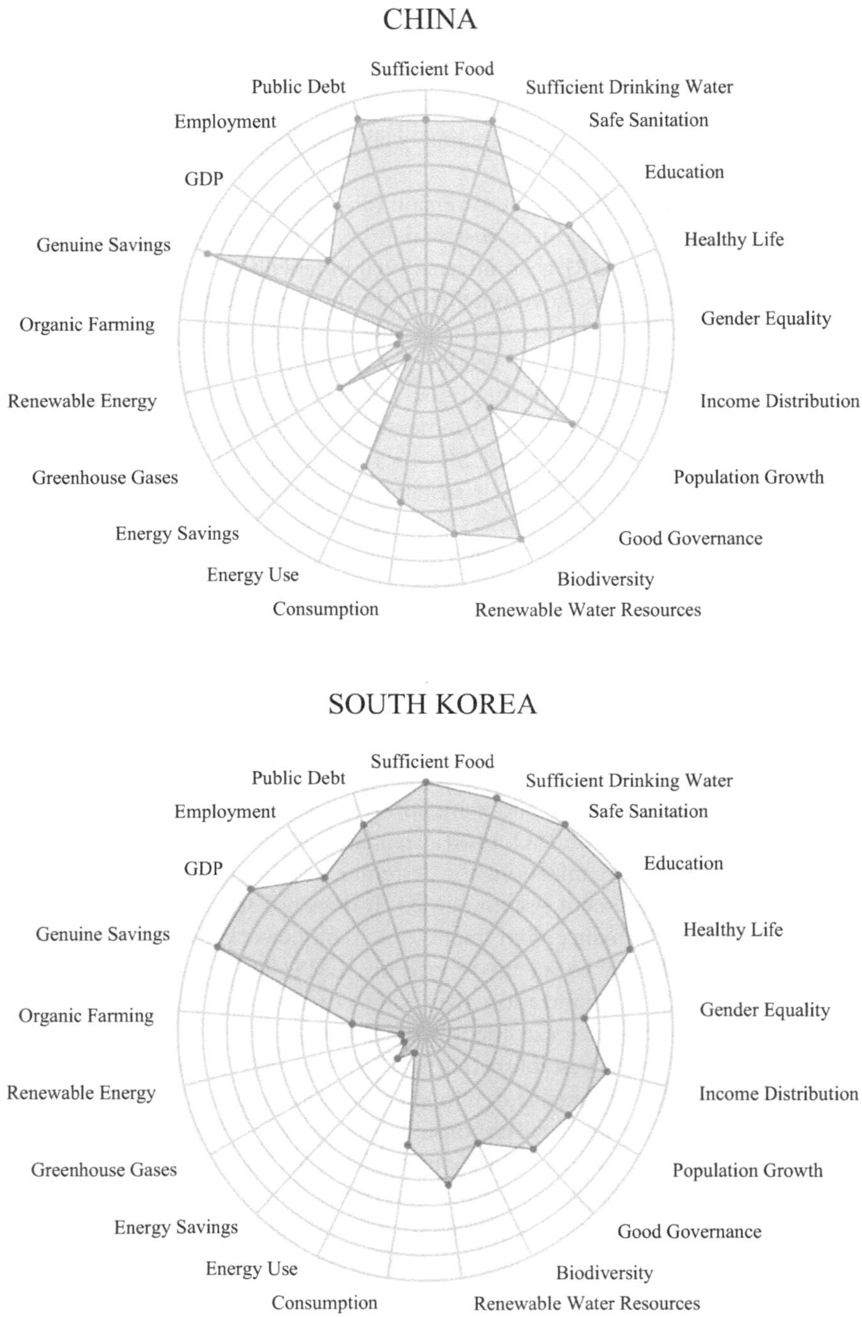

Figure 2.4 Sustainable Society Index maps for China and Korea

Source: Sustainable Society Foundation (http://www.ssfindex.com/). Accessed on Sept. 3, 2015.

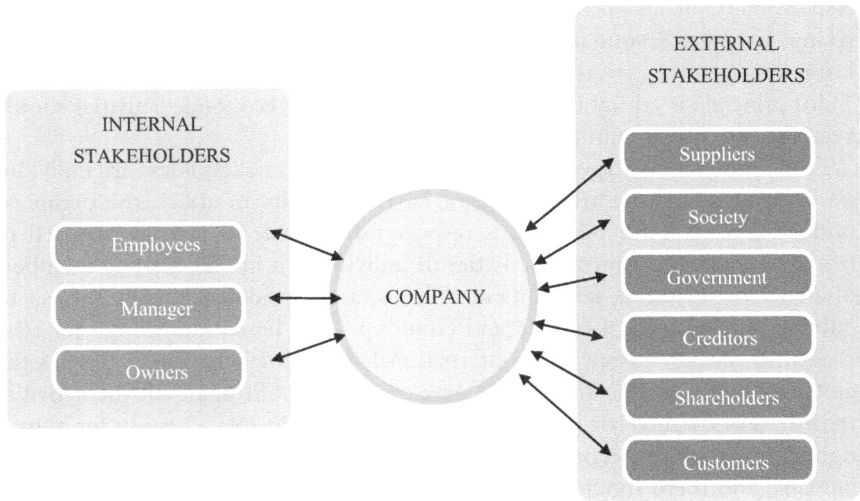

Figure 2.5 Composition of Global Reporting Initiative indicator

Source: "Stakeholder (en)" by Grochim. (https://commons.wikimedia.org/wiki/File:Stakeholder_(en).png#/media/File:Stakeholder_(en).png). Accessed on Aug. 15, 2016.

it has become widely accepted and applied by 157 countries since 2001. Sustainable management for organizations means not only providing products and services that satisfy the customer, and doing so without jeopardizing the environment, but also operating in a socially responsible manner.

Up to this moment, we analyzed the paradigm shift from a self-sufficient agricultural classical economy to assembling of networking. At present, the soft economy emphasizes the invisible values coming from this networking management. Just consider Nike. Is this company a manufacturer? No, Nike has never made its sports shoes by itself. Instead, it just managed all the global supply chain companies as the network manager. Nike exemplifies the role of network managers to create *values*. The performance of a company depends on the numerous groups of people that help the growth of the company, and the company should regard them as network partners, not simply as helpers, to collaborate for sustainable performance. A single manufacturer cannot make all items, parts, and modules by its own innovation potential, and thus, it is best for the company to seek the best partners in this collaborative networking and to organize them to create values by innovation and share these created values among the partners. This means all manufactures are assemblers from the core competence perspective of its sustainable performance, and thus, the decisions of the company should be transparent and fair for all. Then who are the partners, and what is "fair" for the sustainable performance? ISO 26000 shows seven key principles for socially responsible or *fair* behavior for the *partners*, as follows [20].

First principle is accountability in the governance perspectives; it implies responsibility, blameworthiness, and the expectation level for specific account-related activities. Second principle is transparency in the governance perspectives; it implies openness, trustful communication, and predictability of the activities. Third principle is ethical behavior; it implies that the economic activities should keep the social and cultural ethics.

Forth principle is respect for stakeholder interests; stakeholders are individuals or groups who are affected by, or have the ability to affect, the organization's activities. Fifth principle is respect for the rule of law; as opposed to being governed by arbitrary activities of individual, it implies that all members of a society, including government officials, are considered equally subject to publicly disclosed legal regime and common-sense-based knowledge for all.

Sixth principle is respect for international norms of behavior; it implies the global standard on the sustainable development should guide all the activities regardless of codified law or common law. Seventh principle is respect for human rights. Most of the economic activities should promote the healthy life of humans, and there should be equal rights for all humankind.

Based on these seven principles, ISO 26000 has seven core subject fields, which are almost the same as the other indicators of sustainable management: organizational governance; human rights; labor practices; environment; fair operating practices; consumer issues; and community involvement and development.

2.3 *The role of sustainable development paradigm on the traditional studies*

In the previous section, diverse indicators for sustainable development in governments (SSI), companies (GRI), and all organizations (ISO) are reviewed. These indicators support at least the optimal directions for future challenges to quantify the intangible values of the sustainable performance. Even if all these measures are unclear about quantifying the degree of sustainability, it is quite certain that these efforts will improve the quality of our lives in the long term. Unfortunately, even if the paradigm shift toward the sustainable development should be a platform for all existing theories, it is not true in reality due to the lack of the self-consciousness on the sustainable performance. Therefore, it is better to understand the background of this paradigm shift in relation to the traditional theories in conjunction with our daily practices.

Even if the basic methodology in the traditional theoretical framework remains effective for solving many issues, it is so critical that most existing theories should fulfill the missing link to solve unexpected, complex issues related to sustainability. For example, traditional economics is based on the paradigm of efficiency or economies, which means maximizing output while minimizing input. This paradigm is effective only when we deal with the existing old legacy economic system. None of the traditional theories is concerned about the conflicts between contemporary facets of economic issues and their long-term effects. If a firm wants to find an economic way to produce at lower prices, it may disregard environmental byproducts, such as dirty air, water, and waste produced in the production process. If a firm does not produce anything, certainly it can avoid any environmental issue, but if the production process begins, it cannot produce any desirable output without producing additional undesirable byproducts (joint-production hypothesis). In the traditional framework, a firm does not accommodate this kind of external economic variable, such as social responsibility and environmental pollution, and thus, it is put aside as a market failure. However, under the borderless competition of the World Trade Organization (WTO), all firms should expect the production process to be transparent in order to compete with other firms in different countries under a global standard. One of the invisible global standards is the WTO Green Round. If a company does not comply with the environmental protection measures in its production process, such as air filtering and water purification, importing nations could set higher anti-ecological tariffs and taxes or simply restrict these imports. Thus, even a firm in a developing country should comply with the global standard of ecological soundness, certified by diverse indicators. This means market failure arising from an environmental externality could and should be internalized in the traditional paradigm of economics, which should change from the traditional paradigm of maximum output versus minimum inputs toward new paradigm of harmonized value creation by solving sustainable economic issues from totally different perspectives. For example, emission trading system (ETS) is one of the new approaches to solve undesirable output of CO_2 in the production process. It is no longer out of ambit of traditional economic theory. By internalizing the externality of sustainable issues, the emitter should compensate for its environmental degradation by certain investment in green technology and/or additional costs for infringing on the interests of stakeholders.

Similarly, the paradigm of traditional business management, still based on maximizing profits for stockholders, should change its focus from the short-term profit maximization for company owners to the creation of values based on harmonized cooperative networking for all interest groups of people. The traditional approach is unable to handle effectively the diverse requirements of interest groups, such as consumers, society, and government, because their interests conflict with the traditional paradigm of profit maximization on behalf of stockholders. However, the efforts of the company should not focus only on profit maximization in this interdependent networking society. Rather, the efforts should aim for value creation from sustainable network management for all parties. In particular, the rapid development of the Internet and its related technologies and know-how have shifted power from companies and governments to consumers and the public, because now smart netizens want to "participate in" the production process. These "prosumers" (the word is a compound of "production" and "consumer") are proactive consumers who participate in production. They lead the market and their loyalty is extremely important, not only for long-term values, but even for the short-term profit-maximization goal, because they can have strong effects by viral marketing to other netizens. So, instead of profit maximization, CSR type of sustainable governance could be much more important to result in higher values.

All these traditional paradigms are based solely on mechanical approaches to obtain competitive enhancement of efficiency in economics and profitability in business. Sustainability science is not based on competitive zero-sum game, but on harmonizing partnerships among diverse entities, creating opportunity as a new platform for all traditional theories and research, such as human behavioral, social, economic, and even environmental sciences. This platform potential of sustainability science has become a strong motivation for diverse studies to be integrated for a new, innovative way of thinking to open the new frontier of sustainable development.

2.4 *Comparison of the green growth policies in the Northeast Asia*

The global economy has been recovering slowly from the economic crisis that began in 2008. However, each country differs in terms of speed and performance owing to its surrounding circumstances and differences in its policy paradigm. This is especially true from the perspective of sustainable development. Most developing countries could not emphasize the importance of environmental issues. Rather, these countries should place more efforts in the rapid recovery of their low-growth economies. Even so, their individual policy mechanisms and social paradigms differ. Moreover, a country may change its emphasis or paradigm over time. For example, China has been called "the global factory", and "Made in China" was synonymous with lowest prices in the world. However, this is no longer true, because recently the Chinese government has become intensively aware of air pollution and natural disasters arising from environmental degradation, and thus turned around its focus on the environmental policies. Since 2006, the Chinese 5-year economic development plans have begun to put more efforts into establishing the feasibility of decoupling in major industries, and thus, investing more in technological innovation for decreasing energy intensity and increasing eco-friendly productivity. For this purpose, the Chinese government has established new rules and regulations with many more subsidies and promotional policies for sustainable development. It is quite clear that the Chinese government has turned into a new paradigm for green growth by government-led, regulation-oriented policies [21].

Compared with China, the Korean government has adopted a more rigid regulatory regime in the belief that government-led policies should result in much faster and effective performance, by leading green growth [22]. This government-led paradigm in economic development was successful, at least in earlier times, but this is no longer the case in Korea because the economy has expanded enormously in volume, and thus, has become much more complex than before. In particular, the Korean economy has suffered sluggish growth of employment and capital investment and is experiencing zero growth at present. Input-promoted quantitative economic growth in Korea can no longer be sustainable. Instead, innovation-oriented qualitative economic development is necessary for the country's aging society [23]. Moreover, major companies in

Korea, such as Samsung and Hyundai, are conscious of global competitiveness as well as local political pressures on the eco-friendly issues, because the Korean economy is based on international trade with an export-oriented economic structure. Therefore, the regulatory regime for green growth is no longer effective for Korea's innovation-oriented and complex economy [1].

Nonetheless, the Korean government hosted the GCF at Incheon in 2012 and has promoted green growth policies strongly since 2008. Based on the Framework Act on Low-Carbon Green Growth, the Korean government inaugurated a greenhouse gas and energy target management system (TMS) for 470 large companies in 2012 and a nationwide carbon ETS in 2015. The political paradigm for green growth is so firm in Korea that the market should follow the optimal path toward green growth. It is noteworthy that most Korean companies and the public have adapted to the new trend and/or policies, and thus, there is optimism that the Korean economy will promote green growth strategies in more proactive ways [24].

Compared with China and Korea, Japan has established the strongest government-led paradigm for green growth. This comes from the society's cultural background. Most private sector participants in Japan tend to harmonize with the networking society, and thus, political leaders and some business intermediaries may have strong impacts on social activities and economic decisions. Even if the Japanese government does not clearly or significantly regulate the details of green growth strategies, as long as the government propagates the objective goal of green growth, most companies and the public follow without much question [25]. In particular, the Japanese government led the Kyoto Protocol, one of strongest measures to curb global CO_2 emissions, and thus, without many visible regulatory measures, the Japanese economy has been transforming slowly but effectively toward green growth. However, the Japanese government may face a dilemma between normative leadership and the practical burden of green growth. Although the Japanese government led the Kyoto Protocol, and successfully achieved its commitment to decrease carbon emissions by 6 per cent compared with 1990 levels, becoming the leading Annex I country, the exit of the United States from the Protocol and the passive attitudes of many other major countries, such as China, made the Japanese government hold back from a more active role in the post-Kyoto regime. Now, the Japanese government faces extreme fatigue from the Kyoto Protocol, and thus, needs stronger leadership for more voluntary partnerships, not only with other countries, but also with local companies and the public to re-adopt the challenging path of green growth [26]. Before we proceed further, it will be better to look over the case studies of sustainable development conditions and government-led policies in this dynamic, yet too much complicated region to clarify the successful internalization of environmental externalities.

First of all, China is the world's largest consumer of coal, using about 45 per cent of the global total. It is also the largest emitter of CO_2. Thus, China's energy policies will be crucial to limiting the damage from climate change. The Chinese government could do a lot more to encourage industry and consumers to use energy more efficiently. Unfortunately, the Chinese economy still uses more energy to generate each unit of output than the world average, and the government would struggle to catch up to advanced countries, resulting in a trade-off between rapid growth and public health. However, China itself, much like Europe and some states in the United States, has recently initiated regional ETS pilot projects because its environmental difficulties have become too serious not to emphasize such policies. Air pollution is gauged by a measurement known as particles (particular materials or PM) per cubic meter of air, abbreviated as PM2.5 because it measures particles smaller than 2.5 micrometers. The higher the PM2.5 rating, the more dangerously high are the particle levels, and the worse the air is for health. Recently, these PM2.5 and other GHG levels have been seriously high in China. Berkeley Earth released a study showing that air pollution kills an average of 4,000 people every day in China, or 17 per cent of all China's deaths. For 38 per cent of the population, the average air they breathe is "unhealthy" by US standards [27]. The most harmful pollution, PM2.5, penetrates deeply into the lungs and triggers heart attacks, strokes, lung cancer, and asthma. Reducing PM2.5 levels in Beijing could be very difficult because the city itself is only a moderate source of PM2.5 – much of its pollution travels from distant industrial areas, particularly Shijiazhuang, 200 miles to the southwest. In addition to the impact on Beijing, there are too many large cities having terrible air conditions due to rapidly growing local industries.

Because of these dangerous nationwide air conditions, the Chinese government has been making an effort to solve the dilemma between the urgent need for economic growth and deteriorating environmental conditions since 2005. It has launched seven pilot carbon trading systems, starting with Shenzhen, a vibrant city of 15 million with a 2012 GDP growth rate of 10 per cent on June 18, 2013. Together, these seven regions have a CO_2 inventory of more than 1.5 billion tons and populations of approximately 250 million in a geographic area of 481,000 km^2, which is much larger than the Korean Peninsula. The sum of the economies, where the seven pilots were launched, exceeds 29 per cent of China's GDP. Based on the experience of Shenzhen and the other six provinces, the Chinese government will decide when and how it will introduce a nationwide ETS. The Shenzhen ETS covers about 40 per cent of the city's total CO_2 inventory. Its primary goals are to cap enterprise emissions and reduce CO_2 intensity by 25 per cent. In 2013, the Shenzhen ETS included 635 enterprises and 197 large buildings. All other cities have a similar plan, as shown in Figure 2.6. During the course of the ETS, covered enterprises must first measure and report their CO_2 emissions, and then, use qualified third-party verification bodies to verify their emissions. The enterprises must aim to keep their emissions at no more than their allocated carbon intensity, either via efficiency upgrades or by additional investment to innovate green technology. Those enterprises that are able to operate below their caps may either reserve the surplus for later use or sell their surplus allowances. If firms emit more than the quantity of allowances/CCERs surrendered, then the enterprise must (a) forfeit an equal quantity of allowances and (b) pay a penalty equal to three

Region	Launched Date	No. of Covered Enterprises	Compliance Percentage
Shen Zhen	06/18/2013	Industry: 635; Buiding: 197	40%
Shang Hai	11/26/2013	191	50%
Beijing	11/28/2013	543	40%
Guangdong	12/19/2013	190	55%
Tianjin	12/26/2013	114	60%
Hubei	04/02/2014	138	35%
Chongqing	06/19/2014	242	40%

Figure 2.6 Progress of regional ETS pilot projects in China

Source: ICAP, Factsheet

times the average market price of allowances, which is the same rate as that in Korea. However, contrary to the Korean case of almost no trade, the Shenzhen carbon market trades nearly every business day, with a total volume of more than 120,000 tons and a total value of more than 8 million RMB in the 5 months since its inauguration [28].

Compared with the stepwise approach for the carbon emission trading system in some pilot projects, Korea claimed its nationwide green growth policy paradigm in 2010, when it hosted the G20 summit in Seoul. The green growth paradigm aims to promote future opportunities, mainly by the carbon ETS. The Korean government proclaimed that, based on the ETS, it would cut GHG emissions to 30 per cent below business-as-usual (BAU) levels over till the year 2020. For this purpose, Korea's ETS was launched at the Busan headquarters of the Korea Exchange (KRX), the state-run bourse, in January of 2015. In the carbon derivatives market, only 525 companies, including global companies such as Samsung Electronics, Hyundai Motor, POSCO, Hyundai Heavy Industries, and Lotte Department Store have been approved by the Ministry of Environment to engage in trading Korean allowance units (KAUs) for the initial stage of the ETS from 2015 to 2017. In 2015, the first year, the total sum of the emissions quotas amounts to 1.59 billion tons. Each company has received a quota of 15.9 billion KAUs from the government, with 1 KAU equivalent to 1 ton of CO_2. During the initial stage, only companies with emissions targets will receive free carbon allowances, without any third-party intervention in the market, to stabilize the initial stage of ETS. Emission rights trading is a pro-aggressive political measure to internalize the undesirable effects of climate change by allocating emission permits to the companies responsible for emissions. By the successful enhancement of green technology, firms whose carbon emissions are less than the permitted amount can sell their emission rights to firms whose carbon emissions exceed a quota set by the government. KAUs started trading at a price of 7,860 won (US$ 7) per ton, and fluctuated up to around 11,000 won (US$ 10) during the first year, without substantial transaction volumes.

ETSs are currently being executed in 34 countries and regions around the world, including members of the European Union, New Zealand, and Switzerland, according to KRX data. For the policy to launch successfully, the KRX plans to encourage the market by diversifying its tradable products. In addition to GHG emission rights, there are plans for the main bourse to list similar environmental rights, such as air pollutant emission rights. "The key objective of trading is not to create a boon in the financial market, but to reduce the country's emissions of air pollutants," KRX vice president Yoon Suk-yoon said at the inauguration conference [29].

As another case study for the waste management in Korea, the Korean government implemented a volume-rate disposal system that requires residents to purchase and use special trash bags from the year 1995, and thus Korea ranked fourth in the world in its nationwide waste implementation policies, after Switzerland, Germany, and Japan. The price of the trash bag is proportional to its volume. All trash must be disposed in state-authorized plastic bags that are available at local stores. The price differs according to municipality and district, with Seoul City levying 413 won (0.4 US dollars) per 20 liters of trash on average. Busan imposes the highest rate, at 813 won per 20 kilograms as of October, 2015. Since 1995, the amount of Korean household waste has fallen sharply over the past 20 years owing to the introduction of this new disposable system. As of 2013, Koreans threw out about 49,000 tons of waste each day, which is 16.2 per cent lower than before the system was introduced. In addition, the daily trash disposal rate per capita declined 29 per cent to 0.94 kilograms from 1.33 kilograms. As shown in Figure 2.7, the recycling rate rose 59 per cent, implying that 29,000 tons of daily waste disposal are recycled. Between

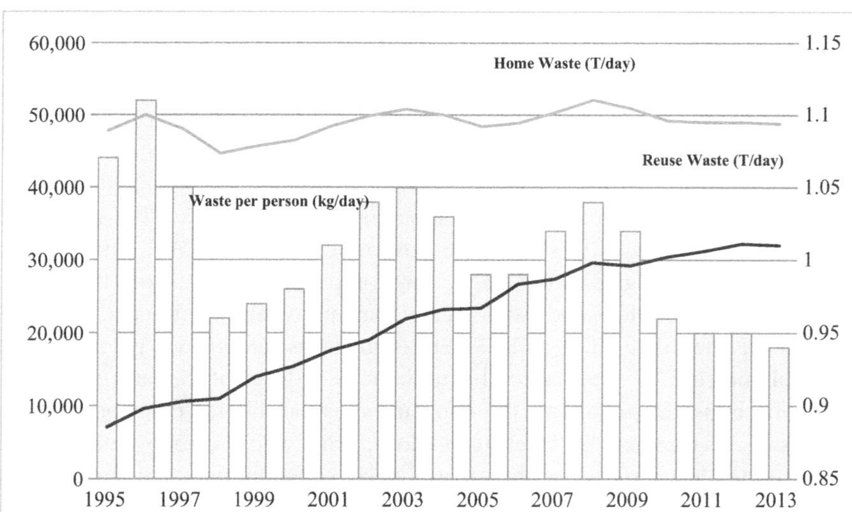

Figure 2.7 Trend of waste disposal and reuse in Korea

Source: Ministry of Environment of Korea, (http://www.me.go.kr/home/web/index.do?menuId=10265), Accessed on Sept. 7, 2015.

1994 and 2013, the daily recycling rate soared by more than 220 per cent, while the landfill rate and incineration level dropped dramatically. The daily landfill rate plummeted 83.3 per cent to 7,600 tons. According to the Ministry of Environment in Korea, the volume-rate garbage disposal system has contributed about the US$ 21 billion in accumulated economic value [30].

Nonetheless, after 20 years of the system, concerns about waste management remain as landfill sites are approaching its full capacity. As of 2010, about 18 per cent of Korean waste went into landfill, while many European countries, such as the Netherlands and Germany have kept the figure at less than 1 per cent, implying that more proactive public participation in the government-led system is desperately required. In the beginning, the system worked effectively for the public to dump less waste and reuse more, but over the long term, most Koreans have developed strong reluctance to continue this system. Therefore, like for most sustainable development policies, the active participation of the private sector is necessary to maintain the system [31]. It implies that the government-driven policies are not sustainable unless the private parties participate more proactively.

In 2005, Korea launched the Seoul Initiative Network on Green Growth to promote multilateral environmental cooperation projects. The initiative aims to discover and share solutions to achieve sustainable development tailored for Asia-Pacific countries. The main programs of the Seoul Initiative include an annual policy consultation forum and workshops that target government officials from the Asia-Pacific, as well as pilot projects in which member countries select applicable technologies and policies. Korea hosted the initiative's 10th policy forum in 2015, with countries from across Asia-Pacific in attendance, giving them a chance to share their environmental policies and experiences related to climate change, under the theme of "enhancing climate resilience for sustainable development". The main topic was the lessons from the inauguration of Korea's ETS policies, and many countries expressed strong support for the ETS and future cooperative projects. In addition, Korea has contributed to diverse international projects with the GCF since 2013.

Japan, due to lack of natural resources, such as coal, has depended heavily on nuclear energy for the past half century. Since nuclear energy is more beneficial than fossil fuels in terms of carbon emissions and lower unit production costs, Japan was the third biggest user of nuclear energy, with 54 commercial reactors nationwide. Japan had depended on nuclear reactors for one-third of its energy. Unfortunately, the tragic Tōhoku earthquake and tsunami on March 11, 2011, destroyed and damaged 17 of these reactors and due to increasing panic about nuclear instability following the meltdown at the Fukushima Daiichi nuclear plant, the Japanese government proclaimed a zero-nuclear economy. Experts say the Fukushima accident is the biggest nuclear crisis after the Chernobyl disaster in 1986. Switching to other energy sources was not an easy task for the government to deal with because other energy alternatives are very expensive and environmentally harmful. The Japanese government is in a dilemma about whether to import more expensive fuels to generate the lost one-third of energy from nuclear reactors, but at the same time, it is really difficult to convince the public to accept a new nuclear safety standard and to agree to the resumption of nuclear power generation. Junichiro Koizumi, the ex-prime minister of Japan who chose Shinzō Abe as the new Prime Minister, made a public statement to urge the government to take a stand against using nuclear power. Unfortunately, the new prime minister supports nuclear power and has stated that leaving the plants idle was costing the country JPY 4 trillion per year in higher costs for alternative energy sources. It seems unavoidable for the Japanese government to restart nuclear power plants, albeit this time more cautiously with a higher safety standard. Due to these unforeseeable policies, Japan lost the global as well as local leadership toward the green growth. The Japanese government should recover its partnership with private parts in more trustworthy way.

2.5 Global perspectives on the green growth policies

As northeast Asian countries take their government-led regulatory regimes toward green growth, the extreme opposite case can be found in the United States. The basic paradigm of the United States may come from the passive intervention on the market by the government with more market-friendly promotion of green technologies. Diverse economic policies related to green growth are not exceptional. Thus, the United States did not enter the Kyoto Protocol on the basis of strong opposition by the private sector to the government decision to follow green growth. Nonetheless, some state governments and global companies, such as California and Wal-Mart, respectively, have taken strong measures to utilize new global opportunities of green growth. Overall, most of the economy is experiencing slow but steady steps toward green growth. Despite the existence of several environmentally friendly protective measures on the part of the government, most of the green growth strategies are not yet ready for an eco-friendly market platform. Unfortunately, the market cannot respond effectively to the green growth paradigm, and it takes too much time for the market to establish the correct way to meet the global standards. Therefore, it is a great task for the US government to lead the market effectively for eco-friendlier practices, yet, the United States is afraid about its potential huge loss when it loses leadership of the global green growth revolution. For this reason, it may need to consider its proactive connection with the private sector to actively lead the global trend toward green growth.

On the contrary, the EU has adopted a paradigm on the opposite extreme with regard to the role of government. With the successful implementation of the Kyoto Protocol, the EU Commission set up the Directorate-General for Climate Action to lead the European Commission's efforts to fight climate change at the EU and international level. It runs the European EMS with the mission of formulating and implementing climate policies and strategies, to take a leading role in international negotiations on climate, to implement the EU ETS, to monitor national emissions by EU member countries, and to promote low-carbon technologies and adaptation measures. The EU is at the forefront of dealing with green growth activities with diverse efforts to promote the development of low-carbon technologies and adaptation measures, especially by creating regulatory frameworks to guide the deployment of these technologies and by providing diverse financial support. However, the regulatory platform is rather passive, and is related more to promotional policies that incentivize areas of green growth through green financing. Therefore, the paradigm of the EU is promotional, even if somewhat government-led, although the financing approach by the EU is noteworthy [32]. It introduced the first carbon ETS in the world, which expanded much more aggressively than those in other parts of the world, even during the global economic crisis. The strong support for the ETS internalized environmental issues from external factors. Even if the ETS is characterized by fluctuating prices and there are questions about its future, it continues to affect almost all economic decision as well as the daily life of the public in the EU. Their positive reinforcement of green financing and indirect government leadership suggests that attempting to achieve non-forced compliance can influence the motives, incentives, and decision making of companies and individuals, at least as effectively – if not more so – than direct enforcement of green growth. Moreover, the paradigm of nudging by finance brought a strong partnership between the local government and private companies in diverse projects for the enhanced adaptation of green growth. This public–private partnership (PPP) is the core paradigm of the Organization for Economic Cooperation and Development (OECD) as well, and it helps to clarify the future direction of the green wave for all countries [1, 33].

A PPP is a government service or private business venture funded and operated through a partnership of government and one or more private sector companies. Since sustainable development is a long-term process with complex outputs, it is very difficult for a firm to compensate all its undesirable outputs from environmental degradation in a short-term production process. In particular, most undesirable GHGs, dirty water, etc. from the production process of a firm may result in toxic effects for the public in general. Therefore, government regulations applicable to firms may require fair evaluation and compensation for these detrimental byproducts. Since most PPPs handle public issues, they are known as the "third sector". For example, the European PPP Expertise Centre is a representative third sector in the EU between the European Investment Bank, European Commission, member states, and even candidate countries of the EU. Its primary mission is to strengthen the organizational capacity of the public sector to engage in PPP transactions by allowing PPP taskforces in EU member and candidate countries to share experience and expertise, analysis, and best practice relating to PPP transactions. One of its major roles is to promote eco-friendly public services [1].

The OECD has taken the lead in the international cooperation for green growth, since sustainable development has transformed into green growth with much more emphasis on the decoupling feasibility between urgent economic needs and long-term environmental protection. The OECD published a series of green growth strategies and best alternative policies for the optimal path toward green growth. In particular, its emphasis on the PPP regime cannot be overestimated in the area of green growth. The government should provide the seed money and strategic platform to counter the fear of investment in green business, invention of new technology, or even the adoption of new technologies. In this way, private companies might be aware of these challenging new initiatives of the government and participate in the new frontier of green growth more proactively (pumping policy). The feedback from these economic entities should guarantee innovative ways for new standards, platforms, and ways of business activities by government concession. This type of PPP requires not the role of helpers but partners' own to enlarge the share for all in a challenging future. In particular, the government should not lead without considering partners, and the private sector should provide more feedback for a market-oriented and performance-oriented paradigm of the green growth under this PPP mechanism [1].

As shown in Figure 2.8, the highly regulated government-led paradigm of green growth policies in northeast Asian countries should decrease the leading role of the government, while increasing the partnership with the private sector. On the contrary, the US government should implement more regulations for

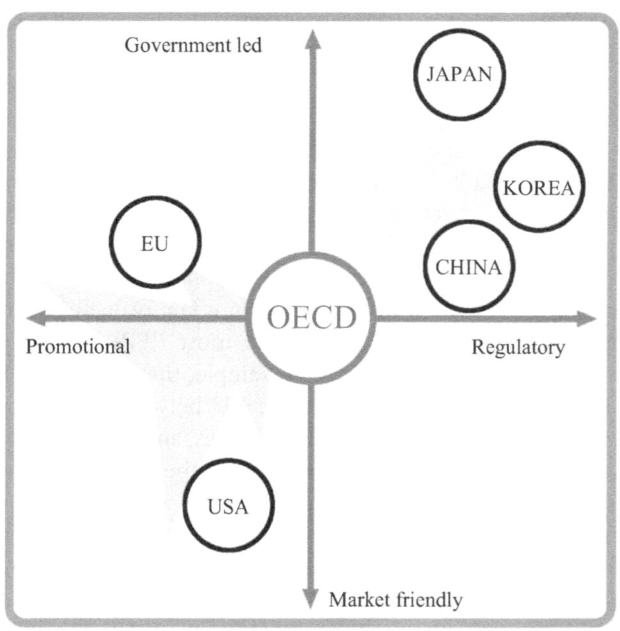

Figure 2.8 Paradigms of the green growth policies by governments

Source: Choi, Yongrok, "Intermediary Propositions for Green Growth with Sustainable Governance", *Sustainability* 2015, 7(11), 14785–14801; doi:10.3390/su71114785.

green growth and prompt active participation by the private sector more effectively in a short time. In this way, the new PPP paradigm could work effectively to create a new global standard for green growth in which every economic entity would be willing to participate in this new standard to create values by the proactive adaptation of the standard. Based on Figure 2.8, it is safe to conclude that the new paradigm for green growth should be based on active partnership between the public and private sectors for sustainable governance [17, 24]. Even so, the spectrum of this PPP mechanism is too diverse – from loose, indirect nudging strategies by governments to strong, direct intervention by governments with the "help" of private partners. It suggests that we need more appropriate role of PPP in these two extreme spectrums.

Up to now, a comparative analysis of policy paradigms has been examined from a global perspective on a country-by-country basis. Since we concluded that PPPs are not optional, but necessary for all countries to promote green growth, it is necessary to examine more practical issues about the appropriate roles and functions of the PPP mechanism for green growth. Because the most important issues for green growth are categorized by the three determinants of green financing, green technology, and green strategies to be handled by the integrated third party (PPP), we use the well-known SWOT Matrix approach in the next chapter to establish optimal propositions for the performance-oriented governance of the PPP mechanism in more detail.

3 Paradigm shift toward the performance-oriented governance

1. Consultocracy in the green growth policies

Even if many theories argue how to use public resources to manage climate change, most research has concluded that there is some missing link between the implementation of these theoretical suggestions and resulting performance because of the lack of harmonized, workable partnership in the process. Since most of green growth policies result in invisible values in the long term via a very complex process with the involvement of diverse interest groups, these policies may have diverse pitfalls and missing links. Policies may *effectively* achieve the quantitative objectives of green growth in the short term, but unfortunately most of these short-term missions are achieved instantaneously, resulting in show-up only achievements without any sustainable performance [1, 31].

It may be the case that nobody wants the achieved outputs, and/or there is no guarantee that this performance will be maintained. Therefore, sustainable performance over time is key for governance in green growth. There are many exemplary case studies whose recommended policies have been implemented successfully, but nobody wants the outputs due to the one-way operation of the government [17, 31]. Therefore, it is also necessary to organize efficient and policy-effective intermediaries for the harmonized PPP system to promote feedback between the government and private sector, resulting in sustainable value creation. In particular, it is extremely difficult to develop or even innovate new green technologies with the lack of partnership under a government-led economy. Moreover, most newly developed technologies are inventor oriented, and thus, it is quite difficult to match them with the right partners, even under a market-friendly economy. Small and medium enterprises, which comprise more than 60 per cent of the business of all countries, cannot easily find where and how to obtain the best support provided by the government, and/or the right technologies newly developed in the market. Thus, intermediation for matching partners to technologies in the challenging new frontier of green growth is core for successful and sustainable governance. Likewise, for feasibility analysis and to follow short- and long-term plans, third parties in new green growth projects are definitely required to search for the right information, evaluate the information, and implement this new project.

Unfortunately, there are too many operational missing links to obtain sustainable performance. For example, a government undertakes a PPP project, such as a forest business to plant trees to avoid deforestation. This policy could be implemented effectively by the PPP in only a short time. However, there is no guarantee that the trees will grow well because the PPP has no concern for them in the long term after its services are completed. All these operational missing links between public policy and market performance require a survival tool for intermediation under the green growth regime, but unfortunately, it is extremely difficult for companies and even for governments to work out solutions for all interest groups and/or cooperative solutions with the best potential partners. Therefore, it is necessary to establish the appropriate roles and functions of these intermediaries to fill the missing links among cooperative networking partners for the governance of sustainable performance [34]. It is especially true that, as the OECD has pointed out, the PPP system is operating over the time by the best intermediary for the internalization of all externalities of interested groups and of their related future challenges.

Most countries use intermediaries for the implementation of government policies on green growth. In Korea, for example, there are several voluntary schemes for PPP projects for green growth, such as those for agreement on energy savings, certification for environmentally friendly agricultural products, certification for use of environmental certification, designation of environmentally friendly companies, green building certification, and voluntary environmental management agreements. However, most of these intermediaries have serious *consultocracy* problems, and thus, many of their programs and projects have only show-off effects. Here, consultocracy means that the supplier-, developer-, or policymaker-oriented intermediaries argue over and confirm the feasibility of new systems, new methods, and new strategies for the market without sufficient consideration for market factors, thereby resulting in the lack of economic efficiency, company capacity, and technical interface with the legacy system due to autocrat decision making [31, p. 38]. Thus, consultocracy causes an enormous waste of resources and time due to the lack of a governance-oriented mediating role [1]. Unfortunately, consultocracy comes from the x-inefficiency of large organizations, such as government-led policy implementation [35]. In the following subsection, we attempt to examine the environmental conditions surrounding the PPP to find out the roots of consultocracy.

2. Environmental conditions for the optimal green growth

Most Asian countries are promoting government-led green growth policies, because there are some conflicts of interest between the public and private sectors, at least in the initial stage of green growth. Since the government cannot intervene in the market in a direct way effectively, most government-led projects can be implemented by intermediaries, such as the independent official authorities (public companies), business associations, and academic third parties. The PPP is the best platform for this kind of economic third sector to handle cooperative challenges in general. When the government cannot perform effectively but wants to intervene in the private sector using the indirect nudge strategy, it may use diverse PPPs to invite a diverse spectrum of participants, from government-owned public companies with minority shares to private companies with majority shares [1].

The motivation for these diverse PPPs can be found in strategic political considerations. Since the green wave requires the utmost participation by almost all economic entities, it is not easy to convene the right signals by policies only. Fortunately, there is global consensus on the pressure for green growth, and this global consensus may encourage the public and private sectors to cooperate with each other. Due to the complex process of PPPs and vagueness in measuring them easily and effectively, green growth should be supported through strong participation by all. The public should be aware of the long-term effects of eco-friendly strategies and, thus, be willing to apply invisible pressure on companies to transform in the direction of green growth; this may result in unexpected new business opportunities for the potential partners from the private sector. For example, POSCO, the steel manufacturer, is under great pressure from the government and public, and thus, has concentrated on greening strategies in the entire manufacturing process. The company noticed there was too much steel scrap thrown out during the manufacturing process as waste, and thus, it invested in decreasing and collecting its scrap. At the end, the waste steel scrap brought POSCO substantial extra profit, as well as brand loyalty as an eco-friendly company. When the company such as POSCO found that new efforts toward green growth did not cost it financially, but that such investment resulted in both visible and invisible value, it was able to participate more aggressively in proactive partnership with the government. However, companies have to harmonize short-term profits with long-term values created by the loyalty of their interest groups, and it is not easy and comfortable for the stockholders as well as the business leaders due to their time limits unless the government promotes it. Therefore, the government should utilize PPPs as the vehicle to initiate new challenges in innovation, new technology adoption, and new green strategies, as well as to obtain the feedback and voluntary, but necessary participation of companies [1].

There are many opportunities for these PPPs to be handled more effectively to create values in cooperative networks. Since PPPs obtain indirect support of governments, it is easy for them to enter new markets, innovate new technology, and undertake new project fields. Moreover, private partners may provide better resources to examine the feasibility of projects, provide more efficient solutions for possible bottlenecks, and implement green missions more effectively. Most of all, the PPP could be a third part of the project, meaning it can avoid the subjective mistakes of either governments or the private sector. In addition, it provides a flexible approach to handle projects by which all participants can contribute to each of their strategic strengths. It can receive strong indirect guarantees by government participation, while it can recruit the best partners to mobilize their best resources. In particular, green growth is an area for multilateral cooperation, and thus, government participation is very important for other project partners to obtain transparent and predictable mechanisms for their major tasks, and to harmonize with global standards and concessions by other countries [1].

However, the conditions surrounding PPPs do not seem to be very effective for the sustainable operation of cooperative networks by all participants, mainly due to uncertainty about policies or policy risks. PPPs require quantitative performance to measure objectives, generally in the short term, and thus, they do not care about the future feedback of users and markets. If policies give good signals about the predictable, transparent operations of PPPs, it would be very beneficial for private companies to participate in such guaranteed opportunities. Unfortunately, government policies tend to be geared toward the short term, and thus, private partners may not invest more when the government is an unsustainable partner. Instead, the private sector may take more passive positions to obtain advantage without making much contribution. In particular, when there is some conflict of interest between the partners, the third-party PPP may not effectively harmonize their interests, and thus, may choose the second best outcome for the government; as the political situations changes, this could result in worse performances for governments than private competitors. Unfortunately, there are so diverse potential conflicts of interest, and thus, it is not easy for each and every partner to participate in this collaboration network proactively to create value for all. Thus, voluntary, proactive partnerships for all members of collaboration networks are required among the interest groups, and only when governments adopt market-oriented strategies can PPPs, as network managers of collaboration networks, fill the missing links.

3. Internal capacity for the optimal green growth

The most competitive factor for a PPP as an intermediary to find and fill a missing link in the collaboration network can be found in legitimate strong support for the PPP by the participating government, and thus, its performance is guaranteed, at least in quantitative terms, in the short run. Government participation makes the PPP more active in promoting policy goals. It could bring the best combination of partners in the field, due to strong incentives and support by the government. For example, Korea experienced insufficient telecommunication in the 1980s. In addition, it had great challenges in telecommunications research and development capacity. When the Korean government established Korea Telecom (KT) as a kind of PPP strongly supported by the government, KT was able to establish the Time Division Exchange system as the world's fourth new inventor. Moreover, the efficient installation of a nationwide telecommunication network by KT made Korea one of the leading IT countries in the Internet era. This kind of PPP could easily access diverse resources with dynamic flexibility and the best partners in their collaboration network, and thus, reduce procedural costs [1].

However, as discussed above, the weakest link in the PPP may come from *consultocracy*. Since most of PPPs are based on defined projects with political missions, they tend to stick to the goals of their policy missions, and thus, may easily forget their sustainable performance. Instead, they insist on short-term achievements, because most policies require short-term benchmarks. For example, in order to prevent deforestation, a PPP may simply plant the same kinds of trees. Even if this is done efficiently and effectively, one kind of tree could be at threat of being attacked by harmful insects, and may even be vulnerable to fire. So, the effectiveness of the policy mission in the short run could not guarantee the sustainable performance as shown in the planting tree policies of Korea. The more government controls the management of PPPs, the greater consultocracy will result. By contrast, if there are certain guarantees by the government with flexible operations to meet goals, then there moral hazard could be found easily by non-responsible decision makers. In 2004, the Korean government pronounced a 5-year regional economic development plan to promote the development of selected regions with a total budget of US$ 66.6 billion through 2008. The core policy project was based on a regional innovation system (RIS). To promote the RIS, the government set up 14 RIS boards nationwide. As PPP-based intermediaries of the RIS, the 14 regional boards comprise 725 people in Korea. Unfortunately, most board members are from universities, and 11 of the 14 board chairpersons come from universities. Moreover, most of these intermediaries from universities are not active participants in commercial activities, because they have no obligations. Some RISs in Korea have been renamed simply to deal with traditional brick and mortal industry complexes, such as Kumi, whereas others are newly established in the green fields of remote mountain areas without any infrastructure at all. Because there are no performance-based incentives or obligations for financing of strategic fields, most RIS boards do not give much consideration to the selection or management of the RIS. Owing to the missing links between the 14 RIS boards, their regional operations could not continue their missions, and when the new president was elected, all the PPPs were gone away with, incurring substantial waste of national resources [36].

4. SWOT Matrix and the proposed paradigm for green growth

Based on the above-mentioned surrounding environmental conditions and the internal capacity analyses of the PPP as an intermediary, we can integrate its strengths (S), weaknesses (W), opportunities (O), and threats (T), resulting in the SWOT Matrix model. As shown in Table 3.1, the internal capacity analysis provides facts about the strengths and weaknesses of PPPs as intermediaries, while the external surrounding environment analysis provides opportunities and threats for PPP as an intermediary. From this summary of the facts, we can draw future strategies for market- and performance-oriented governance. It can be called a strategy, because it comes from the current situation and the internal facts, resulting in more dependable, feasible scenarios of the strategic alternatives [1, 10].

First, the PPP should increase its role as a facilitator (SO strategy, facilitator proposition). Based on strong support by the government and global consensus

Table 3.1 SWOT Matrix strategies

Internal capacity / *External environment*		*Strength* • Government support • Best private partner • Flexible management	*Weakness* • Consultocracy (moral hazard) • Low motivation
Opportunity	• Global consensus • New business opportunity	Increasing role for facilitator (SO strategy)	Increasing role for network manager (OW strategy)
Threat	• Low partnership • Policy risk	Increasing role for collaborator (ST strategy)	Increasing role for service provider (TW strategy)

Source: Choi, Yongrok, "Intermediary Propositions for Green Growth with Sustainable Governance", *Sustainability* 2015, 7(11), 14785–14801; doi:10.3390/su71114785.

toward green growth, the PPP intermediary should make an effort to innovate new technology, to transform its business into the green growth platform with more eco-friendly strategies, and to create new products and new business. As an early adaptor to green growth, it should encourage all interest groups to understand that this new direction is much more valuable than any other traditional legacy system. This requires a proactive role to invite potential partners to enter the collaboration network voluntarily using its own contribution of value sharing.

The second strategy to emerge from the weakness and opportunity factors is based on the increased role as the network manager (OW strategy, network manager proposition). As green growth requires a complex process from inputs to finally created values in the long term, there are conflicts from diverse interest groups. The most important role for the PPP intermediary should manage the cooperative network more effectively for sustainable performance and to harmonize their conflicting interests in terms of bearable, equitable, and viable value sharing. Effective networking and the operation of all interest groups is crucial for the sustainable performance of green growth.

The third strategy to utilize strength and overcome threats should be based on the PPP's enhanced role as collaborator (ST strategy, collaborator proposition). There are too many helpers in government-led projects, but in general, there are no partners. The helpers are not responsible for performance, and thus, they provide consulting that is too abstract under ideal conditions. Nor can they provide proactive contributions because of a lack of practical incentives. Therefore, to promote green growth collaboration continuously, all interest groups should comprise not just outsiders, but also inside partners with proactive contributions, and appropriate rights and shared responsibilities. This collaborator proposition would eradicate consultocracy because helpers alone would no longer be able to contribute only verbally, while partners would participate with strong motivation for the value-sharing system.

The last strategy from the weakness and opportunity factors should be based on the increased role of the PPP as service provider (TW strategy, service provider proposition). The PPP intermediary should provide all the necessary information and potential resources for potential partners. The diverse background of the partners in the collaboration network may lack exact requirement or future challenges in detail, and the network manager should give all possible support for participants to communicate more effectively and find out each other's needs. For example, a technician develops only innovation by his or her own idea, and this green technology may not match the demand of other companies because of lack of market information, time, and funds. In this case, the network manager should provide diverse options to match this new green technology to the partners demanding it [1].

5. Measurement and methodologies of sustainable development

5.1 Basic modeling of data envelope analysis (DEA)

Sustainable development is basically very abstract, and thus vague in its performance, and thus the monitoring and measuring for the sustainable performance became one of the key issues for the researchers as well as the practitioners such as policy makers and business managers. Especially, as there is an increasing concern on the mitigation of climate change, a number of empirical researches have employed diverse methodologies to identify and evaluate the sustainable performance, especially in energy and environmental (E&E) modeling because E&E issues are key factors in sustainable development. Among the wide spectrum of E&E modeling methodologies, data envelopment analysis (DEA) has drawn much attention because it is a nonparametric method in operations research and economics for the estimation of production frontiers. In its more general terms, DEA modeling is used to empirically measure "relative" productive efficiency of decision-making units (or DMUs). Although DEA has a strong link to production theory in economics, the tool is also used for benchmarking in operations management, where DMU measures are selected to compare with benchmark for their performance. In the circumstance of benchmarking, the efficient DMUs, as defined by DEA, may form a "production frontier", (or best-practice frontier). Nonparametric approaches have the benefit of not assuming a particular functional form/shape for the production frontier. It implies that they do not provide a general or theoretical relationship (by equation) relating output and input. There are also parametric approaches that are used for the estimation of production frontiers. These parametric approaches require that the shape of the frontier be guessed in advance by specifying a particular function such as Cobb-Douglas production technology relating output to input. DEA allows a best-practice relationship between multiple outputs and multiple inputs to be estimated. It could also include diverse outputs such as desirable outputs and undesirable, but necessarily combined outputs of greenhouse gases [37].

Among the family of diverse DEA approaches, the directional distance function (DDF) has drawn much attention. One possible reason is because it can model good and bad outputs (pollutant emission) simultaneously. In addition, unlike the cost function, it does not require abundant amounts of price-specific data and information. Given only the quantity data of inputs and outputs, using the DDF, anyone can model diverse vital characteristics, such as environmental technical efficiency, environmentally sensitive productivity growth, and the shadow prices of pollutants.

To introduce the basic DDF, which is a production frontier methodology in E&E studies, we first need to explain the term "environmental production technology". Assume that there are $j = 1 \ldots, N$ decision-making units (DMUs). These can be decision-making units (DMUs) such as manufacturing firms. Assume that each DMU uses inputs vector $x \in \Re_+^M$ to jointly produce outputs vector $y \in \Re_+^S$ and bad or undesirable outputs $b \in \Re_+^J$. The multi-output production technology can be expressed as

$$T = \{(x, y, b) : x \text{ can produce } (y, b)\} \tag{3.1}$$

where T is often assumed to satisfy the standard axioms of the production theory [38]. For instance, inactivity is always possible, and finite amounts of inputs can produce only finite amounts of outputs. In addition, inputs and desirable outputs are often assumed to be strongly or freely disposable. For a reasonable model of joint-production technologies, as described in Färe et al. [38], the weak disposability and null-jointness assumptions need to be imposed on T. Technically, the two assumptions can be expressed as follows:

1 If $(x, y, b) \in T$ and $0 \leq \theta \leq 1$, then $(x, \theta y, \theta b) \in T$, and
2 If $(x, y, b) \in T$ and $b = 0$, then $y = 0$.

The weak disposability assumption (1) indicates that reducing CO_2 emissions is costly, and thus, it entails an opportunity cost measured by the proportionate reduction in desirable outputs. The null-jointness assumption (2) implies that the production of CO_2 emissions is inevitable in production process, and thus, the only way to remove all undesirable outputs is to stop production. After specifying the environmental production technology T, we can use the parametric distance function or the nonparametric DEA to construct an environmental production technology. After specification of the technology, we can use distance function to calculate efficiency.

Before we introduce distance function, it could be better to explain DEA as the convex production possibility curve (PPC) in the Figure 3.1. OABC is assumed the environmental production technology based on weak disposability. A DMU could decrease desirable output and undesirable output simultaneously to move from B to A, while PPC with strong disposability of ODBC do not allow moving from B to A, which results in a stricter movement from B to D.

Under the weak disposability, the direction function for substitution between desirable and undesirable outputs is very important. For this purpose, two kinds of distance functions are widely used in E&E studies: the Shephard distance function

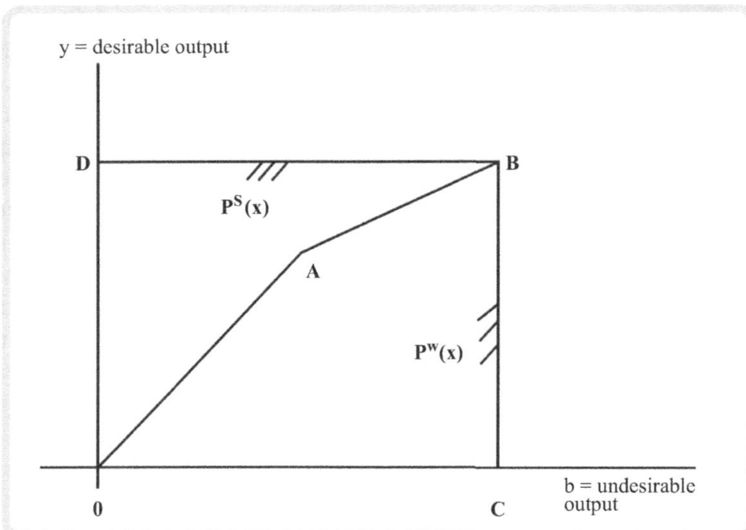

Figure 3.1 Weak disposability technology of production possibility curve

[39] and the DDF [40]. The Shephard distance function expands the good and bad outputs proportionally, to the extent feasible, C to A in the Figure 3.2. Therefore, this method does not credit reduction of bad outputs, since all outputs are expanded at the same rate. On the other hand, the DDF is capable of expanding desirable outputs and contracting inputs or undesirable outputs simultaneously by giving the desirable direction weights on the input and output variables, such as the weight direction of the distance between C to B. Therefore, DDF became a more suitable approach in energy and environmental (E&E) studies with high popularity.

Here, the traditional directional distance function (DDF) can be defined as it maximizes desirable outputs, while reducing undesirable ones at the same rate simultaneously:

$$\vec{D}(x,y,b;\vec{g}) = \max\{\beta:\ (x-\beta\vec{g}_x, y+\beta\vec{g}_y, b-\beta\vec{g}_b)\in T\}, \tag{3.2}$$

where $\vec{g}=(\vec{g}_x,\vec{g}_y,\vec{g}_b)$ is the vector of the directions in which the inputs and outputs should be scaled. β denotes a vector of scaling factors representing the inefficiency measure. The DDF allows for a range of direction vectors, depending on the purpose of the study such as policy targets. From the equation (3.2), one can estimate the DDF to measure environmental inefficiency of each DMU [37].

The DEA-based DDF estimation relies on mathematical programming, and it is based on the construction of a piecewise linear combination of all observed outputs and inputs. A major advantage of the DEA approach is that it does not need the imposition of a functional form on the underlying technology (that means "nonparametric!"). Therefore, DEA can easily provide an estimate of efficiency and

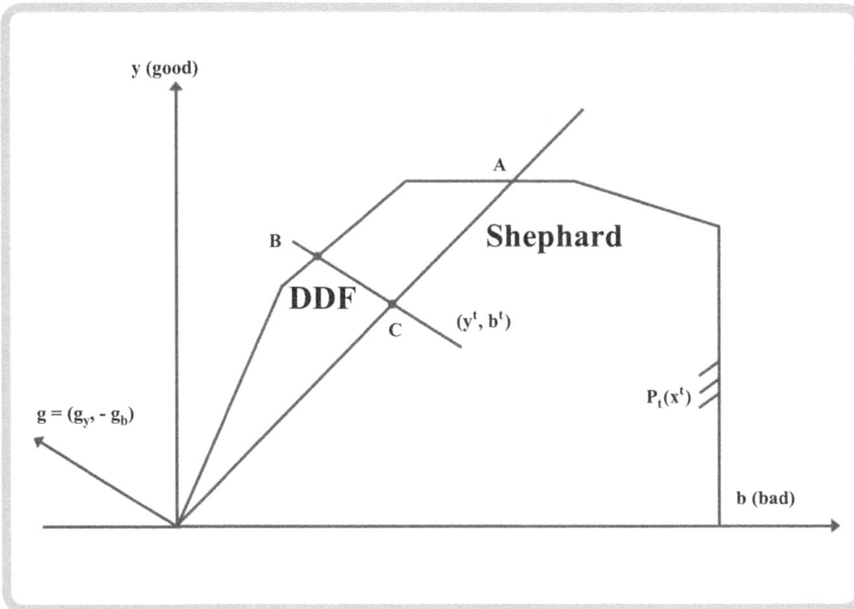

Figure 3.2 Shephard distance function vs. directional distance function

productivity. The parametric approach, which is not as widely used as DEA, requires the use of a functional form for the distance function. It has the advantage of providing an estimated parametric representation of the technology that is everywhere differentiable and easy to manipulate algebraically. Therefore, the parametric method is usually used to estimate shadow prices of undesirable output such as pollutants.

A major advantage of the DEA approach is that it does not need to impose a functional form on the underlying technology; therefore, we introduce the non-parametric DEA piecewise linear production frontier more easily to construct the environmental production technology. Now, we can express production technology, T, for N DMUs exhibiting constant returns to scale as,

$$
\begin{aligned}
T = \{(x, y, b) \ :& \sum_{n=1}^{N} z_n x_{mn} \le x_m, m = 1, \ldots, M, \\
& \sum_{n=1}^{N} z_n y_{sn} \ge y_s, s = 1, \ldots, S, \\
& \sum_{n=1}^{N} z_n b_{jn} = b_j, j = 1, \ldots, J, \\
& z_n \ge 0, n = 1, \cdots, N\}
\end{aligned} \tag{3.3}
$$

where z_n is an intensity variable for constructing the environmental production technology by the convex combination [37].

5.2 *Malmquist–Luenberger productivity index*

The DDF described above can be used to measure relative eco-friendly efficiency across the companies, industries, and the countries in a specific period, as a static efficiency measure. As a dynamic extension of the analysis for a certain period, there are two kinds of productivity index that are widely used; Malmquist–Luenberger productivity index (MLPI) and Luenberger productivity index (LPI). MLPI is used in a ratio way, based on the geometric mean of the DDFs, while LPI is used in an additive way by using the arithmetic mean of the DDFs in two periods to measure environmental productivity growth over time. To define the productivity index, we assume the contemporaneous environmental technology between t and $t+1$ periods for both dynamic index approaches. In the empirical studies, MLPI is more widely used than LPI. One possible reason may be Malmquist type productivity index has had a longer application history than the LPI, and it is easier to show the trend of the decomposed indexes of the efficiency.

Zhang and Choi proposed a Malmquist–Luenberger productivity index (MLPI) based on the DDF to measure environmentally sensitive productivity growth using time-series data [37]. To define the MLPI, contemporaneous environmental technology is expressed as $T^t = \{(x^t, y^t, b^t) : x^t \text{ can produce } (y^t, b^t)\}$, where t = 1,2. . .T. The contemporaneous environmental technology is constructed from DMUs of specific time t.

Let t and s $(t < s)$ denote two time periods. Assume that $D^t(x_n^t, y_n^t, b_n^t)$ and $D^s(x_n^t, y_n^t, b_n^t)$ are the DDFs of firm n based on its inputs and outputs for the environmental production technology at t and s, respectively. Further, assume that $D^t(x_n^s, y_n^s, b_n^s)$ and $D^s(x_n^s, y_n^s, b_n^s)$, respectively, are the DDF of firm n based on its inputs and outputs for the environmental technology at periods t and s. The MLPI is defined as [37],

$$MLPI_n(t,s) = \left[\frac{1 + D^t(x_n^t, y_n^t, b_n^t) \cdot 1 + D^s(x_n^t, y_n^t, b_n^t)}{1 + D^t(x_n^s, y_n^s, b_n^s) \cdot 1 + D^s(x_n^s, y_n^s, b_n^s)}\right]^{1/2} \tag{3.4}$$

$MLPI_n(t,s)$ can be used to measure the environmentally sensitive productivity growth of DMU n from period t to period s. $MLPI_n(t,s) > 1$ (or $MLPI_n(t,s) < 1$) means that the productivity has improved (or deteriorated). Similar to the Malmquist productivity index (MPI), MLPI can also be decomposed into two components: *efficiency change and technological change*. As shown in (3.4), MLPI measures productivity growth in a ratio and based on the geometric mean of the DDFs. An alternative way to measure productivity growth is to use the Luenberger productivity index (LPI), which measures productivity growth in an additive way by using the arithmetic mean of the DDFs in two periods. Based on Chambers et al., the LPI is defined as [40],

$$LPI_n(t,s) = \frac{1}{2}\left[\begin{array}{l} D^s(x_n^t, y_n^t, b_n^t) - D^s(x_n^s, y_n^s, b_n^s) \\ +D^t(x_n^t, y_n^t, b_n^t) - D^t(x_n^s, y_n^s, b_n^s) \end{array}\right] \tag{3.5}$$

5.3 *Extension of DDF and MLPI*

The conventional DDF described above reduces undesirable outputs (and inputs) and increases desirable outputs at the same rate β, as a radial efficiency measure, with the several limitations. A radial measure may overestimate efficiency when some slacks exist. Figure 3.3 visually explains why the radial DDF overestimates efficiency. The OABCDE area is assumed to be an output set corresponding to the environmental production technology defined above. For the point K located near the left side of the frontier, if the direction *g* is taken and the traditional radial DDF is used, then the point F is the benchmark point for evaluating K. However, if the non-radial DDF is used, then the benchmarking point is B because it produces a smaller quantity of undesirable outputs, while generating the same quantity of desirable ones as F. Therefore, the distance BF is the slack in the radial DDF and is referred to as "slack-bias" [41]. Because the radial DDF does not take this sort of slacks into account, it has the potential to reduce inefficiencies and thus may overestimate the efficiency score.

The conventional DDF is a radial efficiency measure that may overestimate efficiency when the slack exists. Non-radial efficiency measures are often advocated to overcome this limitation in measuring energy and environmental performance because of their advantages handling the slacks more effectively. Based on the

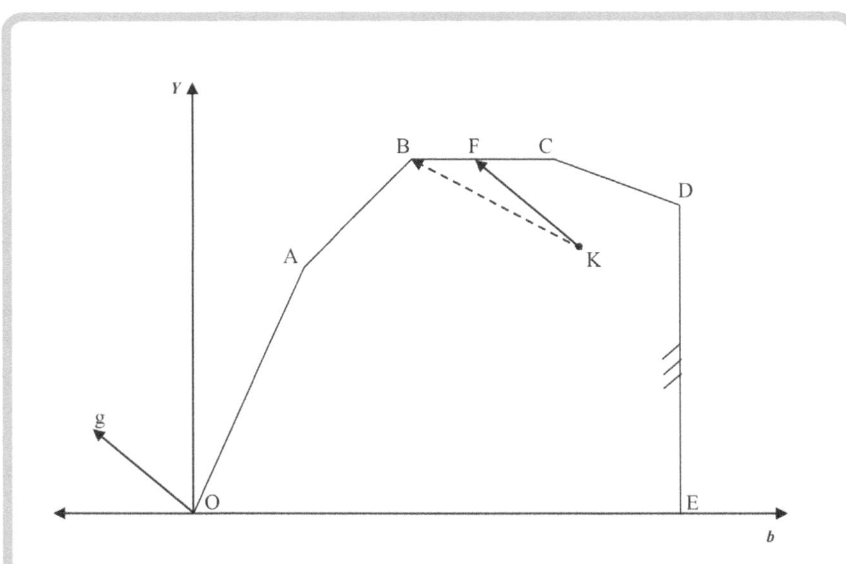

Figure 3.3 Radial vs. non-radial DDF

Source: Zhang N.; Y. Choi, "A note on the evolution of directional distance function an d its development in energy and environmental studies 1997–2013", *Renewable and Sustainable Energy Reviews*, 33(2014), p. 52.

Zhang and Choi (2013), the non-radial directional distance function (NDDF) can be defined as follows [42]:

$$N\vec{D}(x,y,b;g) = \sup\{\mathbf{w}^T\boldsymbol{\beta} : ((x,y,b) + g \cdot diag(\boldsymbol{\beta})) \in T\} \tag{3.6}$$

where $\mathbf{w} = (w_m^x, w_s^y, w_j^b)^T$ denotes a normalized weight vector relevant to numbers of inputs and outputs, $g = (-g_x, g_y, -g_b)$ is an explicit directional vector, and $\beta = (\beta_m^x, \beta_s^y, \beta_j^b)^T \geq 0$ denotes the vector of scaling factors. Combining (3.2) and (3.6), we can compute the value of $N\vec{D}(x,y,b;g)$ by solving the following DEA-type model.

$$\begin{aligned}
N\vec{D}(x,y,b;g) = {} & \max w_m^x\beta_m^x + w_s^y\beta_s^y + w_j^b\beta_j^b \\
\text{s.t.} & \sum_{n=1}^{N} z_n x_{mn} \leq x_m - \beta_m^x g_{xm}, m = 1,\dots,M, \\
& \sum_{n=1}^{N} z_n y_{sn} \geq y_s + \beta_s^y g_{ys}, s = 1,\dots S, \\
& \sum_{n=1}^{N} z_n b_{jn} = b_j - \beta_j^b g_{bj}, j = 1,\dots J, \\
& z_n \geq 0, n = 1,2,\cdots,N \\
& \beta_m^x,\ \beta_s^y, \beta_j^b\ \geq 0
\end{aligned} \tag{3.7}$$

If $N\vec{D}\,(x,y,b;g) = 0$, then the DMU to be evaluated is located on the best-practice frontier in the direction of g, considering the slacks.

Another extension in the dynamic analysis of DEA can be found in the Global MLPI (GMLPI). The conventional MLPI is defined in a geometric mean form and, thus, has the disadvantage of not being circular. Moreover, it faces the potential linear programming infeasibility problem in measuring cross-period DDFs. The GMLPI is constructed based on the global Malmquist index in Pastor and Lovell (2005) [43]. To define the GMLPI, we need the global environmental production technology, which is defined as $T^G = T^1 \cup T^2 \cup \dots T^T$. That is, the global environmental production technology envelops all the contemporaneous environmental technologies into a single environmental technology. The GMLPI is then defined as the ratio of the two DDFs based on the global environmental production at periods t and s, respectively. Figure 3.4 illustrates the concept of GMLPI, the two interior solid lines are the contemporaneous environmental technologies for time periods t and s, respectively, and the interior thick solid line is the global environmental technology.

Although the conventional MLPI is a powerful tool for measuring environmentally sensitive productivity growth, it has a shortcoming in that it does not incorporate group heterogeneities in the productivity analysis. One cannot directly compare the performance of DMUs operating under different production technologies [44]. The Metafrontier MLPI (MMLPI) could be a suitable method to consider group heterogeneities in a conventional MLPI. It constructs a group-frontier and a metafrontier separately to measure productivity growth.

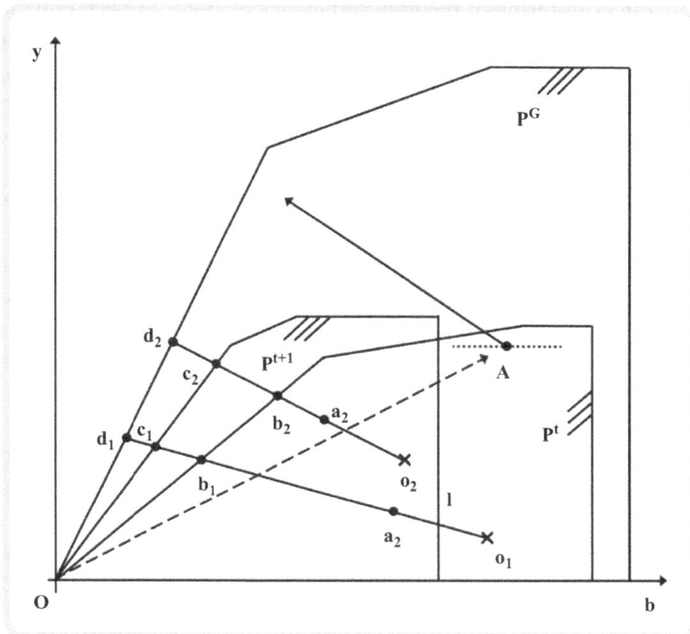

Figure 3.4 Illustration of Global MLPI approach

Source: Zhang N.; Y. Choi, "A note on the evolution of directional distance function an d its development in energy and environmental studies 1997–2013", *Renewable and Sustainable Energy Reviews*, 33(2014), p. 53.

Following the decomposition of the Metafrontier Malmquist index in Oh and Lee [45], we can decompose the non-radial Metafrontier Malmquist CO_2 emission performance index (NMMCPI), one of the MMLPI, into various components: a technical efficiency change (*EC*) index of CO_2 emissions, a best-practice gap change (*BPC*) index of CO_2 emission reduction technologies, and a technology gap change (*TGC*) index of CO_2 emission reductions as follows [42]:

$$
\begin{aligned}
MNMCPI(K^s, L^s, F^s, E^s, C^s) &= \frac{TCPI^G(.^{t+1})}{TCPI^G(.^t)} \\
&= \left[\frac{TCPI^C(.^{t+1})}{TCPI^C(.^t)}\right] * \left[\frac{TCPI^I(.^{t+1}) / TCPI^C(.^{t+1})}{TCPI^I(.^t) / TCPI^C(.^t)}\right] * \left[\frac{TCPI^G(.^{t+1}) / TCPI^I(.^{t+1})}{TCPI^G(.^t) / TCPI^I(.^t)}\right] \\
&= \left\{\frac{\left(\frac{1-\beta_C^{C*}}{1+\beta_E^{C*}}\right)^{t+1}}{\left(\frac{1-\beta_C^{C*}}{1+\beta_E^{C*}}\right)^{t}}\right\} * \left\{\frac{\left(\frac{1-\beta_C^{I*}}{1+\beta_E^{I*}}\right)^{t+1} / \left(\frac{1-\beta_C^{C*}}{1+\beta_E^{C*}}\right)^{t+1}}{\left(\frac{1-\beta_C^{I*}}{1+\beta_E^{I*}}\right)^{t} / \left(\frac{1-\beta_C^{C*}}{1+\beta_E^{C*}}\right)^{t}}\right\} * \left\{\frac{\left(\frac{1-\beta_C^{G*}}{1+\beta_E^{G*}}\right)^{t+1} / \left(\frac{1-\beta_C^{I*}}{1+\beta_E^{I*}}\right)^{t+1}}{\left(\frac{1-\beta_C^{G*}}{1+\beta_E^{G*}}\right)^{t} / \left(\frac{1-\beta_C^{I*}}{1+\beta_E^{I*}}\right)^{t}}\right\} \quad (3.8) \\
&= \left[\frac{TE^{t+1}}{TE^t}\right] * \left[\frac{BPR^{t+1}}{BPR^t}\right] * \left[\frac{TGR^{t+1}}{TGR^t}\right] = EC * BPC * TGC
\end{aligned}
$$

The efficiency change (*EC*) term in equation (3.8) is a measure of the "catch-up" effect in terms of technical efficiency changes in CO_2 emissions for a specific group for two time periods (t, $t + 1$). *EC* captures how close a power plant moves toward the contemporaneous environmental production technology. Here $EC >$ (or $<$) 1 means an efficiency gain (or loss). The best-practice gap change (*BPC*) index measures changes in the best-practice gap ratio for the CO_2 emission reduction technology between the contemporaneous environmental technology and the intertemporal environmental technology during two periods [42]. Here $BPC >$ (or $<$) 1 means that the contemporaneous technology frontier shifts toward (or far away from) the intertemporal technology frontier. Because *BPC* measures frontier shifts in a contemporaneous technology, it can be considered an innovation effect, as in the case of the technological change (*TC*) term in the conventional Malmquist index. *TGC* is a measure of changes in the technology gap ratio for CO_2 emission reductions between the intertemporal production technology frontier and the global frontier during two periods. $TGC >$ (or $<$) 1 indicates a decrease (increase) in the technology gap between the intertemporal technology for a specific group and the global technology. Therefore, *TGC* measures the technology leadership change for a given group [42].

Figure 3.5 shows the MMLPI and its decomposed components. This is a case of two groups (R_1, R_2) and two time periods (t, $t + 1$). Here a_1 and a_2 are observed

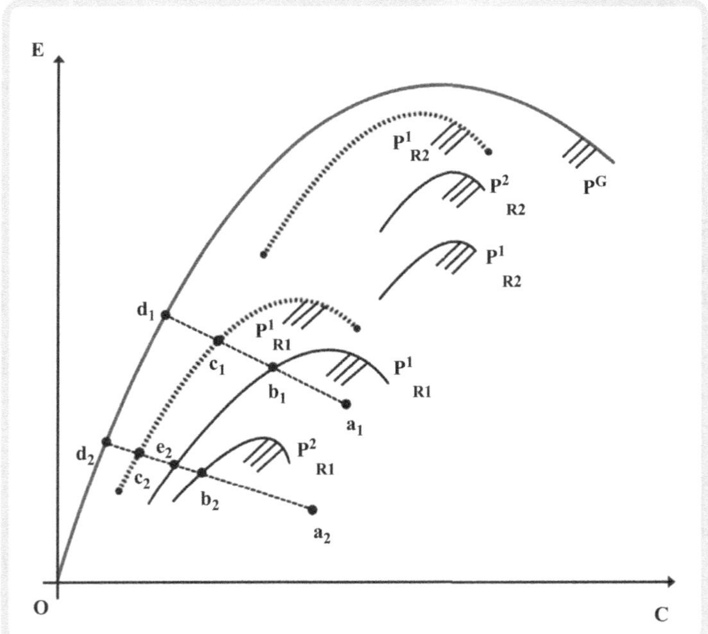

Figure 3.5 Illustration of the Metafrontier MLPI

Source: Zhang N.; Y. Choi, "A note on the evolution of directional distance function an d its development in energy and environmental studies 1997–2013", *Renewable and Sustainable Energy Reviews*, 33(2014), p. 52.

DMUs for the two periods t and $t + 1$, respectively, and P^{t}_{R1} and P^{t+1}_{R1} represent the contemporaneous environmental production technology of group R_1 in periods t and $t + 1$, respectively. P^{I}_{R1} is the intertemporal environmental production technology for group R_1, and P^{G}_{R} is the global environmental production technology for two groups.

The calculation of the MLPI is based on linear programming, and therefore, MLPI is a deterministic approach that measures performance relative to an estimate of the true and unobservable production technology. Since estimates of technology are based on finite samples, the DDF and MLPI based on these estimates are subject to sampling variation of the frontier. Thus, one cannot know whether the productivity growth is statistically significant or not. The bootstrapping method proposed in Simar and Wilson (1999) can be used to provide a statistical interpretation of the MLPI [46]. For a DMU, if one does not contain within the confidence intervals of MLPI, the improvement or deterioration in productivity growth of this specific DMU is statistically different from unity at the desired significance level.

Based on the basic DDF methodology and its various extensions, we could draw a figure of methodological structure of DDF model. Figure 3.6 is the comparative

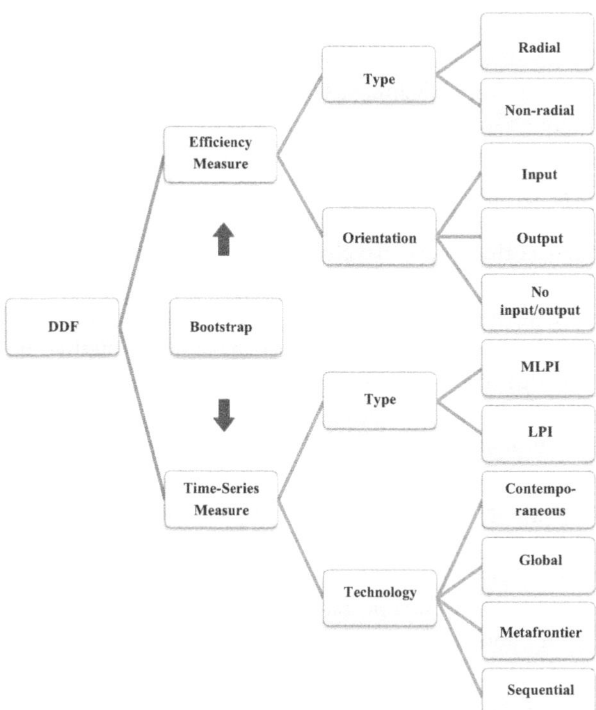

Figure 3.6 Methodological types of DDF model

Source: Zhang N.; Y. Choi, "A note on the evolution of directional distance function an d its development in energy and environmental studies 1997–2013", *Renewable and Sustainable Energy Reviews*, 33(2014), p. 53.

diagram of the DDF family. First, we should decide the efficiency measure of the DDF that consist of measure type and orientation. Then, if the time dimension is considered, the various time-series measures should be employed. Bootstrapping technology could be used for both efficiency measure and time-series measures.

6. Concluding remarks

Recently, we have experienced an increasing world temperature and many natural disasters worldwide. Almost every country in the world had the hottest summer in 2016, and many countries at the same time had terrible floods and drought. Many people die every day directly and/or indirectly due to the unforeseeable disaster coming from the terrible smog, dirty water, and huge mountains of waste. Unfortunately, the situation on the news seems to be aggravated over time, and now, we should do act to overcome this global warming and climate change. Even some of the developing countries such as China proclaimed that eco-friendly sustainable development or green growth is one of the most important fields of policies.

The United Nations established the World Environment Day on June 5 every year to celebrate the inauguration of the third green wave in Stockholm in 1982. Since then, there have been numerous efforts from the local as well as the international field of eco-friendly activities. Among them, the United Nations Framework Convention on Climate Change (UNFCCC) is the most important international venue for the governments to cooperate with each other to promote the sustainable green growth in COP meeting every year since its first meeting in Rio in 1992.

To promote sustainable development, many international organizations and professional entities have developed methodologies to measure, monitor, manage, and control the economic activities of economic entities from the macro-government perspectives, to the micro-firm-level or individual-level of sustainability indicators. Even if these efforts have not brought a universal global standard yet, at least, these indicators shed a light on the right direction for the optimal control for the future.

Likewise, green growth policies worldwide have promoted new challenges to protect the environment, find and develop new green technologies and business, and integrate all possible interest groups for equitable, viable, and sustainable development. Followed by the second revolution of the Internet, this third revolution of green growth has clearly made all economic entities aware of environmental impact and sustainable resource utilization. However, there is still a high level of doubt about green growth, especially from companies' perspectives. Most companies regard the new green growth paradigm as an additional burden with unbearable costs, resulting in the weakening of international competitiveness. There is still hot argument on the characteristic of green investment, that is whether these efforts are extra burden to increase the brand image of the company, or they result in higher values. Many private sectors as well as the governments from the developing countries may consider these green efforts as a kind of huddle for the economic development, transferring the future-generation debt of developed countries into the developing countries. Nonetheless, all the countries and private sectors worldwide agree now that environmental issues are not optional, but are key to survival of humankind. Altruism and self-sacrifice is the core spirit that all these economic entities should propagate worldwide.

And thus, to transform the passive attitude of the private sector and some governments of developing countries toward the new frontier of green growth, PPPs could be the best alternative as intermediaries to fill the missing links in collaboration networking. However, PPPs, as harmonized third parties, may not obtain successful governance due to internal bottlenecks as well as surrounding external difficulties. To utilize opportunities and strengths from the ever-rapidly changing environments, and to overcome threats and weaknesses of intermediation, this Chapter suggested four propositions for PPPs as appropriate intermediaries: facilitator, network manager, collaborator, and service provider. Even though these propositions were able to explain in more detail the roles and functions of the PPP, the study nonetheless did not provide further details about these propositions using comparative case studies. These remain as tasks of the future research.

Since sustainable development is a very complex process with regard to harmonizing all partners, it is much more important to organize collaborative networks, and to enhance the roles of network manager for good governance of continuing performance. Here, the collaborative network implies that each and every member of the cooperative network should communicate with each other to create value and share its created values among all partners in the networks such as consumer, worker, outsourcing other companies, local society, even in the people worldwide, using the synergy effect of diverse partners, not just helpers. Therefore, the organization and operation of sustainable development networking is extremely important for the future.

References

1 Choi, Yongrok, "Intermediary propositions for green growth with sustainable governance", *Sustainability*, 2015, 7(11), 14785–14801, doi:10.3390/su71114785.

2 Lerner, Michael. *Yellow Dust Storm Carries Chinese Pollutants to Korea* (Accessed on 24/02/2015: http://blogs.blouinnews.com/blouinbeatsciencehealth/2015/02/24/yellow-dust-storm-carries-chinese-pollutants-to-korea/).

3 Reuters News. *China to 'Declare War' on Pollution, Premier Says* (Accessed on 04/03/2014: http://www.reuters.com/article/2014/03/05/us-china-parliament-pollution-idUSBREA2405W20140305).

4 WCED (World Commission on Environment and Development). *Our Common Future*. Oxford: Oxford University Press (So-called Brundland Report), 1987.

5 OECD, *Towards Green Growth* (Accessed on 09/09/2015: http://www.keepeek.com/Digital-Asset-Management/oecd/environment/towards-green-growth_9789264111318-en#page4, doi:10.1787/9789264111318-en).

6 Chen, Shiyi; Zhen Xie, "Is China's e-governance sustainable? Testing Solow IT productivity paradox in China's context", *Technology Forecasting & Social Change*, 2015, 96, 51–61.

7 Fankhauser, Sam; Bowen, Alex; Calel, Raphael; Dechezleprêtre, Antoine; Grover, David; Rydge, James, *Who Will Win the Green Race? In Search of Environmental Competitiveness and Innovation*, Centre for Climate Change Economics and Policy, Working Paper No. 111, 2012.
8 Du Pisani, Jacobus A., "Sustainable development – Historical roots of the concept", *Environmental Sciences*, 2006, 3(2), 83–96.
9 Munir, K.A., "Competitive dynamics in face of technological discontinuity: A framework for action", *The Journal of High Technology Management Research*, 2003, 14(1), 93–109.
10 Choi, Y., *Global e-Business Management: Theory and Practice*. Seoul: Bomyoung Books, 2014.
11 *UNFCCC Report* (Accessed on 09/09/2015: http://report.mitigation2014.org/drafts/final-draft-postplenary/ipcc_wg3_ar5_final-draft_postplenary_chapter13.pdf).
12 Tax treaty issues related to emissions permits/credits. *OECD Report* (Accessed on 03/09/2015: http://www.oecd.org/tax/treaties/report-emissions-permits.pdf).
13 Background note: Emissions trading schemes around the world. *Parliament of Australia Report*, 06/06/2013 (Accessed on 03/09/2015: http://parlinfo.aph.gov.au/parlInfo/download/library/prspub/2501441/upload_binary/2501441.pdf;fileType=application/pdf).
14 Grubb, M., "The Economics of the Kyoto Protocol", *World Economics*, July–September 2003, 4(3), 143–189. http://ynccf.net/pdf/CDM/The_economic_of_Kyoto_protocol.pdf (Accessed online at 25/03/2010).
15 UNFCCC. *Transitional Committee for the Design of the Green Climate Fund*, 2011 (Accessed on 24/04/2016: http://unfccc.int/cooperation_and_support/financial_mechanism/green_climate_fund/items/5869.php).
16 Doyle, Allister; Lewis, Barbara, *World Seals Landmark Climate Accord, Marking Turn from Fossil Fuels*. Reuters, 2015 (Accessed on 12/12/2015: http://www.reuters.com/article/us-climatechange-summit-idUSKBN0TV04L20151212).
17 Choi, Y.; Zhang, Ning, "Introduction to the special issue on 'the Sustainable Asia Conference 2014'", *Sustainability*, 2015, 7, 1502–1695.
18 *Sustainable Society Foundation* (Accessed on 03/09/2015: http://www.ssfindex.com/).
19 Willis, Alan, "The role of the global reporting initiative's sustainability reporting guidelines in the social screening of investments", *Journal of Business Ethics*, 2003, 43(3), 233–237.
20 *ISO 26000* (Accessed on 20/04/2016: https://en.wikipedia.org/wiki/ISO_26000); ISO, *ISO 26000 and the International Integrated Reporting* (Accessed on 20/04/2016: http://www.iso.org/iso/iso_26000_and_ir_international_integrated_reporting_en_-_lr.pdf).
21 Gao, P., "Government in the catching-up of technology innovation: Case of administrative intervention in China", *Technology Forecasting & Social Change*, 2015, 96, 4–14.
22 Kim, K.; Leipziger, Danny M., *Korea: A Case of Government-led Development*, World Bank Report Series (The Lessons of East Asia), 1993.
23 Rim, C., "Korea's age boom: How South Korea is addressing the reality of low fertility and a rapidly aging society", *The Journal* (Accessed on 24/07/2015: http://journal.aarpinternational.org/a/b/2013/02/Koreas-Age-Boom-How-

South-Korea-is-Addressing-the-Reality-of-Low-Fertility-and-a-Rapidly-Aging-Society).
24 Choi, Y., "Introduction to the special issue on 'Sustainable e-governance in northeast Asia: Challenges for sustainable innovation'", *Technology Forecasting & Social Change*, 2015, 96, 1–3.
25 Kobayashi, Hideyo, *Corporation Japan* (Written in Japanese, Translated Edition of Korean). Seoul: Ihlsin Sa Publishing Co., 1998.
26 Light, Andrew, *Has Japan Killed the Kyoto Protocol? Even If It Has There's Still Hope for a Climate Agreement* (Web-article), 08/12/2010 (Available online at: https://www.americanprogress.org/issues/green/news/2010/12/08/8733/has-japan-killed-the-kyoto-protocol/).
27 Berkeley Earth Publishes, *KILLER AIR: Study on Air Pollution in China* (Accessed on 07/09/2015: http://berkeleyearth.org/wp-content/uploads/2015/08/Press-Release-Killer-Air-August-2015.pdf).
28 *Emission Trading System in Shenzhen* (Accessed on 08/09/2015: http://www.cerx.cn/inventorEducation/364.htm).
29 Korea Herald Newspaper dated on January 6th 2015, *Emission Rights Trading to Kick Off Next Week* (Accessed on 07/09/2015: http://khnews.kheraldm.com/view.php?ud=20150106000853&md=20150106210142_BL).
30 Korea Herald Newspaper dated on October 30th, 2015, *Korea's Systematic Recycling Drive Boosts Sustainability* (Accessed on 20/04/2016: http://khnews.kheraldm.com/view.php?ud=20151030001070&md=20151102003653_BL).
31 Choi, Y., "The role of intermediation on the international aid for the governance of technical training program", *Technology Forecasting & Social Change*, 2015, 96, 32–39.
32 Tax treaty issues related to emissions permits/credits. *OECD Report* (Accessed on 03/09/2015 http://www.oecd.org/tax/treaties/report-emissions-permits.pdf).
33 Background Note: Emissions trading schemes around the world. *Parliament of Australia Report*, 06/06/2013 (Accessed on 03/09/2015: http://parlinfo.aph.gov.au/parlInfo/download/library/prspub/2501441/upload_binary/2501441.pdf;fileType=application/pdf).
34 Choi, Y.; Yu, Y., "The influence of perceived corporate sustainability practices on employees and organizational performance", *Sustainability*, 2014, 6, 348–365.
35 Leibenstein, Harvey, *General X-Efficiency Theory and Economic Development*. New York: Oxford University Press, 1978.
36 Choi, Y., "Optimizing risk management for the sustainable performance of the regional innovation system in Korea through met mediation", *Human and Ecological Risk Assessment*, 2009 15, 270–280.
37 Zhang, N.; Choi, Y., "A note on the evolution of directional distance function and its development in energy and environmental studies 1997–2013", *Renewable and Sustainable Energy Reviews*, 2014, 33, 50–59.
38 Färe, R.; Grosskopf, S.; Lovell, C.A.K., "Multilateral productivity comparisons when some outputs are undesirable: A non-parametric approach", *Review of Economics and Statistics*, 1989, 71, 90–98.
39 Shephard, R.W., *Theory of Cost and Production Functions*. Princeton: Princeton University Press, 1970.
40 Chambers, R.G.; Chung, Y.H.; Färe, R., "Benefit and distance functions", *Journal of Economic Theory*, 1996, 70, 407–419.

41 Fukuyama, H.; Weber, W.L., "A directional slacks-based measure of technical efficiency", *Socio-Economic Planning Sciences*, 2009, 43, 274–287.
42 Zhang, N.; Choi, Y., "A comparative study on CO2 emission performance change of fossil fuel power plants between China and Korea", *Energy Policy*, 2013, 62, 324–332.
43 Pastor, J.T.; Lovell, C.A.K. "A global Malmquist productivity index", *Economic Letters*, 2005, 88, 266–271.
44 Oh, D., "A metafrontier approach for measuring an environmentally sensitive productivity growth index", *Energy Economics*, 2010, 32, 146–157.
45 Oh, D.H.; Lee, J.D., "A metafrontier approach for measuring Malmquist productivity index", *Empirical Economics*, 2010, 32, 46–64.
46 Simar, L.; Wilson, P.W., "Estimating and bootstrapping Malmquist indices", *European Journal of Operational Research*, 1999, 115, 459–471.

Part II

Green of IT industry

Overview

As the sustainable development made outstanding paradigm shift from the traditional profit-oriented economic activities toward the harmonized creation of the values based on the network management, IT revolution promoted by Internet changed all the existing theories into the interdependent networking paradigm. This chapter examines the historical background of Internet revolution based on the paradigm shift of the terminologies from the e-commerce, via e-business, toward the social or smart e-business. There has been wide consensus that the netizens, the Internet users as a group, made a huge change in our society, economic structure, and all the technological bases of the industries. The power of netizen led to a rapidly changing environment in the sustainable development as well. However, it is certainly noteworthy that the IT applications and e-business became the platform for all the existing theories as well as the strategic decision by all the economic agents of government and the private sectors. Therefore, this part of the book shall explain the green platform as an integrated part of two important mega trends in the history and its promotion strategies on behalf of the information and communication technology (IT or ICT) industries. It is called simply "the green of IT". Now, let's navigate the new era of green IT for the future of mankind in the history.

4 Internet revolution and the new frontier

1. Background: collabonomics in soft economy

1.1 Collabonomics: from manufacturing to assembling

What the Apple does for their profit? Do they produce any iPhone by itself? Is Apple a manufacturer? The answer is no. The Apple company never made iPhone by itself for sale. They just *assembled* all the business functions with strategic alliances and outsourcing partners with some "fancy gadgets" on their products. They never *manufactured* even a single product for commercial use. They just developed new items such as Apple computer, iPhone, and iWatch, and organized all the production and marketing procedures to maximize their own profits from these new items based on the outsourcing and strategic partnership over the world.

Not only the Apple company, but there is no single manufacturer in the world that can produce all the modules and parts of the final product without the support from other business partners. For example, even the micro business of a small fish cake baker in the street of Korea should buy the black soybean paste from China, because the soybean paste in Korea is too expensive to put a very cheap fish cake in the street. Thus, even this single fish cake seller does collaborate with many partners such as soybean farmers in China, an international carrier and importer, and many, many other parts and material suppliers. Likewise, all the companies in the world should depend on each other on their production and distribution process. There is no single manufacturer that provides all the parts and materials alone in its production process. This kind of collaboration network could enhance the comparative efficiency much, much better, because all the participants of this collaboration network are professionals in their fields. Any company on the collaboration network should concentrate on its own core competence, and thus any failure of the company in its core field of competence could bring the failure to all network members, as shown in the Toyota car recall mishap worldwide in 2009. Toyota wants to keep decreasing its manufacturing costs and maximizing the profits in the short run, and thus the brake parts outsourcing company has to use brakes of a lower quality with a hole to keep the floor mat tightened missing. Due to this mismatching brake pad and floor mat, there have been several car accidents and several consumer complains. But Toyota hesitated to listen to these voices, and finally, these consumers published their claims on the web. Soon an enormous number of complaints followed, resulting in the government intervention and inspection of these complaints and global "recall-gate" of Toyota car in the year 2009. From this lesson we can learn that the profit maximization for just the owner of a manufacturing company can lead to loss of loyalties of its workers, consumers, outsourcing partners, local society, even the global world itself!

Now, all the businesses in the world have changed their paradigm of business competitiveness *from manufacturing to assembling*. The paradigm shift from manufacturing to assembling implies that the most important success factor of the global business depends not only on its own core competence, but on all the partners in its global collaboration networking. Instead of profit maximization based on the zero-sum game, the win-win type of voluntary participation on the innovation became the core governance factor for the sustainable management in this new era, because the assembler, not a manufacturer, gets the highest portion of profits from the new innovation, while all the other partners certainly get more by value (not just simple profits) sharing. In this kind of interdependent economy, therefore, the network manager gets the best portion of values, because it guarantees the satisfaction for all the partners in a sustainable manner. We call this kind of value creation and sharing structure *soft economy*, compared to the traditional *hard economy* led by the manufacturers.

Moreover, this kind of efficiency from collaboration network is so-called *collabonomics*, a compound noun made of "collaboration" and "economics". Collabonomics implies we live in the world of interdependent economy, and the group intelligence or group economies of networking are much more important for the sustainable success under the rapidly changing market environments. What you produce and consume certainly depends on the impact that others have on the production and consumption. All a single assembler, not a manufacturer, needs is the core competence in the collaboration network. This core competence could come from the manufacturing of main parts or module, or just logistics management with private brand by a competitive distributor. The other professional partners in the field support all other business functions. This interdependent economy created the collabonomics as the new way of innovative decision or activities by group intelligence. When the author visited Microsoft in 2002, as part of the Korean government sponsoring project, a leader of Microsoft told a group of the Korean professors that Microsoft is no longer a software producer, but that it just wants to be a service provider with the new business platform Dot Net, an Internet platform for self-developed web services. Well, it is true that even Microsoft could not lead the innovation of the global business world every day, and thus they just want to recruit the partners for the innovation frontier for their new business. Microsoft wants to be considered a service provider or just assembler in the collaborative innovation platform.

Now, who gets the maximized profit from this collabonomics network? Sometimes, it could be the final assemblers such as Hyundai or Samsung, but sometimes distributers such as Wal-Mart and JC Penny stores when they create their own brand (called Private Brand or PB product) could get the leadership of the networking. Internet provided these companies with strength to these companies to overcome any time and space limits for their cooperation with other partners. Of course, the government could get the benefits from these interdependent Internet-based activities as well. The government utilized Internet to communicate with the private sectors and do business with private sectors, such as open Internet procurement with companies and tax collection with the consumers. But, most of all, consumers are the winner to utilize the strongest power to initiate, and modify the production procedures by *smart* group intelligence. As a group of consumers on the Internet, the power of netizens made many outstanding performances for companies to recall their products and to promote the diverse social responsibilities of the companies. Now, the market has changed in its leading role from the manufacturing companies to the smart consumers, and thus, this smart consumer as the leader of the market got the maximum benefits from the *soft economy*, and the major mission of a company is now to make these smart consumers their *business partners*.

Terminology: private brand or PB product

Private brand is defined as a brand placed on products that a large retailer has created for smaller manufacturers. The leading retailer places their own brand label on the final good which was created by a third-party manufacturer. Private branding is a cost-effective way to produce a product without a large manufacturing or design team. It is also known as private label. Many private brands became successful due to the flexibility in production and very little capital required to start (no need to build manufacturing plants). For the manufacturer, the benefit of selling private brands is the increased sales volume and stable supply contracts. Even if this private brand product is based on the win-win game rule with the harmonized interests of more sales to manufacturers, more customers to the retailer, and lower price (or higher quality) to the consumer, it may bring risks associated with relying on outside partners. But in general, these firms are well established and specialized in product manufacturing. PB products are directly based on the demand from the market. If the customers want the lowest price, the PB could fit this demand through the no-brand marketing, while if the customer demands a certain quantity, it also fits this kind of special demands. In Korea, many large retailers develop PB based on the quick response on the market. For example, most of Korean customers buy toilet paper as a gift when their friends move into a new house, implying no worries about things such as smooth toilet paper in the future. Due to this special purpose, toilet paper is the most popular PB products in Korea, not too expensive and easy to carry in hands. With this kind of PB, the customers are the leaders in the collaboration network between the manufacturers and distributors.

1.2 Soft economy with Web 3.0

In any case, the collaboration network requires a proactive participation from all network members for their best performance. This kind of interdependent business structure is called *soft economy*. The original meaning of soft economy was defined as the low level of economic development status where the national resources or infrastructure is too low to take off. Recently, however, the soft economy has changed its meaning due to much different perspectives of market governance. In this book, soft economy is defined as the invisible value-oriented network (or interdependent) economy for the sustainable and performance-oriented management when the largest part of created values goes to the network manager of collaboration network. Soft economy is defined as the collaborative business network to create and share the values among the interdependent partners of the network.

The core of the soft economy comes from the network manager to initiate the collaboration with the best partners in their fields, harmonize their conflicting interests, and finally share the created values based on the proactive participation of all the partners. The soft economy depends on diverse network managing companies under the different collaboration networks. The network manager for the *collabonomics* requires not just passive assemblers, but more innovative facilitators in the product development and promotion of it. The network manager is a more proactive economic agent in seeking the appropriate business partners to promote the best teamwork for all. In terms of this network manager, the soft economy can be characterized by several paradigms as follows.

First of all, the soft economy could be characterized with the emphasis on the fusion and integration. The innovation should be promoted by open collaboration network instead of monopolized, closed network inside of a big company. As seen in the case of Sony, a monopolistic video manufacturer in the world in 1990s, if the major player on collaboration network insists on its leading role and does not allow other partners to participate in the innovation process, the continuous successful innovation is not sustainable. And thus, Sony lost its video market even if it produces the best-quality video tapes in the world. JVC, Samsung, and many other video tape-manufacturing companies won the market not by their own competitiveness, but by their interoperability. In the soft economy, the network manager should make all other members partners, instead of just simple helpers. On this open innovation network, the network manager should "create the value" from innovative operation of networking by new product, new functions of old product, new approaches to the market, etc. In this regard, the most important feature for the open innovation could come from the integration of diverse business functions and fusion of different concepts and approaches. Collabonomics was first used to describe cooperation by makers of luxury electronics and automobiles. But now, the meaning is extended, so it is spreading to food and fashion in different ways. The most representative case for this fusion type of collaboration could be found in "LG-Prada Phone". Through "LG-Prada Phone", LG extend their customer filed from early adapter to fashion people, which can trigger other people to enter this kind of new business for collaboration.

The second characteristic of the soft economy can be explained with the concepts of Web 2.0 and Web 3.0. The role of Internet in our daily life has changed from just information sharing (Web 1.0) to the reciprocal participation of the information fabrication (Web 2.0). When the mobile phone was introduced, most of mobile phone users got entertainment from the phone through Internet games or simple information search such as stock market price or latest news. This initial stage of information-oriented Internet use is called Web 1.0 era. Soon, the Internet users started to share information from their experiences and professional education background, and this rich information made the Web 2.0 era through the participation and Internet feedback. There are too many hidden heroes in our daily life on the Internet and too diverse, yet so many funny or interesting videos on the Internet. Such user-created contents represent examples of the Web 2.0 era.

Recently, the explosive distribution of smartphones made the users not just participate in the creating of information, but also the values by their own mobile applications (so-called smart apps). These apps soon gained the popularity among the users, and then they lead to profits and advertisement commissions or higher loyalties from the app users. This kind of value-creating web utilization on the Internet is called Web 3.0, and we shall discuss latter the conceptual characteristics of Web 3.0 in more detail. Now, we are in the era of Web 3.0. Everybody can create his or her own Internet business such as commercial apps without much difficulty, and these applications may lead to an unexpected dream of success come true. That is the true meaning of Web 3.0. Therefore, do dream for your future!

2. Paradigm shift in e-business

2.1 Historical background of the paradigm shift

Before we analyze the beginnings of e-businesses, a historical overview of the paradigm shift could contribute to the in-depth knowledge about the background of the Internet revolution. In general, there was almost no historical change in the classical economy for about 3,000 years, beginning approximately in 1,000 BC until the middle of the eighteenth century. All these years could be described as an agricultural economy and could be classified within the basic paradigm of a self-sufficient economy. As Say's law says – the law of markets in classical economics indicates – aggregate production necessarily creates an equal quantity of aggregate demand in the self-sufficient economy. If you produce, you or your neighbor shall consume it. Supply creates its own demand! Just imagine the manorial system of medieval times, when the agricultural farmer produces what he or his small society wants to consume for a certain period. If there is a surplus of one good, there must be unmet demand for another product, and these items could be bartered in this small society. There should be no surplus or shortage of the product at the end of any period. Therefore, a shoemaker produces just the shoes that the citizens in the manor want at any given time. The son and grandson of the shoemaker become shoemakers because the self-sufficient society requires all the producers to produce as expected in that society over time.

However, the *Industrial Revolution* changed the *self-sufficiency* paradigm of the classical economy and replaced it with the new paradigm of *economies of scale*, which implies that the more you produce, the lower the unit (or average) costs. As Adam Smith says in his famous book *The Wealth of Nations* (1776), larger production returns cost advantages that enterprises obtain owing to scale and standardization of operation, with the cost per unit of output generally decreasing with increasing scale because of the division of labor. This neo-classical economy under *industrialization* became so powerful in capital-intensive mass production that mass production afforded the leading power of the social structure to the company owners and government, resulting in a supply-oriented society. The *economies of scale* paradigm made companies persuade the passive consumer through the mass media to buy their (oversupplied) products: mass consumption was the result. Even so, producers could not sell all of their products, which was a result of the innovative manufacturing capacity under industrialization. Therefore, during 300 years of the industrialization era, all the countries looked for overseas markets, such as colonies, and this battle for the markets, so-called imperialism, made World Wars I and II consecutively in the one generation period of the twentieth century.

Since then, the world has wanted to open up mutually beneficial economies and protect against another world war. Thus, the United States developed and utilized the computer, and this computer-led information society has brought diverse changes to our societies globally. The information society (or economy) resulting from this new paradigm of *informatization* places much more emphasis on information, implying that information is money and power. If you just get out of the subway and feel thirsty, then you may just run into the closest convenience store to buy a Coke or other drink. Unfortunately, as soon as you begin to drink it, you may find another big discount store just around the corner with the advertisement, "Buy one get one free!" If you had the information available, you would certainly buy from this store, not the previous one. Unfortunately, you need to spend all of your time and effort to find the "right" information, and thus, white collar workers with the support of information, lead the whole society. All of these white collar workers emphasized the productivity that comes from having the information. Higher quality with better productivity has replaced simple economies of scale. In this information era, supported by computers and other electronic tools, "information is money and power."

However, this information society could not be sustainable after the advent of the Internet, because the Internet provided too much information, well a flood of information, and you may have much more difficulty finding the right direction in a sea of information. Now, the problem is not the lack of information, but the confusion that comes from too much information. After 30 years of the information society, the world has finally entered the Internet era. This has made the whole society change rapidly. We will analyze more in detail the role of the Internet in this rapidly changing society.

2.2 Conceptual change from e-commerce to social business

The origins of the Internet reach back to research commissioned by the US government in the 1960s to build robust, fault-resilient communication via computer networks to protect the defense information system and data from the potential attacks during the Cold War period. The funding of a new US backbone by integration of the Alpha defense network and education network of the National Science Foundation in the 1980s, as well as private funding of other commercial backbones, led to worldwide participation in the development of new networking technologies, and finally the grand merger of many networks in early 1990s.

The terms Internet and the World Wide Web are often used interchangeably; it is common to speak of "going online" when invoking a web browser to view web pages. The World Wide Web (abbreviated as WWW or W3, commonly known as the web) is a system of interlinked hypertext documents accessible via the Internet. With a web browser, one can view web pages that may contain text, images, videos, and other multimedia and navigate between them via hyperlinks. Tim Berners-Lee of CERN, a European research organization, wrote a proposal in March 1989 for what would eventually become the World Wide Web. Experts generally agree that a turning point for the World Wide Web began with the introduction of the Mosaic web browser (later it became the first commercial web browser of Navigator), a graphical browser developed by Marc Andreessen in 1993. But it could be more safe to say that the Internet has begun in 1995, when Amazon.com introduced a new way of Internet business utilization, and soon it became extremely popular.

Although there are still arguments about the first official application of the Internet, it is safe to say that the Internet became open for commercial use in 1995. (Frankly speaking, when Internet begun its first commercial use, the author of the book worked at Korea Telecom, which is the largest national backbone telecommunication company in Korea. But the author never heard about the Internet during those three and a half years of employment, until February 1995, when he transferred to university. For this reason, the author personally argues that the year 1995 is the first year of the Internet open to public!)

In the initial stage of Internet for commercial utilization, the electronic commerce (EC or e-commerce) is the only single type of Internet-based business. E-commerce is defined as *the commercial transaction of buying, transferring, or exchanging products, services, and/or information via computer networks, especially on the Internet.* E-commerce has shown great potential from many perspectives, including business process, service, learning, collaboration, and community activities. E-commerce is often confused with e-business. However, we need to understand why the terminology changed from e-commerce to e-business, because the change of the terminology implies the shift of major function of Internet utilization from simple maximization of profit by e-commerce toward the value creation by e-business.

Of course, e-commerce was the first and the only type of commercial use on the Internet. It started with business-to-consumer type (B2C, or BtoC) of the traditional transaction on the Internet such as Amazon.com. In the initial stage of EC, as the terminology implies, it is just the same as traditional commercial transaction using Internet as a tool to promote the smooth transaction without any time and space limits. Therefore, the purpose of Internet use is exactly the same as the traditional business management: ***profit maximization***. The traditional company could gain the market access much more easily via Internet and effective communication with consumers via Internet. All the efforts by the companies focused on this easy and effective communication with consumers to maximize their profits from the commercial transaction on the Internet. In this traditional marketing perspective, the B2C type of e-commerce needs to be differentiated with ones of other traditional brick companies, but for different marketing purpose only. It has the same purpose as traditional commerce, but it uses the new tool of Internet for the marketing channel only, which resulted in the new concept of *e-commerce*.

However, as e-commerce grew increasingly popular in the world, many companies tried to extend their commercial use of Internet to the backhand office management such as warehouse control or automatic ordering system for materials and parts, or even with the automatic connection with banking system for payment. This kind of fulfillment of sales contracts requires the participation of many partners in the collaboration network. As more and more members participate in the single commercial transaction, the need to standardize all the information sharing as well as the punctual synchronization based on the cooperative, and/or simultaneous procedures of the commercial transaction and its diverse supporting business activities, is increasing. In this case, e-commerce may not be appropriate to describe all these extended activities surrounding B2C. This kind of new business that started in 1998 is called the business-to-business (B2B, or BtoB) type of Internet-based business. Moreover, the diverse application of B2B made the new trend of the Internet use.

The purpose of Internet is not limited to the commercial use, but it includes the internal company intranet collaboration such as automatic cooperation between diverse departments like accounting and financing units, as well as the outside of business functions such as e-tax payment (government to business, G2B). Clearly, these intranet activities, such as the enterprise resource planning (ERP) system and extranet e-tax payment, are related to each other through a mission more diverse than just profit-maximization commercial transaction activities. Such newly created business functions from the extensive Internet use could yield a higher quality of services or better user satisfaction, undoubtedly including a higher profit. These excellent results of the new Internet use could be termed "*the value*", and the activities to create these values are not anymore traditional e-commerce. Therefore, they changed the name and invented new name of "e-business", because now the Internet is widely used inside of the company (intranet such as ERP) and outside of the company (extranet such as Supply Chain Management, SCM) not only for commercial use, but also for "*creating values*". Especially, intranet and extranet are not open networks, but closed Internets for only certified members, and these "closed-Internet" users need the standardized general format such as

Electronic Data Interchange (EDI) as their automatic synchronization activities. Based on EDI, the automatic concurrent engineering (CE) between the departments of the inside company, as well as the synchronized collaboration among the partner organizations such as banks and outsourcing companies, is widely utilized e-business on the Internet to create values.

Electronic business, or e-business, is the application of information and communication technologies (ICT) in support of all the activities of business functions such as marketing, financing, accounting, and manufacturing management. E-business constitutes the exchange of products and business services between businesses, groups, and individuals and can be seen as one of the essential activities of any business. Electronic business focuses on the use of ICT to enable the external activities and relationships of the business with individuals, groups, and other businesses. Electronic business or e-business enables companies to link their internal and external data-processing systems more efficiently and flexibly, to work more closely with suppliers and partners, and to better satisfy the needs and expectations of their customers and all other partners such as outsourcing companies, other departments of the same company and the government. The Internet became much widely acceptable to the traditional businesses through the new way of standard EDIs. Companies use more private and hence more secure networks for more effective and efficient management of their managerial or business functions. In practice, e-business is much more in its applications than just e-commerce. While e-business refers to more strategic focus with an emphasis on the functions that occur using electronic capabilities, e-commerce is a subset of overall marketing strategies. E-commerce seeks to add revenue streams using the World Wide Web or the Internet, to build and enhance relationships with clients and partners, and to improve efficiency, while e-business enhances the quality of business functions, services, as well as the higher, but invisible values for all the members of its own business network.

E-business involves business processes spanning the entire value chain: electronic purchasing and supply chain management (SCM), electronic order processing, handling customer service, and cooperating with business partners. Special technical standards for e-business such as EDI facilitate the exchange of data among companies. E-business software solutions allow the integration of intra- and inter-firm business processes. E-business is conducted using the web, the Internet, intranets, extranets, or some combination of these. Thus, *e-business means the new activities to create the value based on the network management.*

Due to growing popularity of the e-business, there has been explosion of expectations in the early 2000s, starting the burst of bubbles in such an e-business model without a specific revenue source in the real world. Most people thought the ideal innovative idea could make money because Internet was becoming more and more popular, and some e-businesses such as Google made a great success not from its revenues, but from diverse sources of revenues such as advertising sponsorship. Well, it seemed like the dreams could come true! However, it was just an exception. Without detailed business strategies, ideal models of web site businesses such as "I love school.com" in Korea could not make any tangible revenue, and thus many people realized that the value of e-business should be based on the commerce-related one-source, multi-use type of diverse business activities of its core competence. E-business should also include the commercial success at least in the long-term and thus many web companies in the Asian countries as well as in the United States had bankrupted at the beginning of the twenty-first century.

Terminology: Internet, intranet, and extranet

The ***Internet*** is a global system of interconnected computer networks that use the standard Internet protocol suite (TCP/IP) to serve billions of users worldwide. It is a "network of networks" that consists of millions of private, public, academic, business, and government networks, ranging from local to global in scope, connected by a broad array of electronic, wireless, and optical networking technologies. An ***intranet*** is a computer network that uses an Internet protocol technology to share information, operational systems, or computing services within an organization. This term is used in contrast to Internet, an open network between organizations, and instead refers to a network within an organization. Sometimes, the term refers only to the organization's internal web site, but it may be a more extensive part of the organization's information technology infrastructure, and it may be composed of multiple local area networks (LANs). An intranet can be understood as a private analog of the Internet, or as a closed extension of the Internet confined to organizational members. The most representative intranet is enterprise resource planning system (ERP). The ERP is business management set of software, typically a suite of integrated applications, that an organization can use to collect, store, manage, and interpret data from many business activities such as product planning, manufacturing, and marketing management. The ERP facilitates the information flow between all business functions and manages all the resources of the company using the integrated intranet. The ERP systems manage all the business resources of cash, raw materials, production capacity, as well as the status of business commitments on these resources. The ERP provides an integrated view of core business processes, often in real time, using common databases.

Intranets are sometimes contrasted to extranets. While intranets are generally restricted to employees of the organization, extranets may also be accessed by customers, suppliers, or other approved parties. ***Extranets*** extend a private network onto the Internet with special provisions for authentication, authorization, and accounting. An extranet is a computer network that allows controlled access from the outside, for specific business or educational purposes. In a business-to-business context, an extranet can be viewed as an extension of an organization's intranet that is extended to users outside of the organization, usually partners, vendors, and suppliers, in isolation from all other Internet users. The most representative extranet is supply chain management system (SCM) for the participating member companies out of the specific manufacturer. The SCM is defined as the planning, execution, control, and monitoring of all the supply chain activities with the objective of creating integrated value, building a dynamic infrastructure with outsourcing partners, leveraging worldwide logistics, synchronizing supply with demand, and measuring performance globally. Thus, the SCM is the management of the flow of goods and services based on the extranet, a closed Internet outside of the company among the partners. In many organizations, intranets and extranets are protected from unauthorized external access among the members only by means of a network gateway and firewall.

2.3 Structural factors of e-business

In the initial stage of the B2C type, the Internet was just used as a tool to differentiate competing products in the limitless time and space cyber market. To maximize its profits in the cyber markets, the company could make more effort to differentiate their web site's performance from others. To differentiate their web site-based marketing, they needed to differentiate their business strategies with more uniquely customized technologies, and to utilize policy incentives as well as the regulatory frame. These kinds of differentiated activities using Internet as e-commerce in the first generation is sometimes called Internet marketing or cyber marketing. The major direction or paradigm of the Internet marketing emphasizes, therefore, the differentiation. In order to successfully separate one's own business from others, the three factors of business strategy, technology, and policies are the most important core factors. Business strategy for differentiation is important in that it gives a unique position or concept to the public. Technology could be one of the core competencies to differentiate its Internet use in its reliability, creativity, and easy and effective use. Of course, the policy factors also make a great influence on the successful operation of e-business. If a policy prefers regulation rather than promotion, it is crucial for the e-business does not have to go far for new innovation. Therefore, these three factors of business strategy, technology, and policies are the structural factors of e-commerce or web marketing of the e-business.

The e-business, from the perspective of cooperative transactions in the value-creative network, is based on a procedural approach, an approach extremely different from other social science perspectives, such as the structural approach in economics, or the functional approach in business management. Based on the procedures involved, e-business consists of marketing activities to conclude legal contracts, and the implementation procedures after the contracts are signed. The former is called *web marketing or front-office management* and differs significantly from the latter, because of its paradigm of differentiation. In order to win in a competitive market, the companies should transform their web sites into marketing tools as unique and customized as possible for the "prosumer", a proactively participating consumer in the production process. The latter is called *e-automation or back-office management* because its activities are focused on the paperless and/or automatic implementation of the contract among the interrelated partner companies and other organizations. This may include those involved in automatic procurement by the subsidiaries for the supply of parts and modules, financial transactions with the bank, automatic delivery orders to the transporter, custom clearance of international trade, or tax payments with government agencies.

All these automated or inter-cooperative activities are based on the EDI in general, and thus the structural factors of the EDI could be considered as the factors for cooperative standardization as well. As with all machine friendly information-sharing systems, EDI should be based on the standard document format to share the information with the diverse partners. For this purpose, the United Nations created UN/EDIFACT (Electronic Data Interchange for Administration, Commerce, and Transport) in 1987 as the ISO standard ISO 9735. The EDIFACT standard provides a set of syntax rules to structure data, an interactive exchange protocol (I-EDI), and standard messages that allow multi-country and multi-industry exchanges. To facilitate cooperation among the partners, EDI worldwide has a standard format at the heart of paperless automation. For example, the "implic.edi" filename implies an import license from the Korean government to the importing company. Unfortunately, EDI is a machine friendly document and thus an EDI user cannot easily handle the file. In order to support this standard format, therefore, a user-friendly system is required as the second structural factor of EDI. The user system consists of the hardware, such as the common carrier leased line and leased terminal, etc., and the software of the input/output system, which transforms the system as well as the transferring system. Using these user systems, the user can input the data more effectively, transform them into a machine-readable file, and transfer them into its own leased line for security. As cooperation among the partners requires the utmost security, this process needs a closed extranet secured by the third party. One of the most representative EDI networks in the world is SWIFT. The Society for Worldwide Interbank Financial Telecommunication (SWIFT) provides a network that enables financial institutions worldwide to handle financial transactions in a secure, standardized, and reliable environment. For this purpose, SWIFT, as the authorized third-party value-added-network (VAN) operator, also provides user systems, such as software and services, to financial institutions, much of it for use on the SWIFTNet Network and ISO 9362. Like SWIFT, all the EDI files should be monitored and managed by a certified third party of value-added-network (VAN) operation. The VAN operator provides the user system, certify and modify the standard form of EDIs, and authenticate the EDI transfer for non-repudiation. It is crucial that the VAN operator, as the network manager, authenticates the contents of the EDI. Finally, all these information-sharing and information-based forms of automation require a legal

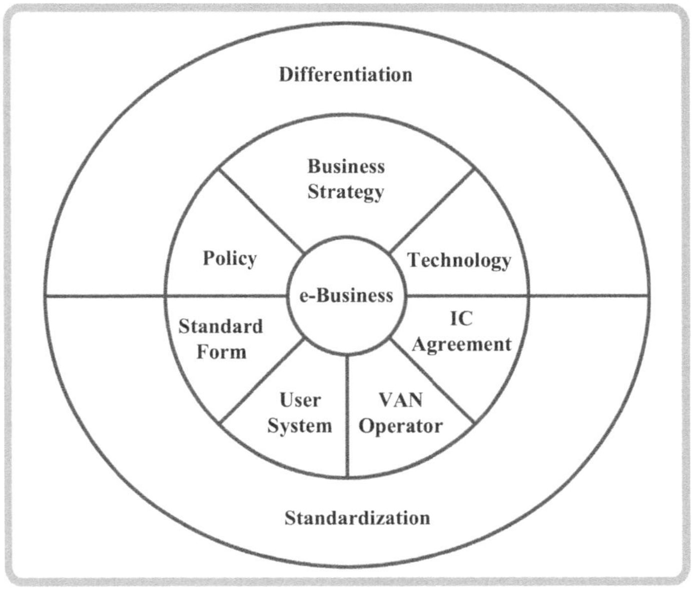

Figure 4.1 Structural factors and their paradigm of e-business

framework for handling possible future claims and making the predictable use of EDI more transparent. Thus, interchange agreement (IA) could be the fourth structural factor for standardization based on EDI. Because EDI members sometimes are involved in diverse arbitrage issues globally, consensus is required on the terminology, and terms and conditions for EDI among the partners; thus, IA could provide a more effective information-sharing environment. All these four factors of the standard format, the user system, VAN operator, and interchange agreement (IA) provide an effective platform for the partners to cooperate with each other more reliably, and secure activities using the Internet. Now, if we combine these four structural factors with the three web marketing factors, the structural factors e-business could have are two dimensions of the paradigm of differentiation in front-office management, and standardization in the four factors for back-office management as shown in Figure 4.1.

2.4 Truth and myths of e-business

There have been too many misconceptions about the Internet-based businesses, and it has been very difficult to distinguish between the myths and truths. To be sure, the Internet is a power tool for opening the way to new markets, customers, products, and modes of conducting business. At the same time, it is prompting newcomers unwittingly to embrace some risky half-truths and to neglect serious tensions beneath seemingly feasible strategies. Rangan and Adner (2001) mentioned the seven misconceptions on this half-truth issue. Some of them are summarized as follows [1].

First, do not believe too much in the "first-mover advantage". Being first can give a company a frontier-pushing aura, as shown by the Amazon.com example, can generate valuable brand recognition, and can provide a bigger opportunity to lock in unattached customers based on the economies of network. However, the first mover should not overvalue these benefits and should be cautious for the durability of the advantage. The new standard made by the first mover could become the barrier not only for the following companies, but for the new users who do not want the change that is too far from the traditional legacy system. Just remember that new or not, the rules are not easily exploitable for everybody.

Second, do not provide too much for the "customer solution". As the customer gets greater convenience, the company gets the higher possibilities for the values in general. The extended service warranties that hardware manufacturers offer are a good example. Just look the Apple iPhone! It aims to provide customers with convenient solutions as a full set from the hardware to software unique to fit them! But this kind of too much reach may result in the failure of the core competence. When the market becomes large enough, it pays off to specialize, and if the market becomes competitive, it will hurt not to do so. That is why Samsung focuses on the hardware only.

Under the interdependent soft economy, the company may want the best partners for their collaboration networking. However, this "best-of-breed-partner leverage" misconception could result in the worse performance when the partners have common goals to participate in, and there are no leaders strong enough to confiscate the major portion of the value created. It turns the partners toward a passive helper or even an enemy in the future.

There is the "born-in global" misconception as well. Most of managers believe that Internet-based business can spread all over the world effortlessly. Well, web sites are accessible from anywhere, and thus it may be true in some part. Even if this born- global is really an appealing perspective, however, it is a risky strategy to go overseas without much consideration on the balancing between the global standard and localization of the services. The company should first be successful at home, then move outward in a manner accommodating the local differences. Many global leaders are not successful in the Asian markets due to this failure of localization. Most of Koreans do not use MS Word; instead they use Han software, because it gives much flexibility to fit the local culture. By the same token, many global leaders have gigantic local competitors in China because they are failed to customize the local users' hidden demand.

Using the exemplary case study of customer relationship management (CRM) software, Rigby et al. (2002) also analyzed the similar misunderstanding in the e-business [2]. CRM is an approach for a company to manage interaction with current and future customers. The CRM approach tries to analyze data about customers' history with the company, to better improve business relationships with customers, specifically focusing on retaining customers, in order to drive sales growth. It is based on the Pareto principle. The Pareto principle, known as the

80 versus 20 rule, states that 80 per cent of your sales (or revenues) come from 20 per cent of your clients. Management consultant Joseph M. Juran suggested the principle and named it after Italian economist Vilfredo Pareto [3]. To manage these loyal 20 per cent of customers, the CRM compiles information from a range of different channels, including a company's web site, e-mail, live chat, customers' sales history, social media, and more. Through the CRM approach and the systems used to facilitate CRM, businesses learn more about their target audiences and how to best cater to their needs. However, the adoption of the CRM approach may also occasionally lead to favoritism within an audience of consumers, leading to dissatisfaction among customers and defeating the purpose of CRM. They argued the CRM is not the panacea for a company to bring and retain much more valuable customers due to the four kinds of misconceptions on the CRM [2].

First, remember that the CRM is not a solution, but just a technology. Many CRM producers claim that they will automate the delicate and sometime mysterious process of creating loyal customers. But, unfortunately, it is not true. Implementing CRM before creating a customer strategy would be like trying to build a house without engineering measures or an architectural plan. A company should make it clear for the future strategic plan before it implements the CRM, because CRM eventually should become part of the solution, but it didn't drive the strategy or the appropriate process by itself. Thus, make sure the strategy comes first, then CRM.

Second, installing CRM before creating s customer-oriented organization could be the most dangerous pitfall. In most of cases, companies do not consider too much for the readiness of the company and just hurry to implement new technology or software such as CRM and ERP. However, a CRM rollout will succeed only after the organization. Its processes – job description, performance measures, compensation systems training programs, and so on – have to be restructured in order to better match with the traditional or old legacy system of the organization culture. Otherwise, CRM may not work, and it may even lead to monster-like disasters. Thus, ensure education first for the organization members so that they are ready for the new technology or new business strategies.

There is another misconception that more advanced CRM technology is better. But it is certainly not true. Merely relying on a technological solution, or assuming that a higher level of CRM is better than a low-tech one, must be a costly pitfall. In fact, companies with well-functioning CRM programs dot all points of the technology spectrum from low-tech, mid-tech, to high-tech. Thus, make sure that the customized CRM are not the expensive and/or most up-to-date technologies.

Finally, using CRM beg with, but not stalk with customers. If the CRM managers push too much for the customers, they do not want to send the "spam" mail to them, and this kind of stalking does not lead to a better relationship, but is just one form of another "push" marketing. These managers often end up trying to build relationships with the wrong customers, or relationships with the right customers in the wrong way. Relationship should be based on a two-way communication, not just one direction of stalking. All these misconceptions and misunderstandings about the Internet-related businesses brought the serious bubble burst in the middle of 2000s, and thus, many people thought the e-business is no more "the goose that laid golden eggs". Thus, make sure that too much pulling activities could result in the worse effects on the customers.

Therefore, the e-business companies should make sure that e-business solutions are not panacea for all the customers. They need to differentiate between the truth and myth of the e-business strategies and their technological solutions. After the serious market adjustment of e-business industries that resulted from the bursting of fancy expectations of the ideal e-business model, there has been new trend of social network services in the middle of 2000s. It started by Tweeter, and was followed by several groups of innovative business models such as Facebook and YouTube to share the experiences, and following the social trust-based new business. *Social business* is based on the relational marketing, which is a very new concept of e-business, unlike the traditional e-commerce. The group purchase, and the re-purchase based on the viral marketing of the recommendation and experiences of the members on the private social network, made a new frontier for the social business companies to expand the blue ocean of emotional or relational marketing. Currently, the e-business in its widest meaning, includes a rather new trend of social business, and this social marketing could be defined as the new way of value creation based on the relational management, instead of too much emphasis being given to traditional approach to the product and services. It is a revolutionary concept, and thus we will examine more about the web marketing mix and social business in the following section.

3. Web marketing mix strategy

3.1 Environmental change on the market

It is quite striking that the rapid diffusion of e-business changed almost everything in our everyday lives. Even if we still use the traditional approaches of economics or business management, certainly the "smart" use of Internet has changed the surrounding environment as well as the platform of our business and economic activities in totally different dimensions. In the traditional social sciences, the leader of the market was the companies and/or government, because they have superior power with regard to the information on the markets and products. So the paradigm of economies of scale and profit maximization made mass production, mass advertisement on the mass communication, mass consumption all worldwide led by the companies. If a company produces more, it gets lower in its unit costs (*economies of scale*). Based on this massive production, a company will try to "push" the market to buy its product, using the mass communication. This promotion made the customer to be passive to choose its product. The consumers are not the production partners, but just an object of consumption for the product, due to the lack of the product information and to the powerful marketing push by the manufactures. However, all these traditional market environments have been changed by the diverse utilization of Internet.

Clearly, Internet brought more advantages to all the economic agents such as the manufacturers, governments, and the consumers than ever before. Companies are able to expand new markets thanks to the time and space unrestrained Internet, and to reduce its costs as well via synchronized networking of the business functions. Governments also benefited due to the more efficient automation of the public services such as e-tax payment, searching of the legal property certificates, and so on, on the Internet. Nevertheless, best of all, the consumer became the champion of this new marketing environment. Each individual consumer may not have enough power to change the market decision, but netizens, the Internet-connected consumers can create the group intelligence, and the power of netizen made a new environment for the companies and government to "read and follow" the market-oriented smart consumers. The consumers are not any more passive economic agents who watch TV advertisements and buy the items shown on TV, because of insufficient information. The Internet changed these passive consumers into more proactive consumers, and these smart consumers changed the market as well. Now, the manufacturers could not lead the market by the "push" marketing, because even if the companies push the consumers by TV and any other promotional tools, the smart consumers will not just accept the supplier-oriented information. Instead, the smart consumers ask the manufacturers and distributors for what they really want. Now, the leader of the market is not any more the company and/or government, but the smart consumers. The smart consumers do not want the massively produced uniform product, but demand the customized product for their own use! Because the market and consumers changed, the traditional marketing is useless, as we shall see later. That is the reason to find out a new paradigm of marketing for the smart consumers.

The traditional market under the industrial economy as well as the digital economy has emphasized the importance of information, saying that "information is money and power". If you just came out from the subway and feel thirsty, you just enter the convenience store in front of the subway exit and buy a drink at a little higher price. Then you just turn around the corner and find the hyper discount store such as Wal-Mart or Carrefour. You may feel sorry you spent much money on a drink because you did not have "*information*" about the store location. Well, certainly you understood the information "*is*" power and money in this case. Under this digital economy, the marketing activities of the company, as a leader on the market, should concentrate the diffusion of information to the consumer, and thus their major approach to the consumer is based on the "push-marketing". Before you enter the market, you never thought you wanted to buy an instant coffee mix, but when the company does promote this item as being on a special sale with many promotion coupons and discounts at the aisles inside of store, you may buy it without thinking too much. It is a usual concept of push-marketing based on the information asymmetry.

Terminology: ubiquitous society or economy

Omnipresence or *ubiquity* comes from the Latin word for the property of being present everywhere. Ubiquitous (computing network) society is based on an advanced computing concept where computing is made to appear any time, any place, anything, and any way. And thus, sometimes it is called "4 any" system society. In contrast to desktop computing, ubiquitous computing can occur using any device (freedom in access; anyway), in any location and time (limitless time and space; anytime and anyplace), and in any form or style of activities (freedom of action, it implies not only the sharing of information but utilization of the information to initiate some actions. For example, we may turn on the air conditioner before we enter the house by mobile phone; anything). A user interacts with the computer, and/or computer-interconnected any electric items which can exist in many different forms, including laptop computers, tablets, terminals, and phones. The underlying technologies to support ubiquitous computing include Internet, advanced middleware, operating system, mobile code, sensors, microprocessors, new input/output devices and user interfaces, networks, mobile protocols, location and positioning, and new materials.

However, the business environment has been changing so rapidly. Now, if you want to buy a toner for your printer on the Internet, you will never look around other sale items on the same web sites such as coffee mix at half price. There is no effect of sales promotion on Internet web site unless the consumer have plan to buy it a priori. Even with the sales promotion, an online shopper may compare too much information for right decision. He wants knowledge instead of just a flood of information. For his knowledge, the information from the manufacturers is not very effective. Instead, he may depend on the recommendation by his friend or the experience from other Internet users. Their satisfaction with the product will be the key of knowledge for you to buy a product. Therefore, the knowledge is the key for the demand-oriented "pull-marketing". Here, we define ***knowledge*** as the information to activate your decision.

Not only the market changed from information-push marketing to the knowledge-pull marketing, but the consumers changed as well. The smart consumers are not anymore passive to buy the products. They ask for the companies to make "what the consumer really wants". The demand from the market is based on the knowledge which influences the decision or activities directly, and thus companies have to listen the voice from the market and smart customers. That is the core for the pull-marketing. Therefore, the customers are participating in the production process with any type of knowledge. This kind of consumer is called a prosumer, a synthesized acronym of producer and consumer, and the private brand (PB) product is the most representative product from these prosumers.

Now, the proactive prosumer and the demand-pull knowledge-based market made the traditional marketing mix useless and require a new paradigm for the prosumer, a new leader of the market, to get the emotional satisfaction in very diversified ways. This change of the market and consumers became the background of inauguration of web marketing mix.

In the traditional market approach, the marketing mix was a business tool used in marketing to maximize profits. The marketing mix is often synonymous with the 4Ps: price, product, promotion, and place because the core of business is to maximize the profits, and to maximize profits, it is crucial to choose 4Ps appropriately at the same time. Since these 4Ps are not separated, the decision maker should combine or mix the 4Ps altogether. For example, the low price for more sales should match with low quality of product with street market channel without any special promotion, because all 4Ps are related to get the maximum profits by the price advantages in this case. Unfortunately, this 4P marketing mix cannot hold its effectiveness to maximize the profits anymore, because all 4Ps lost their strategic importance on the e-business era. Let's look this change more in detail.

First, the price could not be the core in the e-business. Can you think about the feasibility to sell the "product" under the production costs? In traditional marketing concept, it is impossible to sell the product at the lower cost than its production or procurement costs. But, in e-business world, it is always possible because we may bring one-source multi-use for any specific product. For example, a company can sell the product at the lower price than its production costs when there is some additional source of profits from the web sites advertisements for other products. You can find diverse source of profits using one-source, multi-use paradigm, and thus the price of the product could be just one of the sources of profits as a reference. Sometimes, you may have a product even free of charge or you may quote your own price for the product or services. It implies that an e-business company could have very diversified price strategies and thus price for some specific item is no more important to maximize the profits under the one-source multi-use paradigm.

Second, the decision on the product also lost its importance to maximize the profits. In traditional concept, the product should have integrated functions altogether for the massive-consumption to lower costs. However, e-business created pull-marketing instead of massive push-marketing, and thus instead of a standardized product at "lower price than its production costs". The sales item on the web sites should have many differentiated items for "only you". This customized way of product made a new way of niche market for new concept of product. Instead of general refrigerators, e-business companies created "Korean Kimchi refrigerators", wine refrigerators, and even cosmetic refrigerators. All these "new" products could be differentiated from the traditional products, and thus the positioning of the products became much more important than just the basic or general function of the product.

Terminology: mass-customization and Mezzotiege strategy

Mass customization is defined as producing goods and services to *meet individual customer's needs with near-mass production efficiency*. The mass customization strategy is a strategy that creates value by some form of company–customer interaction at the fabrication and assembly stage of the operations level to create customized products with production cost and monetary price similar to those of mass-produced products. Mass customization is the new frontier in business competition for both manufacturing and service industries. At its core, there is a tremendous increase in variety and customization without a corresponding increase in costs. At its limit, it is the mass production of individually customized goods and services. At its best, it provides strategic advantage with reasonable economic value. Since the mass-customized products are very similar with mass-produced general product at its price, while the quality is higher due to the customized differences, it is sometimes called the ***Mezzotiege product***. The term "Mezzotiege" comes from the combination of mezzo-production (instead of mass production) with prestige quality (due to the customization).

Third, traditional places or distribution channel strategy in the marketing mix is no more useful to maximize profits in e-business era, because the distribution channel and the role of middleman on the distribution channel has been changed so differently in e-business. In the traditional concept, the middleman (or intermediary) was a very important match-maker to bring the market demand and supply to get the equilibrium. For example, a real-estate broker was important in the real-estate market, because without a real-estate agent, the house sale transaction cannot be handled easily. So the distribution channel management was very important in traditional marketing. But the e-business broke the time and space limits by 24 x 365 web sites order with limitless delivery. It means there is no more simple middleman required for a web site transaction. So, the traditional intermediary should evolve into the information-equipped intermediary or just *infomediary*. They need to provide more information than just for match-maker. Moreover, the online shopping web sites should make more proactive role for the buyers and sellers to know each other by auto-mailers and/or certified monitor for the delivery and payment as the big brother for all commercial transaction manager. These kinds of diverse value-added activities are crucial for e-business intermediation. We call this kind of proactive multi-tasking intermediary *metamediary* ("meta" is from the Latin word "many").

Finally, the promotion strategies in the traditional marketing mix should be changed because they are based on the push-marketing. As explained before, the traditional consumer may buy unwanted product from the sales persons in the aisles of the supermarket who promote the special sales with discount coupons or some additional bonus. However, a prosumer will never buy any other item on the web sites even if there are many pop-up advertisements on the web sites. He just wants to search for the item that he planned to buy on the web sites and buy it only for what he wants, regardless of the push-type of promotional events. So, the promotion for the item that he never thought to buy is useless even with many pop-up advertisements. Therefore, the new type of promotion in pull-marketing on the Internet should be based on the appropriate knowledge for the potential customers. That is the background of pull-marketing. Do not beg the consumer to buy your products by pushing promotion. Instead, you had better find out what they really want and let them feel your product just as a customized product for them. You should remember that the best product gives the satisfaction, but best service gives the emotional touch, that is the spirit of pull-marketing promotion.

As discussed above, no traditional marketing tools of 4Ps to maximize the profits could maintain their importance anymore. Therefore, it is the time to replace all these old marketing tools for the creation of values. That is the web marketing mix.

3.2 *Definition of web marketing mix*

Web marketing is defined as the relationship marketing to create value on the network management in the long term via standardization and differentiation by personal marketing, cyber marketing, and database marketing [4]. The traditional marketing focused only on the short-term profits, and thus once a sale was done, there was no feedback provided. In the web marketing, however, the long-term relation is much more important than just one instantaneous deal. The web marketers should "buy" the consumer's mind before they "sell" the item. This philosophy on the web marketing created relational importance represented by the degree of loyalties.

First of all, to create the relation, it should be characterized by the personal marketing on its marketing target perspectives. Instead of mass-marketing, it just emphasizes the customized contents of the web sites and due to the individualized contents, it can create emotional loyalties in the long term. Second, web marketing is cyber (or tele-) marketing. There is no limit or difference between the local and global markets at least on web sites. Therefore, the global sourcing made a fierce competition among all possible sellers and thus born-in global marketing strategies are so essential on web sites. A company should provide its products and related services in any time, at any place by seamless automated e-business functions.

The WTO made a new paradigm of borderless competition on the unified global market, and this paradigm of WTO has been realized on the Internet. There is no arbitrage trading for the same product on the local and global market anymore, and it is much more difficult to keep the championship position on the global market because the competition becomes more and more severe on this global market. Because of this severe competition among the potential producers worldwide, the differentiation on the web sites are so much important, and that is the core contents of the web marketing mix as we shall discuss later. Contrary to the differentiation strategy on the web marketing, the e-business is different than traditional marketing in terms of the simultaneous collaboration on the Internet. For the fulfillment of the sales contract, many partners should cooperate with each other to check the payment, transportation, etc. simultaneously. In the broader concept, web marketing includes the fulfillment of marketing on the transaction automation procedures. The latter part of automation procedures requires the standardization of all the related information formats and even some contents among the partners as well. This harmonization between the differentiation and standardization for the collaboration is the key for cyber marketing.

Third, the web marketing is based on database marketing. For the customized marketing, the most important efforts of the web business should be based on the data search, processing, and utilization of the sea of information and data. If you log in, and the web site greets you with a messages such as, "How is it going, Prof. Choi (your name)? You visited twice today. I really appreciate your second visit today," then you may feel much more friendly and want to stay longer. Customization should be based on the data that the user provided directly and indirectly such as your visiting time and frequency. Sometimes, very seemingly unrelated groups of data may result in the innovative idea for the web marketing, and thus the data mining with the big data is crucial for the effective web marketing. Data mining is the computational process of discovering patterns in large datasets involving methods at the intersection of artificial intelligence, machine learning, statistics, and database systems. The overall goal of the data-mining process is to extract information from a dataset and transform it into an understandable structure for the special use. This special use will bring the more customer-friendly environment of the web marketing and thus the utilization of the database is very unique in the web marketing to create and maintain the relationship in the long run.

All these characters of web marketing are based on the creation of values not from the instant and direct sales, but from the relational management with network members. It is so crucial to understand the difference of web marketing from the traditional marketing. The purpose of web marketing is not the (short-term) maximization of profit. Instead, it aims to create the "relationship" and maintain it for the long-term loyalties. Note that we are focusing not on the (short-term) profits, but on the relationship. The relation-oriented web marketing is based on the Pareto principle [3]. The Pareto principle (also known as the 80 versus 20 rule) states that, for many events, roughly 80 per cent of the sales (or revenues) come from 20 per cent of the customers. Based on Pareto principle, the web marketers should treat the loyal customers with much emphasis and benefits as well, because they will bring in much more profits and other values. They may recommend the web sites to his or her friends, and this kind of viral marketing is so important in the no-face-to-face marketing via Internet. For the win-win game to enlarge the pizza in the future, the relational long-term loyalty is the core factor on the web marketing. Especially, the loyalty from the customers will not

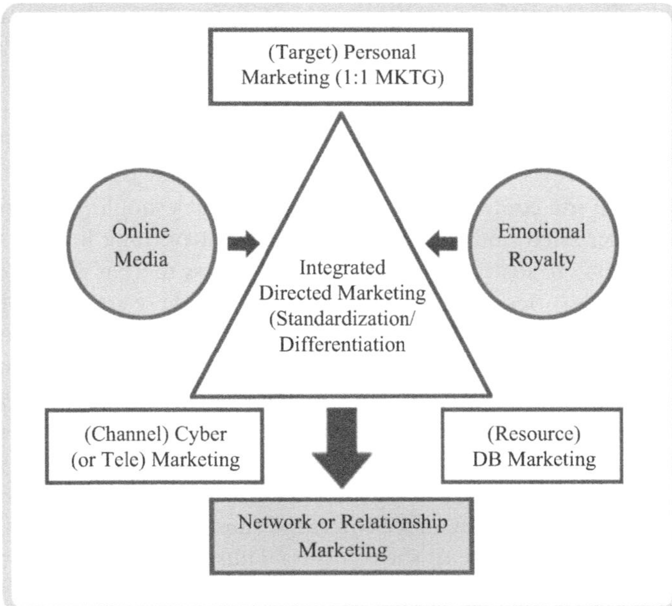

Figure 4.2 Conceptual characteristics of web marketing

only enlarge the future sales volume by themselves, but also effectively convey it with the viral marketing. Viral marketing is based on the buzzwords referring to marketing techniques that use pre-existing social networking services (SNS) and other technologies to increase a brand awareness or to achieve other marketing objectives (such as product sales) through self-replicating viral processes, analogous to the spread of viruses or computer viruses. It can be delivered by word of mouth or enhanced by the network effects of the Internet and mobile networks.

Therefore, the relationship management is crucial to create values for the network manager, and thus the web marketing should emphasize how to create the relations, how to maintain them, and how to create value from the relations. To answer all these questions, we need to understand the procedural strategies of web marketing mix and its components of 4Cs [4].

3.3 Components of web marketing mix: 4Cs

The web marketing is a totally different from the traditional sales-oriented marketing, in that it is based on the purpose of creating the values of the network management. The tool of web marketing is not based on the product, but on the web sites. It may or may not get its profits from the product, and thus it is clearly different from the traditional approach to the customer. Therefore, the first step toward the web marketing comes from the creation of relation. That is, for this relation via web sites to be created, the consumers should get the easy and effective access to the network. This easy and effective access to the network is called the *communication strategy*. Here, the communication implies the information sharing to begin to create the relationship between the Internet user or web site visitors and the web marketer as a network manager. The web sites should be easily accessible in terms of their loading time as well as easy instructions to search around the web site contents. Especially, the web sites should be more reliable for user to enter safely and validly. If the web sites have long loading time, the users will not stay to load all the web contents unless there is already a reliable relation. The web surfer may not show any interest if there are no feedback mail functions with the web site manager. On the contrary, if there is some certification of the web sites such as local community guarantee or an award for the safe or best practice, etc., then the user certainly wants to visit and stay longer because of the psychological effect of trust. Even if the content is well organized, if it takes longer than 5 seconds to load the web content, nobody wants to wait to enter the site, especially in Korea. So, make your web site content as clear and as condensed as possible. When a user enters the sites easily, he or she only spends time on the activities that he or she wants to. Thus, if the homepage starts with some moving pictures for the better understanding or difficult menus to search for, it could be a waste of time for the user, and he or she may not come back again. Therefore, the easy and reliable access to the web sites is the first step for the user to enter the web sites without any psychological or practical restraints. This easy and effective access strategies are certainly the core of the communication strategies for web marketing.

When the consumer enters the web sites, now the web marketer should make the user stay longer and visit frequently. In order for the visitor to get accustomed to the web sites, the web marketer could provide an interesting game and/or real-time information such as the latest news or weather/stock market information. This kind of strategy for fun or for knowledge (not information!) is called the *contents strategy* in a narrowest concept. This usefulness of the web site contents is important for the user to maintain the relational loyalties with web sites. In general, contents are broadly defined as information or experience provided to the user in a customized manner. But in a narrowest meaning, the contents are some pieces of information or something to create an interesting experience (such as free online game) in terms of knowledge or fun. Contents are very important for the consumer to stay longer and visit often because a web marketer needs to get the mind of the consumer before he or she sells the final product or services. For example, on most game sites, the initial stage of the game or e-book is free, but later the consumer needs to pay because this free-but-not-free strategy lets the user get accustomed to visit more on the web site and finally agree to pay for the identified value.

After the consumer enters easily by communication strategy and visits more frequently by contents strategy, it is time for the consumer to spend some money on the web sites. That is the *commercial strategy* of the third stage of web marketing.

The commercial strategy means the way to make a profit from the web sites. Note that we are not just talking the invisible values. Without short- or long-term profits coming from values, the e-business is not sustainable, but at the same time remember that there are diverse types of making profits by the one-source multi-use on the web sites, which is a totally different approach from the traditional marketing concept. There are six types of commercial strategy even on the same product or services [4].

First, the commerce certainly could be based on the profit margin at a little lower price for the same product as offline one because it costs less. For this classical B2C type of e-commerce, a web marketer should make more differentiated strategy for the same product to the new niche market using many supplements such as e-purchase coupon or mileage rebates for the next purchase.

Second, the commerce could be based on the other sponsor source of funds such as advertisement commission, instead of profit margins on the sale item. In case of Gomtv.com in Korea, a web marketer may give the premium movies for free. The source of profits may not come from the movie itself, but from the advertisement before the movie starts. This is a kind of free-but-not-free sponsor strategy.

Third, customers may not pay for each specific item; instead, they just pay lump sum membership fees. The most representative case of the membership fees can be found on the e-learning. If you pay for the e-lecture, you can visit as much as you want based on the initial membership fees, or monthly payment.

Fourth, a web marketer could get some commission fees from the visit or purchase of the customer on other web sites via its own web sites as a middle hub for commercial transaction. For example, a consumer wants to buy a cheapest airline ticket via price comparison sites. Then, these price comparison hub sites provide many services and receive some commission when the customer finally purchases airline ticket via this comparison web site. The commission is one of the best compensations for the infomediary, and it is quite important in the open market and international e-trade.

Fifth, the web sites rental could be one of the profit sources as well. Like in an open market, a web marketer provides one-stop services for the small producers to get good design of the web as well as the periodical feedback and update of web sites in return for the rental fees for this partial use of web sites. This rental could be found more easily in a field of hardware and facility providers such as data hub rental or mall-in-mall web sites management.

Finally, the commercial strategy sometimes could take the click and brick type of integration on the services. The consumer may take the initial stage of consulting online, and the consulting fee may cover the offline lectures in the second stage. Likewise, there are many possible ways to combine the online and offline commercial activities together to maximize consumer's satisfaction.

Of course, all these six types of commercial strategies could be combined for the better values with one-source multi-use purpose. For example, the free movies of advertisement sponsor may give another business opportunity on the movie character utilization for sale in offline toy shops to the movie maker.

Figure 4.3 Web marketing mix: 6Cs

"Once a customer, forever a customer!" is the slogan for the web marketing relationship management. So, if a customer purchased some items from the web sites, then let him or her visit over and over again to take the follow-up for the expanding its relation with other users. This *community strategy* is crucial for the customer to participate in the web sites updating and self-management by user group. New contents by the customers such as the experiences from the purchased item and new ideas for the use of the existing item may have a strong pressure for the potential customers to purchase that item. Therefore, the Bulletin Board System (BBS), which is an online system that allows users to participate in the community and update his or her own information or experiences, is essential for the community strategy. Once logged in BBS, a user can perform functions such as uploading and downloading software and data, reading news and bulletins, and exchanging messages with other users, either through e-mail, public message boards, and sometimes via direct chatting. Many BBSs also provide chat rooms, allowing users to interact with each other. This kind of user-friendly environment is crucial for the customer to maintain his or her loyalties, and his or her loyalty in the community will enhance the loyalty of other members as well.

The above-mentioned communication, contents, commerce, and community are the core for the web marketers to create the value, including short-term profit and long-term loyalty. These 4Cs are not independent and cannot be separated from each other, because all these strategies should be well performed in on same page of a web sites. Rather, they should be complementarily integrated in the procedural approaches. Therefore, 4Cs need to be interdependent on the web sites and thus the expression the *web marketing mix*.

However, sometimes 4Cs are not enough to create the value and loyalty. Thus, two more components could be complemented on 4Cs. These are connection and customization strategies. *Customization* is important for the consumer to think that they are intimately communicating with the web marketers on the personalized web sites. If you enter a convenient store to buy soap, but a shop employee strongly recommends the cleansing cream instead of a soap, you may not buy anything and get out of the store. That is the background of customization strategy. Once you logged in, the web sites start with a comment, "What a nice morning, Prof. Choi (*User's ID*)!" and show you a lot of soap-related items once you purchased soap on the web site. Then, this intimate call will lead you to buy the next item.

The web sites provided by a web marketer cannot cover all the information that the customers want. Then, the web sites could take a role of an online guide to connect the related information. All you need is to put some more frequently visited web sites or strongly related other portals. The appropriate *connection* will make your web sites more condensed and for the customer to get through your linked other sites. Sometimes web marketing mix could be 6Cs instead of 4Cs, including *customization* and *connection*. But in general, the latter 2Cs are complementary strategies rather than core strategies for the better web site environment, and thus we could still stick with the 4Cs for the core strategies of web marketing mix.

3.4 *Procedures for the web marketing mix*

All the e-business-related activities could be analyzed on the procedural approach integrated with structural and functional approaches on stepwise plan. As shown in Figure 4.4, the strategic process of web marketing starts with the proposal for new business, and this stage of making proposal is called the pre-feasibility stage, because it requires the business idea on to the feasible design with an object specification of TCP. First of all, the new business should initiate to whom and how it can be started. The new business object should be clarified with target (T), broad meaning of concept (C) and positioning (P) differentiated from other existing businesses. Here, target implies the major object of value creation with the definition of the right customers and right products (sales item). The more "specific" object on the target is, the more feasible the successful operation becomes. To clarify the right product and customer, concept and positioning will give better

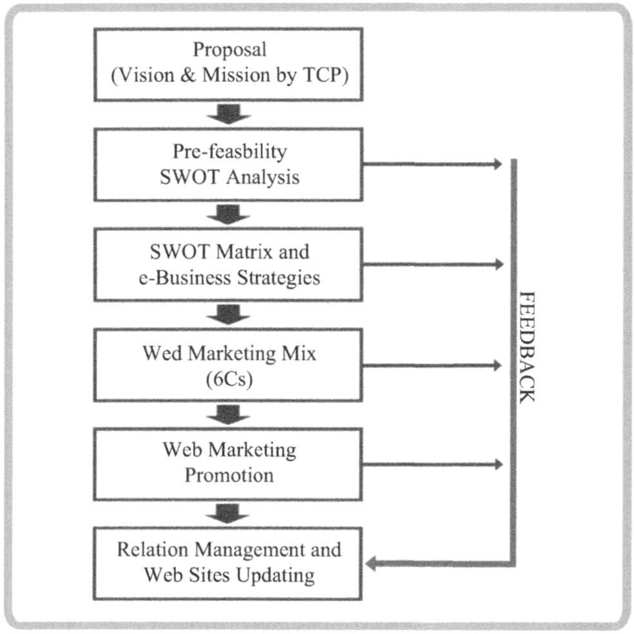

Figure 4.4 Strategic process of web marketing

basic guideline of the business model. For the concept of customers, differentiation is the core for the new concept on the customer's perspectives. To make it more specific, for example, instead of women web sites, focus on web sites only for the ladies in the early 20s. It is the key for the niche market concept. Now, make the sales item more differentiated in terms of positioning criteria. For example, the beer could be characterized by its taste (bitterness) and the degree of alcohol. If you can find these criteria for the existing items, then you may try to find out the best niche market from the positioning chart of all the competitive items on the market. It will give you the guidelines to distinguish your product and customers from other competing items.

When the choice of right customers and products is explained in details, now the basic direction of how to operate the business should be based on the SWOT analysis and its matrix. SWOT analysis (alternatively SWOT Matrix) is a structured planning method used to evaluate the Strengths and Weaknesses for the internal capacity analysis of the company, and Opportunities and Threats for the environmental analysis surrounding the new business involved in a project or in a business venture. Identification of SWOTs is important because they can inform later steps in planning to achieve the objective.

- Strengths: competitive and/or strong points of the business giving an advantage over others
- Weaknesses: weak point or disadvantage relative to others

- Opportunities: elements that the new business could exploit to its advantage from the environment
- Threats: elements in the environment that could cause trouble for the new business

Remember there is no neutral information. All the information could be pros or cons in your future business perspectives, and thus you should find out all the bright side as well as dark sides together in these environmental and internal capacity analyses. After the specification of all the details of SWOT elements, a web marketer should make the combination of all these elements to get the basic direction of the business by SWOT Matrix, which is called the *business strategy*.

After a web marketer sets up the basic direction of the business or strategies, we need to put these strategies on the web sites using the web marketing mix of 4Cs. To make the web sites 4Cs, it is quite important to harmonize the strategic factors of the web sites content among information factors (content in broader meaning, C), art factors (design, D), and technical factors (technology, T). If the sites are good to look at, but without much information, then these are not well-organized web sites. Therefore, the harmonized CDT should result in the well-organized web marketing mix. Of course, web marketing mix could be more specific to characterize all the details according to the target, positioning, and all the detailed SWOT strategies. After the creation of web sites, a web marketer should enroll the web sites on the Internet via value-added information service providers. In most of countries, you should get the telecommunication line with its telephone number first, then using your telephone number, you can enroll into the authorized international network information center of global domain sites (www.internic.org), or your own country's domain (for China: www.cnnic.cn; for Korea: www.krnic.kr; for Japan: www.jpnic.jp, etc.).

Now, the web sites are ready to make a profit in short term, as well as to create the value in long-term simultaneously. After a successful introduction of web sites on the Internet, a web manager should promote the diffusion of the web sites information, and at the same time, he or she should sensitively respond to the web site visitors. The former activities are called web promotion, and the latter represent

Table 4.1 SWOT Matrix and the strategies of e-business

Environment analysis		*Opportunities*	*Threats*
Internal capacity analysis		*Detailed lists of factors*	*Detailed lists of factors*
Strength	Detailed lists of factors	SO strategies (in details)	ST strategies (in details)
Weakness	Detailed list of factors	WO strategies (in details)	WT strategies (in details)

web management and it is the key activities for the web sites vividly updating by the visiting users.

Web management or web operations is a domain of expertise within IT systems management that involves the deployment, operation, maintenance, tuning, and repair of web-based applications and systems. In terms of bilateral communications with the customers, the feedback from the web site search and information on the web is very much important. To analyzes the web data for the web business management, a blog is the key item to be analyzed. A blog, a compound of the words "web" and "log", is a discussion or informational site published on the World Wide Web, consisting of discrete entries ("posts") typically displayed in reverse chronological order (the most recent posts appear first). Until 2009, blogs were usually the work of a single individual, occasionally a small group, and they often covered a single subject. More recently, "multi-author blogs" (MABs) have developed, with posts written by large numbers of authors and professionally edited. The most important logs are Access_log, Error_log, Agent_log, Referer_log, etc., and these logs gives a good guideline for the network manager to make feedback for the customers on the customized way.

Log analysis is an art and science seeking to make sense out of computer-generated records (also called log or audit trail records). The process of creating such records is called data logging. Web log analysis software (also called a web log analyzer) is a kind of web analytic software that parses a server log file from a web server, and based on the values contained in the log file, derives indicators about when, how, and by whom a web server is visited. Usually, reports are immediately generated from the log files, but the log files can alternatively be parsed to a database and reports generated on demand.

Terminology: data mining and big data

Data mining is defined as the computational process of discovering patterns in large datasets involving methods at the intersection of artificial intelligence, machine learning, statistics such as database, and database systems. The overall goal of the data-mining process is to extract information from a dataset and transform it into knowledge, an understandable structure for further use. Data mining comes from the big data analysis, because the Internet contains too much data and information, and thus the appropriate filtering for knowledge is essential.

Big data is defined as a collection of datasets so large and complex that it becomes difficult to process using available database management tools or traditional data-processing applications. The challenges include capture, storage, search, sharing, transfer, analysis, and visualization. Big data require massively parallel software running on many servers at the same time (cf. cloud computing).

3.5 *Cultural and emotional factors in social business: case study of the Hallu (Korean wave)*

The web marketing has been transformed into the social business with the emotional and cultural factors in the social network service (SNS). The most outstanding feature in the social network business or social business is the integration of the emotional group intelligence, instead of the knowledge, as group intelligence in the e-business. The social business is the enhanced version of e-business in terms of the more emphasis on the importance of the emotional and/or experience-based loyalties of the user group. At the beginning of the social business or social business model, it was defined as the e-business based on the social media tools and social networking services such as Facebook and Tweeter, across functional areas for communicating and engaging with external audiences, including customers, prospective customers, prospective employees, suppliers, and partners, which fully involves these members in the organizational business process and increases customer intimacy and trust. It began with a type of group shopping for the better deal with other members of the group, then expanded diverse areas of field- and performance-oriented activities with the strong support of other netizens. Most of members on SNS are proactively contributing with their feelings and experiences regarding the products and these experienced recommendations are crucial for new customers to decide whether to buy a product or not. Soon, it expanded diverse location-connected services with the support of geographical location services of the Internet, such as nearest shops and the best dining services in the region, etc.

The most important factor in the social business comes from the loyalties of the other users' recommendations for the final decision. Due to a rapidly increasing popularity of the social business, the advanced, or enhanced e-business should take a consideration about the loyalties coming from the recommendations of other users. These recommendation-based *emotional marketing* is called the viral marketing. Viral marketing is a marketing technique that use pre-existing social networking services and other technologies to increase brand awareness or to achieve other marketing objectives (such as product sales) through self-replicating viral processes. It is in general, delivered by the word of mouth and/or enhanced by the network effects of the Internet and mobile networks. Therefore, the loyalties from the ex-users are crucial for the purchase intention of new customers. This kind of emotional factor in online and offline business can be found easily in the Hallyu (Korean wave) in diverse field of industry.

The Korean wave or *Hallyu* literally means "the flow of Korea", a neologism referring to the increase in the popularity of South Korean culture since the late 1990s. First driven by the spread of K-dramas televised across Asian countries during its initial stages, the Korean wave evolved from a regional development into a global phenomenon due to the proliferation of Korean pop (K-pop) music videos on YouTube such as "Gangnam Style". Currently, the spread of the Korean wave to other regions of the world is most visible among teenagers and young adults in almost all the countries in the world. The growing popularity of

Korean entertainment services such as K-pop, K-drama, K-movies in the world has prompted the Korean wave as a tool for soft power, facilitating its creative sector to enhance the country's burgeoning economy as well as fulfilling the nations ambitious goal of becoming the world's leading cultural exporter, a niche that the United States has cornered for nearly a century.

The most outstanding features of the Korean wave can be found in the cultural factors in the Korean entertainment sectors and other creative industries. This Korean wave can be found in the e-business as well. All the cultural factors in e-business can be identified with the Pumsae, a basic form of Taekwondo, Korean traditional martial sports, consisting of agility, flexibility, and diversity. These cultural factors of Taekwondo worked as successful factors even in the e-business of Korea [5]. The first cultural factor of the Korean wave, shown in the Pumsae of Taekwondo, is based on the agility strategy. Taekwondo is much proactive, offensive martial sports, compared to the Japanese Judo. Nonetheless, it emphasizes the "you-attitude" of the attack, because the agility means the quick response to your next move. Before you attack the competitor, you should be sensitive enough to feel the move of other competitor a priori. That is the key for the agility strategy. In many K-dramas, the viewer can feel more favorable story proceedings, because the drama synopsis is always changing based on the feedback from the field. If the viewer wants some talented role more, the story will change with the more favorable seen for this role in the drama. This kind of interaction with the viewers certainly will enhance the popularity of the K-drama and will bring much more emotional involvement in the ongoing story of the newly edited drama.

Therefore, the agility of the e-business should not only depend on the speed of the response, but the degree of emotional sharing with the users or potential customers. For example, Microsoft has experienced lots of difficulties in the Korean market, because the local companies of GOM player provide not only video tools such as Window Media Player, but also a lot of its free movies and TV programs, by virtue of the advertisement sponsorship. In the same manner, the MS Word has had difficulties to penetrate into the Korean word processor market, because it took more time for the special demand for the local alphabet, than the local word processor of Hangeul.com. Hangeul.com not only provided the unique characters of Korean language faster and better, but with a more flexible mechanism of the file opening. A user can open the MS word file in Hangeul, but not vice versa. This agility strategy is the key for the Hallyu (Korean wave) to gain the worldwide popularity, because all that is K-made is based on the real-time feedback from the market. If you see any Korean tour groups in your country, you may hear "*ppali, ppali* (hurry, hurry)!", implying that one should make his or her decision or activities faster. They are risk-lovers to make challenges for any new product and new services more aggressively. That is the reason why many global IT companies and even the cinema industry do take Korea as the test-bed market.

The second factor of the Korean wave, shown in the Pumsae of Taekwondo, is flexibility. As mentioned before, the Korean web companies provided many flexible software systems such as free-but-not-free strategy. Lots of Korean software is free because the Korean people are so sensitive to price differences; it is much more difficult to provide web services that charge money. Therefore, Symantec, an anti-virus software company, and many other global companies could not be successful in Korea, because most of other local competitors provide similar services for free. This comes from the one-source multi-use strategy to make a profit. A local company may get the source of profit not from the product or service itself, but from the advertisement sponsorship, and some lump sum type of membership fees. Sometimes, they are really free, especially during the introductory period of the game, a few pages of new e-book, etc. This kind of free-but-not-free strategy showed much flexibility in user recruiting, sales, and other Internet activities, resulting in a very low entry barrier for the new entrants in the business. Most of Korean people use Alyak, which is free-of-charge anti-virus software with the best updating capacity. Of course, the source of the profits for the Alyak comes from the advertisement sponsorship, and thus it seems very flexible for the user to try this service easily and effectively.

The third strategy of the Korean wave comes from the diversity strategy in the Pumsae of Taekwondo. The potential customers always want to get the one-stop services from the web portal sites to try diverse activities, and most of Korean portal sites provide these connectivity services free of charge. In the United States and most other countries, you pay to access to the Internet. There is very little room for the free Internet access, while the users in Korea can access the Internet anytime, anyplace, because most of Internet is free of charge, and Wi-Fi covers almost everywhere all the Internet-related services. Most of portal sites provide web chatting, searching, free games, and much, much other diverse Internet-related activities. For example, *Naver*, one of the most well-known portals in Korea, has the slogan of "You name on it, they (other proactive users) will make it right away" in its knowledge portal.

Unfortunately, all these case studies could not hold their sustainable performance over time. Just remember that the global leading mobile phone manufacturer Nokia could not maintain its successful history of 150 years, dating back to 1865 when a mining engineer created a pulp mill. It has successfully transformed its core competence from the paper manufacturer, to the telecommunication cable manufacturers, and to the mobile phone and other telecommunication networking equipment, until 2011. Nokia introduced its first Windows Phone in 2011, the Lumia 800, and it had been a successful leading telecommunication company in the world. Unfortunately, Nokia had not improved much with the Lumia for a few years, which resulted in consecutive quarters of huge losses. Finally, it transferred its mobile division to Microsoft, and the brilliant success story could not continue any longer.

The competitive dynamics of Korean martial sports, Taekwondo, as the offensive one, compared with the defensive sports of Judo, tells us the Golden rule of trend-setting. To lead the competitive market with sustainable performance, it is necessary to create a new niche market such as new product, new consumers, new marketing channel, etc. The leader should maintain its core competence as the global standard and let other competitors do not copy of your competitiveness by agile movement toward the new niche market of blue ocean continuously. This innovative differentiation proposition is the key for the first company to keep its best position over time. If it is just too proud of itself like Nokia with Lumina mobile phone, it can easily lose all its markets to the fast follower. That is the core of the Taekwondo with the detailed principles of agility, flexibility, and diversity.

It is true that the Internet business is global in nature, but make sure you always harmonize with the unique local culture in your e-business in the local market. If the global leading companies do not respond to the local voices well due to restrictive global standards, they may lose too much potential as shown by many US Internet businesses, such as Google, Twitter, etc., in China.

3.6 *Social network service (SNS) and social business*

Social network service (SNS) is a kind of platform service to build and promote social networks or relations among people who share similar interests, activities, backgrounds, and/or real-life connections. As Web 2.0 Internet-based applications, SNS is based on the user-generated content (UGC) to share the experiences and knowledge. Most social network services are web-based and allow users to interact over the Internet, such as e-mail and instant messaging. The main types of SNSs are those that contain categorical places such as the same school year or classmates, means to connect with friends for live chatting, and a recommendation system linked to trust. There are so much popular examples of SNS worldwide: Facebook, LinkedIn, Instagram, and Twitter widely in America and worldwide; Wechat, Sina Weibo, and Tencent QQ in China; Myspace and XING in Europe; Nexopia in Canada; Badoo and Bebo in Russia; Nasza-Klasa in Poland; Skyrock and StudiVZ in Germany; Tagged, Tuenti in Spain; Hi5 in Central and South America; Cyworld and Cacao talk in Korea, etc. [6]. It is very interesting that even if the global SNS services are so popular worldwide, most of all individual country has its own SNS, because the SNS reflects the virtual society of the users sharing the same cultural background as well as the local knowledge in general.

The background of the SNS comes from the change in the focus of the Internet utilization. In Web 1.0 era, the Internet is used mainly for the information search. Because of the too much emphasis on digital economy, information search was so powerful for the user. Soon, due to the flood of information, we cannot find right information, and thus, the knowledge from the group intelligence became much more helpful for the user to buy some specific product online. Web 2.0 era made this group intelligence possible due to the proactive participation of the other users to fabricate the Internet contents. Now, they want to show their own contents, and it became much more heart-felt for other users because it is easier to feel the same way, and it feels more comfortable to share the experiences. This fabricated contents in Web 2.0 era created more trustful or reliable information than the simple information in Web 1.0 era. That is the reason why these new experiences or field-oriented information is called *knowledge*. Thus, the emotional sharing is more important than just information sharing in Web 2.0 era. Based on this emotional sharing in virtual community of SNS, you may create new services and new business. This kind of SNS-based new businesses comes from the Web 3.0 era. In Web 3.0, you may think your web contents to create values for sharing with others for business purposes, and this kind of emotion-oriented network business is called *social business.*

In Korea, there are many Chinese students who came to Korea to study. Since they are still using the SNS even in Korea, sometimes they never feel they are in Korea, but just in China. Sometimes, if the friend or intimate relatives in China do not want to buy some Korean products in China, they may ask the students in Korea to purchase some products such as Korean cosmetics in Korea for them. Many Chinese students in Korea participate in this type of purchasing agent business for their relatives and friends in China, because many Chinese people cannot trust a Korean product in China, even if the product is labeled "Made in Korea", due to too many illegal copy products of foreign items in the Chinese market. Most of these purchasing agent services are managed via SNS such as QQ, because these SNS services provide a more trustful communication than simple e-mail. This kind of SNS-based services is the most representative example of social business.

These days, there are diverse social businesses emerging based on the SNS platform. If you visit a new city or foreign country, you may need an instant field-oriented knowledge. For example, if you visit Seoul for first time in your life, you may not know where to stay and where to eat. Especially, if you visited some famous place such as *Myeongdong* in Seoul, you may feel hungry after the tour, and if you have a communication difficulty in the street, you just need to open your SNS and ask somebody on your human network for the best restaurant with some special discount "now". You can get the customized knowledge with some special event and/or discount online coupons on your smart web, recommended by your friend instantaneously. All these field-experiences and spot-knowledge requires the concurrent engineering to find out *instantaneous knowledge*. Rapidly changing environment of the mobile infrastructure, terminals such as smartphone and smart watch, and smart app service innovation brought the mobile big bang, and this mobile big bang under the ubiquitous system created new challenges for social network-based social businesses such as Uber Taxi. If you have a car not in use at present, and somebody you know by SNS wants to rent a car "at present", then you go to the Uber taxi apps and ask to rent at very competitive price. This kind of field-oriented spot business is a core competence of emotional marketing concept of social business.

Social business is not yet generalized, but can be conceptually characterized by two core factors of mobile big bang. With hands-free smartphones, we can now easily and effectively access the Internet any time, any place, we can access anything in any way. This ubiquitous society made it possible to fill the missing link between the online and offline fabrication and utilization of the information simultaneously. It brought the field-oriented knowledge more proactively. If you find any disaster in your neighbor or in the street, you just can capture all the vivid information to broadcast worldwide. At the same time, if you need any latest information on the place you are passing by, you can ask the field-experts for the most updated knowledge for your decision. These creation and utilization of the live, vivid information on the smartphone will make you decide more effectively about any issue on the spot. Another important environmental change resulting from the mobile big bang is the synchronized filling of the missing links between information and active decision from that information. This automated synchronization between information and decision will result in the performance-oriented knowledge. If you think you need something to buy, or if you just want to check whether you turned off the gas when you left your home, you just need to push a few more buttons on your smartphone to activate some actions while you are working in other place, even at other time. This synchronized smart way of mobile big bang resulted in a new form of social business with the four social marketing elements as follows.

First, you always want be in the virtual network for communication 24 hours a day, by SNS, because you want to share not just information, but a kind of emotional knowledge to manage your diverse chores in the field spot. Likewise, *emotional* sympathy or identity is so crucial for the governance of the *relational* networking management. Second, the smart decision on the virtual SNS network requires value- and performance-oriented governance. You need to share what is

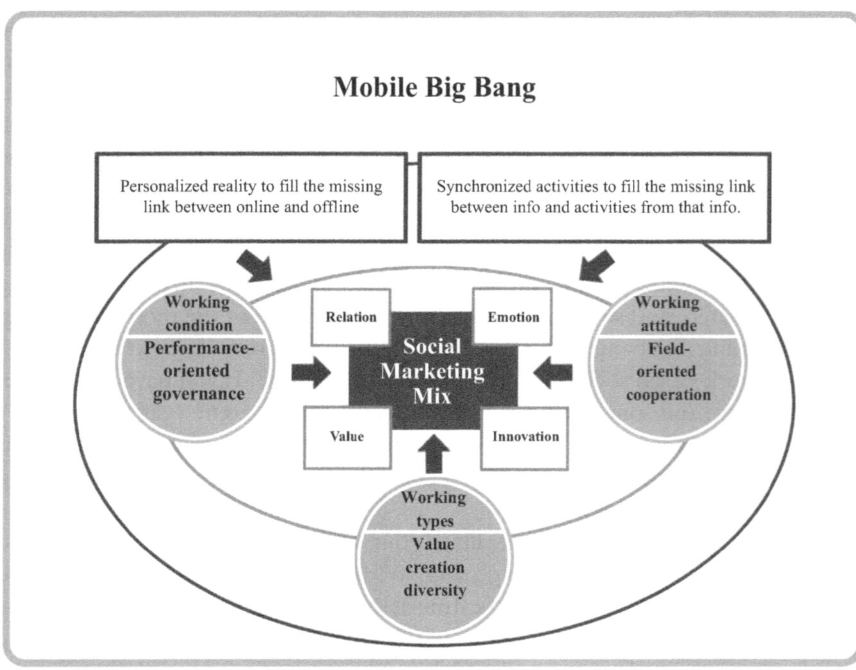

Figure 4.5 Conceptual characteristics of social marketing mix

Source: Choi, Y. *Global e-Business Management: Theory and Practice*. Seoul: Bomyoung Book, 2012.

better in your communication partner in some respect, and these criteria could be the base for the *value*, because this unique value will let you decide something for performance. Finally, social web marketing mix should be based on the *innovation-promoted* business strategies. It needs to be "smart". Otherwise, it is out of the topic for the communication. Your partner on the virtual SNS network will give you the new way of thinking, new product, new usage of that product, additional or complementary idea for the consumption of the product, etc. for you to decide it. All these four factors of *REVI (Relation-Emotion-Value-Innov ation)* consist of the emotional sharing of virtual network activities, altogether, and thus we could consider all these REVI as the social marketing mix, a kind of advanced web marketing mix.

4. Sustainable governance and green IT

4.1 Sustainable development and green IT governance

As the e-business or IT applications became the platform of all the traditional theories, the sustainability science takes the role of another platform for all the existing theories. We cannot even think of any major theories without the connection with ICT application. The sustainable paradigm also provides all the changes in the traditional theories. The platform of e-business gives the direction for all the existing theories not toward its own optimization, but toward the collaborative networking in terms of economies of networking, while the sustainable development or green growth gives another platform for the traditional theories not for the competitive maximizing efficiency in economics or profits in business, but of the win-win type of value creation. The common factor between the e-business and the sustainable development platforms is based on their objectives of harmonization for the governance in the procedural perspective.

Both fields of studies should take the platform for all the sciences and engineering, in terms that they provide innovative approach to solve the traditional market failure or seemingly unrelated complicated issues altogether, and to maintain the sustainable performance over time. That is really different from the traditional studies under the *ceteris paribus* (with everything unchanged, or everything constant) condition. In this rapidly changing environment under interdependent society, there is no optimal solution possible for a specific economic entity at certain time period due to the unrealistic ceteris paribus condition. Therefore, the interdependent optimal path control over time is necessary to meet all the new challenges from the diverse, complicated conflicts coming from the interdependent mechanism of all the studies. That is the background of the new research and study platform of the sustainable e-business or green IT.

Sustainable e-business (or green IT) is an interdisciplinary field that aims to utilize the techniques from economics and business management, computer science, information and telecommunication science, operational research, and applied mathematics to harmonize the environmental, economic, and societal challenges for the sustainable development. We already discussed the sustainable development as an integrating platform of all the traditional theories to harmonize the diverse interests of the stakeholders surrounding the economic structure. In the above section, we described the e-business paradigm or purpose of the e-business study as the creation of values based on the collaborative network management. In the interdependent society, all of our everyday business decisions and economic policies are interrelated each other, and thus there are always the conflicting interests as well as the complicated procedural issues to handle the performance-oriented mechanism of e-business. Since the e-business requires the voluntary proactive participation of all the networking partners, it also has the similar purpose of sustainable development; to harmonize the conflicting interest and to create the better values by the cooperative networking.

In this regard, the sustainable development should be based on the strong platform of the effective and efficient information industries as well as the governance-oriented e-business application toward the green growth. In terms of the environmental perspectives, the former is called as the *green of IT* and the latter as the *green by IT*. In terms of field of activity perspectives, green IT consists of two important pillars of protection of environmental degradation and the enhancement of energy use as shown in Figure 4.6.

Therefore, the sustainable development and green IT have the common factors of sustainable governance, and this governance could be the key directions for the green of IT and green by IT. Green IT becomes the core of the survival kits to meet the rapidly ever-changing economy as a method to reduce environmental pollution, as well as a method to innovate the new frontier of IT industry.

However, the relationship between Information (and Communication) Technology (IT or ICT) and the sustainable development is complex, because of the negative environmental impact of IT production, use, and disposal. And thus, making this effect of greener or environmentally friendly IT has been termed *green IT*. Green IT considers IT's undesirable environmental impact primarily as a problem to be mitigated (green of IT) and another effect involves the positive impact of using IT to improve the eco-sustainability of economy (green by IT).

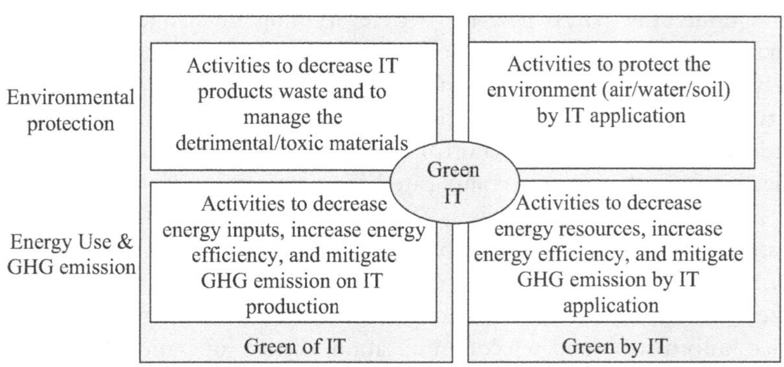

Figure 4.6 Conceptual characteristics of multi-dimensional green IT

In general, green IT should be based on the strong support of the IT hardware industries to provide the eco-friendlier environment for the use of Internet and its related applications. Therefore, these green IT industries consist of green IT infrastructure or green information platform. This platform industry includes the first layer of the computer and other related hardware manufacturers, the second layer of the telecommunication network providers, and the third layer of the middleware providers such as intranet software platform and extranet middleware providers. The major objectives of all these industries are based on the more cost-effective, eco-friendly provisions of the Internet environment. Therefore, their focus is in general on the IT's environmental impact primarily as unsustainable problems to be mitigated. It is rather passive compared with the more proactive application of green IT for the positive impact of using IT to improve the eco-sustainability of economy. Thus, the green IT platform industries with the more basic, yet more conservative objectives could be summarized with their strategy as the green of IT, and all the other green IT applications to find new business opportunities for the eco-friendly sustainable development could be summarized by the green by IT strategies.

The paradigm evolution of green IT can be summarized as shown in Figure 4.7. Like United Kingdom, the initial stage of greening policies may begin with the emphasis on the less carbon dioxide emission, but soon it emphasizes more the basic platform IT industry for the lower energy consumption and higher energy efficiency in digital devices, as Korean government does. As more public pressure imposes on the cognition of the eco-friendly system, not only IT industry, but all the other industries as well should make more efforts toward the green economy as the Japanese government does. The ultimate goal of these green paradigm shifts will be on the green growth, where all the business opportunities are on the greening revolution.

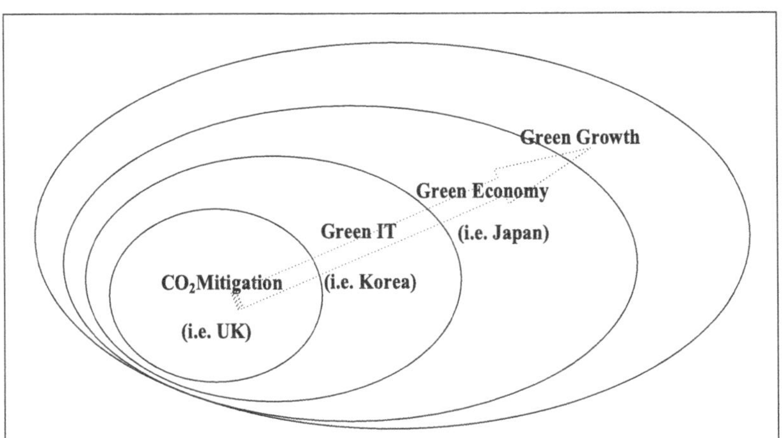

Figure 4.7 Green IT on the paradigm shift

Green IT is based on the sustainability science platform to handle the "green IT governance". In its original meaning, the governance reflects the emergence of de-centered and mutually adaptive policy regimes, which rests on regulation rather than service provision or taxing and spending in political science. Government is defined as the organizational structure to implement the political objectives (policy effectiveness), while the governance, on the other hand, conveys the administrative and process-oriented elements of governing rather than its antagonistic ones in its original meaning (policy efficiency). Soon, it is imported into the wider application in the social science. As mentioned before, we could define the *governance* as the performance-oriented workable mechanism. In this respect, green IT governance primarily deals with connections between business focus and IT management toward the eco-friendly society. The goal of green IT governance is to ensure the investment in eco-friendly IT field will generate a better business value and mitigate the environmental risks associated with green IT projects. Since the governance itself is a procedure-oriented terminology, the green IT governance includes its determinant factors of strategic alliance with IT business, responsibilities on the decision and implementation process, and governance mechanism as a structure and process. There are several definitions about the green IT governance and its related theories, but most of these definitions have a common factor of the sustainable and dynamic process of the green IT strategies over time for all the participating members.

Green IT governance or sustainable IT governance could be explained more in detail through the procedural approach. In the system dynamic perspectives, this

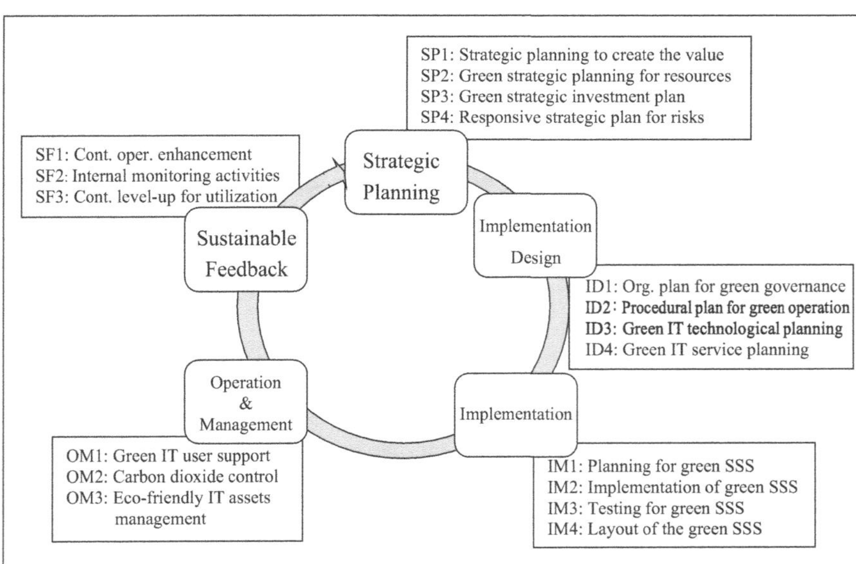

Figure 4.8 Green IT operational process

procedure could be identified with a five-step approach: major field of projects selection, green management target identification, green IT objectives clarification as a subset of green management, management process and project timetable setting-up, and procedural chart mapping in detail.

First, the green IT project target area should be selected taking the legacy system into consideration. It should be interchangeably implementable or interoperable with an existing legacy system. Otherwise, the ideal implementation of green IT could lead to internal conflicts with the legacy system. Before a new project begins, make sure all the stakeholders inside and outside of the organization be ready to adopt and use it. Strategy should be preceded before the technology implemented.

Second, considering the major focus of the new green project, a more concrete target should be identified. What should be provided for the new green IT project, and how can the organization provide this new function? The top manager should make it clear with the strong support of professional expert group who can identify the connectivity for the complicated process of the project, possible outcomes in terms of desirable and undesirable results from the project, value creation from its related social responsibilities, and finally dynamically sustainable performance with the feedback over time.

Third, the green IT objectives could be more scrutinized, in terms of green of IT and green by IT. It should create the value, including long-term profits, with the better images, better working conditions and consuming performance, and the compliances with the regulations in the sustainable area, by green of IT targets. Moreover, it should bring in the more effective implementation process, dependable performance and monitoring system, greener working condition, and better optimization of the IT resources by green by IT targets. Therefore, the green IT governance could be defined as the mechanism to utilize the IT resources for the greener performance (green of IT), and to create the green values by IT utilization (green by IT) on the circular manner. As shown in Figure 4.1, most of European countries such as the United Kingdom have emphasized the enhanced technology development in carbon emission mitigation (green by IT), while Korea has strongly promoted the paradigm of green of IT as the stimulus for the transformation of the economic structure toward the advanced economy. Japan has been proactively invoked to make all the industries green (green by IT), finally leading toward the advanced and enhanced green growth.

The green IT project should be based on the feasible flowchart of the process, with all the relevant structural inputs on the appropriate times. This flow chart-based green IT plan could integrate all the necessary resources and other relevant supports from the partners. Based on these stepwise procedures on the planning of the green IT project, the flowchart type of the functional mechanism of the green IT project could be clarified about the green IT (project) management process. This optimal path control over time consists of five categorical processes on the circular structure in general: strategic planning, implementation planning, implementation, operation and management, sustainable feedback.

The first step of the strategic planning consists of four sub-work processes: strategic planning to create the green value, green strategic planning for IT resources, strategic planning for green IT investment, and the responsive strategic planning for the potential risks of the green project. The second step of implementation design consists of four sub-work processes as well; organization planning for green IT governance, managerial process planning for green IT operation, green IT technological planning, and the green IT service planning. The third step of implementation consists of four sub-work processes; implementation planning for green IT solution, management system and green services (green SSS), implementation of green SSS, testing for the green SSS, and the lay outing of the green SSS. The forth step of operation and management consists of three sub-work processes; green IT user support and management, carbon dioxide control, eco-friendly IT assets management. The fifth step of sustainable feedback consists of three sub-work processes as well: continuing operational enhancement, internal operation control and regulation certifying activities, and the continuous level-up for the green IT utilization.

Green IT governance comes from the totally different approach with traditional legacy system, and thus we showed the green IT governance in terms of its procedural perspectives. As shown in Figure 4.6, green IT issues, such as green of IT industries and green by IT application for all the industries, could not be effectively and sustainably managed by the traditional theories with the legacy system, because the green IT requires the innovative way of value creation in the long term with the harmonized cooperation of diverse partners. Especially, the green of IT and green by IT show very unique approaches toward the sustainable performance. And thus, in the future, it will be better to handle these green IT strategies more in detail, based on the business case studies and relevant policies.

4.2 Conceptual characteristics of green IT

Nowadays, ICT has a significant impact on the economic growth and quality of life. Because of remarkable advances in the adoption of IT, everyone thinks of the benefits of information technologies, including the "right direction" for sustainable development. Unfortunately, most of all traditional production technologies consume huge amounts of electric power, placing a heavy burden on electric grids, and emitting greenhouse gases. However, not only does use of IT also harm to the environment, but its additives, production processes, and disposal activities could also cause a great ecological mischief in IT industries. For the purpose of preventing or reducing harm from IT products' life cycle, many modern companies switch to the concept of greening by IT.

Greening by IT is defined as a regime or mechanism for every computer user, and especially the IT industrial business managers to green their IT systems by reducing the undesirable outcomes of business and production technologies, and thereby creating a sustainable environment by changing the way they use these systems to being eco-friendlier. Greening by IT creates environmental values by improving energy efficiency, lowering greenhouse gas emissions, using less harmful materials, and encouraging reuse and recycling. Factors such as environmental regulations, the rising cost of waste disposal, corporate images, and public perception on the green activities give further impetus to the green IT initiative for all industries as well as all government policies on IT industry.

The IT industry, as the basic platform provider as well as the prompter for transforming the society and its economic structure into one characterized by sustainable development, has its own strong impact on the environment from its production and provision of all the information sharing and communication facilities. The total electrical energy consumption by servers, computers, monitors, data communications equipment, and cooling systems for data centers is rapidly increasing owing to the ever-increasing social demands on IT applications. This increased energy consumption also results in a much higher rate of greenhouse gas emissions. Each computer, data center, and other communication facility in use generates millions of tons of CO_2every year.

Since the industrial revolution began in the middle of the eighteen century, human activities have contributed substantially to climate change by adding CO_2 and other heat-trapping gases to the atmosphere. Unfortunately, the growth rate of CO_2 emission is hyper-rocketing because of the ever-increasing diffusion of IT applications. Atmospheric CO_2 concentrations have increased very steadily since pre-industrial times, until approximately 280 parts per million (ppm) by volume was reached in the eighteenth century. For the first time since we began tracking CO_2 in the global atmosphere, however, 400 ppm was reported when all of our Arctic sites reached that value in the spring of 2012. In 2013, the record at Mauna Loa Observatory in Hawaii first crossed the 400-ppm threshold value for sustainable development. Reaching 400 parts per million as a global average is a significant milestone in the irreversible downturn of climate degradation. Unfortunately, the monthly global average concentration of this greenhouse gas surpassed 400 parts per million in March 2015, according to NOAA's latest results, not at a single time or in a day, but over the whole month [7]. The current CO_2 level is higher than at any other time in history, and the speed of its increasing rate is accelerating over time. These greenhouse gas emissions have increased the greenhouse effect and caused Earth's surface temperature to rise. Most scientists agree that 350 ppm is a threshold value if the Earth is to sustain its atmospheric environment. Therefore, it is crucial that IT and its applications should be more proactive in decreasing CO_2 emissions to preserve the global average temperature.

The materials of which computers, phones, data servers, and other IT-related items are made are very toxic. Often the old, unnecessary equipment and waste parts, including the valuable components, are simply exported to developing countries where they are sorted and collected for reuse. Moreover, all the rest, as a rule, settle on open garbage dumps, turning into toxic e-waste. Every year, 20–50 million metric tons of e-waste are disposed of worldwide. Only 12.5 per cent of e-waste is currently recycled [12]. As the platform provider for sustainable development, many IT companies are making efforts to green their IT products life cycle.

4.3 Definition for green of IT

Green of IT is the study and practice of designing, manufacturing, using, and disposing of computers, servers, and associated IT subsystems, such as monitors, printers, data storage devices, and networking and communications systems, efficiently with minimal or no impact on the environment [9]. Green of IT also strives to achieve economic viability and improved system performance and use, while abiding by our social and ethical responsibilities. Green of IT strategies are based mainly on reducing power consumption by energy saving, and they result in lower costs or higher efficiency. They also strive to ensure lower carbon emissions and environmental impact so as to boost brand image and improved system performance, as well as space saving to enhance the quality of the service. The IT manufacturing companies, which are not doing harm to the environment, have not only a good reputation but also high competitiveness, owing to a visible (i.e., energy efficient) or invisible competitive advantage (i.e., an eco-friendly protection image) over other companies. In many countries, there is an ecological tax, a payment for pollution that is raised from enterprises that are especially polluting the environment, and/or a carbon emission trading system (ETS) for trading emission rights. At the expense of these, many investors will be more interested in the companies that are not doing harm to the environment, namely, green funds. All these visible and invisible pressures on the IT industries make the greening of IT strategies a core competence for the future.

Green of IT does not just imply about creating energy-efficient digital equipment, such as low-power processors and networking equipment, although this is an important component of the strategy, especially as the use of IT proliferates. Green of IT is more than about the application of IT to create energy-efficient processes, such as telework and video-conferencing, which replace energy-intensive activities such as commuting by personal vehicles or air travel. In more detail, green of IT strategies span a number of focus areas and activities, including but not limited to:

- designs for environmental sustainability;
- energy-efficient computing;
- electric power management such as super grid, microgrid, and picogrid;
- data center design, layout, and location;
- server virtualization such as cloud computing;
- responsible disposal and recycling of IT parts and materials;
- regulatory compliance on environmental policy;
- green metrics, assessment tools, and methodologies for sensing and monitoring;
- environment-related risk mitigation;
- use of renewable energy sources; and
- eco-labeling of IT products such as carbon footprints.

The four dimensions of the green of IT paradigm could summarize all these strategic efforts. First, all the IT products should be based on green design. This implies that designing eco-friendly technologies, spare parts, and equipment is the starting point for the research and development of new products. In the second stage of green manufacturing, IT companies should innovate eco-friendly manufacturing technologies, which will have a minimal impact on the environment during the manufacturing process. IT companies should also emphasize the green use of their own products. Green use of IT implies reducing the energy consumption of IT. The final stage of green of IT should be based on green disposal of old electronics through recycling and reuse. The materials and parts of IT products should be easily and eco-friendly decomposable, with minimal e-waste. All these green of IT strategies should be consistently interrelated with each other throughout the product life cycle (PLC) of IT industries.

Of course, most companies want to take on this paradigm in their businesses. However, the main barrier to solving environmental problems is an isolated attitude to ecology in the planning of production tasks and processes. It is therefore necessary to consider reducing the burden on nature caused by human activities to a sustainable level through sound policies, intelligent technology, and intelligent management strategies, which are the core structural factors of e-business. We shall discuss these one by one in the following section on the perspectives of green of IT.

5 Green platforms and smart revolution in IT

1. Green of IT platforms

Green of IT encompasses environmentally effective solutions and the use of IT to contribute to environment preservation. Green of IT focuses on the sustainable governance to initiate and operate the innovative cooperative network. Most of all, the green of IT could bring in the harmonized performance with the three bottom lines of sustainable development by providing the new platform of innovation. Green of IT Technology provides many desirable benefits, including increased eco-friendly efficiency, energy-saving access to IT, and convenient use of IT products. However, the production, use, and disposal of IT equipment requires large amounts of energy and resources as well as the undesirable carbon dioxide (CO_2) emission in general. Green of IT, therefore, is the innovative way to enhance the sustainability of computing and networking industries through manufacturing lower impact materials and products, reduced energy consumption of data centers and computers, and better recycling and longer end of life management. Data centers in the United States consumed 61 billion kWh of electricity in 2006, 1.5 per cent of total consumption, at a cost of $4.5 billion [10]. In Korea, this figure of electricity consumption of Internet data centers (IDCs) goes up to the 3 per cent of total consumption, which is really an energy-consuming area in the IT sector of industries. Moreover, the average computer wastes 50 per cent of its power [11]. Most of computers are connected with too much peripheral machines such as printer, several monitors, and other audio/video equipment, and most of these tools are on the idle mode. All these phenomena require a more proactive approach by the IT industries. Especially, the IT industry does not only consume too much energy and electricity, but it also produces very harmful greenhouse gases (GHGs), including CO_2. Whenever a user searches throughout the Google twice, it produces the 7g of CO_2, and it is equivalent to the amount of carbon of boiling water for a cup of coffee [12]. This is why we need to begin with green of IT industry as the platform for all the sustainable governance of the whole society.

Green IT has three development stages of its development. The first stage of green IT is called the green of IT, because it requires that all the IT industries should improve the energy-intensive structure of their manufacturing and operating procedures for IT, and less CO_2 production with the increase of eco-friendly efficiency. The second stage of green IT is called the green by IT, which facilitates all the Internet and network platforms to apply in our daily life to mitigate the outbreak of GHGs and to promote the eco-friendly enhanced technology development. The last stage of green IT is called the green in IT to new business, because IT takes the more proactive role to find the new business opportunities using the green of IT technology and its applications. There are two misconceptions about the green IT. First, the green IT technology does not give any optimal solution by itself, and thus before we develop the green of IT solutions, we need to have perfect readiness by the well-structured strategies. The IT solution or green of IT technology itself is just a vehicle to mitigate the undesirable output of GHGs and to find the new business opportunity, and thus before we implement the new solution and/or technology, we should certainly be ready to utilize this new technical environment. The green of IT does not guarantee the best performance unless we have appropriate strategies with organizational readiness. Second, green of IT does not guarantee any future by itself. The core for the successful governance of green of IT depends on the organizational readiness. If the organization readiness is not well provided, the green of IT may increase costs only with or without any significant image up. Unfortunately, it is really difficult to quantify these invisible values with ever-increasing costs, and thus it may result in the unsustainable disappointment at last. On the contrary, if the organization readiness is enough to bring in the stimulus for all the organization members, then the green of IT may increase not cost, but investment, because the organization shall evaluate every process of its implementation activities and its resulting performance. It is not easy to quantify all these process, but by the stimulus of the organizational readiness, green of IT can result in the visible decrease in the costs and GHG emission level significantly with much more visible achievement. Therefore, make sure that green of IT is not panacea, but the strategic tools for the future.

2. Green of IT policies

Many countries worldwide have emphasized the importance of the green of IT as a strategic field for the future challenges, and promoted with the diverse political paradigm. Since the green of IT policies became the platform of all the policies in the world, it is very insightful to examine the comparative benefits of the green of IT policies among the major countries. As we will see below, however, every country has a different approach depending on its cultural background of the public and private sectors.

As the other polices always do, the United States has promoted the market-led green of IT policies for a de facto standard. It may take too long to go through the trial and errors to get the popular standard or paradigm of the market. The government did not give the strong regulations and/or promoting incentives on the green of IT industries. Instead, it just emphasizes the importance of the green of IT, especially in the private sector. Nonetheless, the United States is one of the leading countries to promote the green of IT industries, because it has promoted the well-known "Energy Star" program in the Environmental Protection Agency since 1992. This program helped most of equipment as well as the facilities and buildings to save the energies, and enhance the energy intensity of the economy. Electric Power Research Institute (EPRI) has developed and promoted "Inteli-Grid" project as the smart-grid system, the interchangeable feedback management system between the demand and supply of the electricity, with the support of the Department of Energy (DOE) since 2001. Especially, the US Senate asked for a decrease in the level of electricity use of data centers and computer servers nationwide, which was reported at the 1.5 per cent of the nationwide consumption of the electricity in 2006. The urgent problem for the green growth in the United States lies in an ever-increasing speed of the energy consumption and its resulting environmental degradation. Therefore, instead of the government, many global companies in the United States took the major actions toward the green of IT, as we shall see later in more detail [12].

On the contrary, the Japanese government took the leading role to promote the green of IT as the new economic engine for the sustainable development, with the strong support by the private sector. As a leader of the Kyoto protocol, the Japanese government proclaimed the "Cool Earth 50", with the objective of 50 per cent lower carbon emission in business as usual (BAU), based on the year 2008, until 2050. Based on this new objective, the government put a lot of research fund to boost the technological level in the energy efficiency. The government will subsidize millions of dollars to save energy in IT industry, and to find out new business opportunity from the IT application toward the energy saving in all the industries. In 2008, the Japanese government organized the PPP committee of green of IT Initiative, to set up the new global standards, to expand international cooperation, and to find out the best practices and benchmarking case studies to the public. Japan had been acknowledged with its core competence in IT industries, but due to the "lost 20 years of economic stagnation", Japan wants to retake its leading power in the new green of IT area by the promotion of this PPP type of nationwide efforts. With this green of IT initiative, the Japanese government aims to lower the energy consumption by 10 per cent in 2025, with the matching mitigation of the carbon emission [8].

The United Kingdom took the "nudge" policies for the green of IT. The government has led many pumping policies to induce the participation of the private sector in this strategic field. The government has made the PPP with the green growth board, and this PPP requested most of government procurement under the criteria of the green of IT. Unlike Japan, however, the United Kingdom does not place much of the invisible pressure on the private sector to promote the green of IT. Instead, the UK government took the leading position by utilizing the green e-government. The government set up the objective of Sustainable Operations on the Government Estate (SOGE) in 2007 and put the carbon emission target management system (TMS) across all the government departments and agencies. The UK government is operating one of the largest computer systems in the world to provide diverse areas of public information services, resulting in waste of energies with the higher level of environmental degradation. Thus, the

UK government sets up the ambitious plan of "Carbon Neutrality", implying no carbon emissions in the major buildings and other facilities of the government in principle until the first stage of 2012, and then zero carbon emission from all the IT-related activities of the government until the second stage of 2020. The UK government does not put any pressure on the private sector, nor does it follow the market decision as a de facto standard. Instead, it just leads the private sector by the example itself, and this leading role of the government as the best practice is the unique paradigm of the green of IT policies.

Like other North Asian countries, Korea also emphasizes the more proactive leading role of the government in the green of IT policies. Korea established the low-Carbon Green Growth General Law in 2009, and according to the law, it organized the Green Growth Committee under the president of Korea. The committee has promoted diverse laws and policies related to the sustainable development as well as the green of IT since 2009. It published the "National Strategic Plan of Green of IT" in 2009, and organized the PPP type of Industrial Cooperation Committee for Green Growth for the detailed action plan to promote the energy-efficient, eco-friendly technology development. The government set up the national objectives of the green of IT. The first direction of the green of IT aimed to enter the top five of the green technological leading countries in the world in 2020, and the second direction aimed to transform the national economic structure toward the low-carbon eco-friendly advanced economy.

3. Green of IT in data server systems

The continued rise of Internet use and web applications is driving the rapid growth of data centers in IT industries. Enterprises are installing more and more servers or expanding their capacity for innovative e-business activities. These days, especially, "big data" can be considered the source of innovative values, and most companies do handle a lot of internal as well as external data mining; this causes data server capacity to increase. In this case, many companies ask IT companies to handle their data servers as well, as IT companies are professionals in this field. With the energy prices of maintaining data centers increasing explosively worldwide, the operational costs of data centers continue to increase rapidly as well. In addition to the costs, the availability of electrical power is becoming a critical issue for many companies whose data centers have steadily expanded. Consumption at worldwide data centers accounts for 1.5 per cent of the world's total power consumption on an annual basis, with that portion expected to rise up to 3 per cent by 2016 [13].

The social, financial, and practical constraints involved in data centers will force businesses and IT departments to reduce energy consumption in much more professional ways. As experts in the field, IT companies can improve data center efficiency by using new energy-efficient equipment, improving airflow management to reduce cooling requirements, investing in energy management software, and adopting environmentally friendly designs and new measures to curb data centers' energy consumption.

While building a new eco-friendly data center requires complete design control, IT professionals can take measures to reduce heat, add eco-friendly light, and discard materials that contain toxic chemicals in existing data centers. For instance, they can use energy-efficient windows, skylights, and sky tubes, and change the paint and carpets to a variety that involves low-volatile organic compounds (VOC). For example, the Google's Finnish data center at Hamina in Finland utilized its location advantages to "green" its data center. The specific regional advantage from being situated just near the seacoast means that the temperature of the coastal waters is maintained at some degrees above zero year-round. Moreover, this data center is located in a former paper mill where there is already a system of a fence of chilled water. It was necessary to adapt the system to meet the needs of a data center, but most requirements were already in place. There is also a built-in system of cleaning, and the system of return is designed in such a way that harm to the environment is negligible. Utilizing all these traditional ready-made factors, this green data center shows optimal power usage effectiveness (PUE) much more than any other Google data center worldwide. Another Google data center at Zhanghua in Taiwan uses wind power from its own wind power generation stations, to supply electricity for the center. In addition to this renewable energy source, the unusual cooling system uses a cool water circulation system as well. The water used here as a cooler is cooled at night then is brought to the heat-isolated stores, and used as required during the day. With the approach of the day, cold water is used in the cooling system, given the accumulated water during the night, it is just adequate for the length of the day enough. Thus, the data center in Taiwan uses much less electric power than other centers.

Virtualization is another option of the green data center to reduce its power consumption. With virtualization, one physical server hosts multiple virtual servers. Virtualization enables data centers to consolidate their physical server infrastructure by hosting multiple virtual servers on a smaller number of more powerful servers, thereby using less electricity and simplifying the data center. Besides getting better hardware usage, virtualization reduces data centers' floor space, makes better use of computing power, and reduces the data center's energy demands. Many enterprises are using virtualization to curb the runaway energy consumption of data centers. Busan, located on the seaside of the southeast region of Korea, has hosted many local as well as foreign data centers by virtue of its eco-friendly location advantages near the sea and year-round winds.

As it continues pursuing a leadership position in the worldwide cloud services market, Microsoft has been expanding data center capacity in the United States and abroad. High-growth Asian markets have been a particular focus for Microsoft and its competitors, and thus Microsoft is promoting a data center being built in the country's largest port city, Busan. The Microsoft data center will be built on an approximately 1.8 million sq. ft. site near an existing LG CNS data center—an IT services subsidiary of the Korean multinational LG Corp. By either establishing fully fledged cloud data centers in major metropolitan centers or by offering private network connectivity to its Azure cloud from collocation facilities, Microsoft aims to improve the performance of cloud services for Asian users, in a more eco-friendly way. By a similar token, Yahoo also has its data center in Korea, because Japan, the headquarter of Softbank, has been experiencing significant earthquakes and tsunamis recently and thus wants to utilize the location advantages of Busan.

The largest telecommunication operator, KT Corp. and US semiconductor chip giant Intel Corp. jointly developed an energy-efficient technology to reduce power consumption at data centers in Cheonan, 92km south of Seoul, adapting the eco-friendly high technology at KT's data center. Like nearly all of the world's other major telecom companies, KT is focusing on cloud services because of a sluggish wired network business. KT has ten data centers in Korea and it recently expanded in Cheonan with a new annex building. The cooling system of a data center is a big cost for operators. In this new data center, supplying warmer air to the data center floor reduces the amount of energy a cooling system consumes, and subsequently reduces the cost. The new technology enables data center operation at temperatures above 30°C, allowing operators to cut the electricity costs needed currently to keep the temperature between the optimal 18–21°C range. Server rooms in the data center building can be run at up to 30°C, which can save up to 36 per cent on air conditioning, according to KT [14].

4. Green of IT case studies

Green of IT industries are based on the energy saving and mitigated carbon emission on the product life cycle in IT industries. In this field, the leaders of the private sector could be the Korea Telecom in the field of Internet-providing telecommunication, and Samsung electronics company (Samsung) in the field of ICT hardware manufacturing. These companies are well known for their eco-friendly sustainable management, and thus, they could be utilized as one of the best practices as well as the benchmarking case studies.

Korea has experienced so serious bottleneck for the penetration rate of telecommunication network till 1980s. To boost the rapid delivery of the telecommunications, the Korean government separated its information network implementation from the planning department and set up the third sector of Korea Telecom (KT) in 1982. KT has promoted the expansion of the telecom infrastructure so rapidly and effectively nationwide, at much lower costs. Before KT begins its business, the price of a telephone line is almost equivalent with the price of a house, but just 10 years later the price became less than one twentieth, with one of the highest penetration rate of telephone lines nationwide in Korea. KT, as a kind of subsidiary of the government, has developed the fully digitalized Telephone Digital eXchange system (TDX), the 4th in the world, and developed successfully the Code-Divided Multiplex Access (CDMA),the 1st in the world. By these successful research and development, KT has made a miracle of the Internet paradise in Korea since 1995. Korea has the highest penetration rate of Internet in the world, and many global companies enter into the Korean market as a kind of test-bed for the new telecom services, because the Korean people are so adaptive to the new services with highly responsible feedback for the improvement of the new business.

Based on the successful history of the telecommunication industry, KT has launched the "Green of IT Vision and Strategy for the Low-carbon Green Growth" in 2009. This green of IT vision just came out after the government proclaimed the new start of green growth paradigm in 2008. KT emphasizes its role as the metamediary to facilitate the convergence of all the information-based businesses and activities by green of IT in its vision. The vision is driven by three directions, with the core strategy to "Make IT Resources Green in KT". Since KT is the major telecommunication infrastructure provider nationwide, it will make all the resources consisting of the telecom infrastructure, such as national backbone servers, power supply, network lines, etc., be green by the enhanced eco-friendly efficiency. For example, it will convert the power supply of all the Internet data centers (IDCs) into a direct current circuit system, and virtual server system, aiming the increase of electricity efficiency up to 500 per cent, and network efficiency up to 42 per cent. Based on this green of IT infrastructure, the second direction of "Green Productivity Increase" strategy will be promoted. Using all telecom lines and wireless fidelity (Wi-Fi) network, it will increase the green productivity of the services of KT, and enhance the life quality of the public telecommunications with eco-friendly environment promotion. For example, KT will develop the smart traffic information management system, which transform the public transportation structure eco-friendlier, aiming at 1 billion dollars of new business creation, carbon emission mitigation by increased use of the more comfortable smart public transportation, and the 0.2 billion dollars cost deduction in the transfer discount fees. The third direction of KT is to create new business and renewable energy, by the "Embedded with Green of IT" strategy. The strategy is based on the convergence of the next generation green of IT technologies and the smart IT infrastructure.

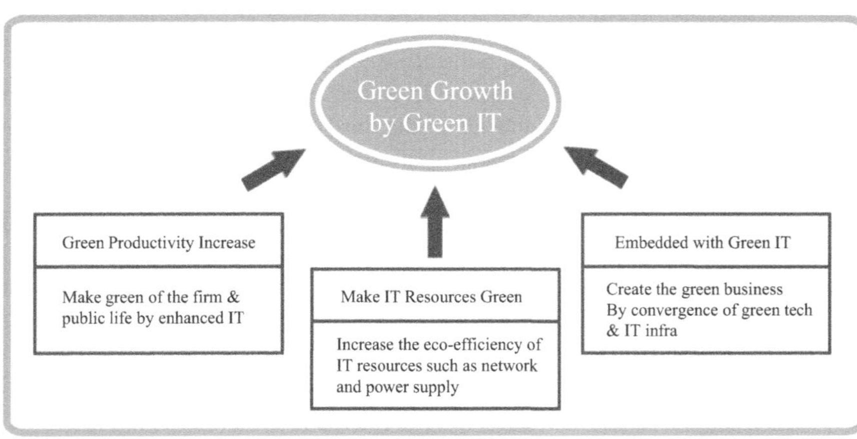

Figure 5.1 Green IT vision of KT

Source: KT Economics & Business Research Center, Green IT Vision and Strategy for the Low-carbon Green Growth, 2009

Samsung, the largest company in Korea, has set up its new vision of "Creative New Value through Eco-Innovation" in 2009. It just reflected the strong promotion policy paradigm by the Korean government. Nevertheless, since then, Samsung has aggressively promoted the green of IT strategies. Samsung won the award of Green Management by the Korean president with its new product of Jipel refrigerator in 2014. It implies that Samsung brought the innovative technologies in its products. This new refrigerator of 9000 liters (*Jipel T9000*) implemented diverse innovation of "the larger size, the less energy with better environment" technologies. It enhanced the 15 per cent of energy efficiency and saved 8.7 per cent of electricity use, and 46 per cent of breakable parts loss potentials. Especially, it used the biodegradable packaging system to reuse up to 40 times of its box package. This biodegradable box package saved 2,742 tons of papers per year with a 99.7 per cent decrease in traditional chemical usage, which is equivalent to a decrease of 9,320 tons of carbon emission and planting of 130,000 trees per year. This eco-friendly box package won many famous awards in the world such as Asia Star Awards in eco-packaging, and 2013 World Star Awards in electronics. Overall, this refrigerator could reuse all its parts and materials up to 78 per cent. Not only this case, Galaxy mobile phone uses the 100 per cent reused paper box package, and 3D glasses uses the biodegradable plastic. Samsung smart air conditioner controls its speed of the wind and temperature automatically depending on the room conditions, using the smart sensor, smart temperature changer, smart inverter and other technology innovations. By all these efforts, Samsung decreased total of 886 billion tons of GHGs between 2008 and 2013, which is equivalent to planting 8 million of trees [15].

The successful factor of this green of IT strategy of Samsung is based on the eco-friendly Life Cycle Assessment since 1995. Samsung adopted the eco-friendly solution and management skills on all the life cycles of the product, beginning from the research and development stage, procurement of parts and modules, production, distribution, consumer's consumption, till the disposal of the product, as shown in the figure.

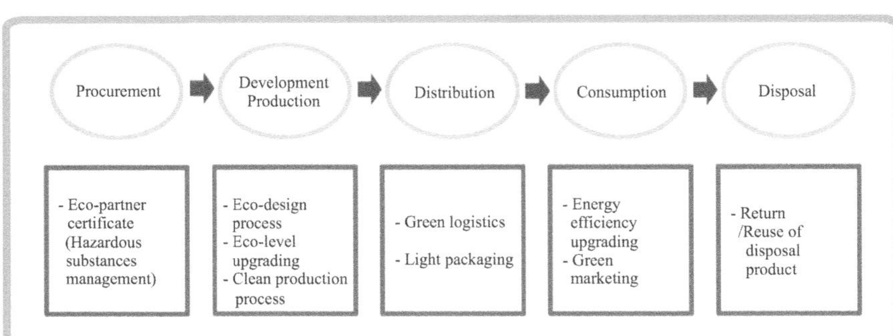

Figure 5.2 Green IT life cycle assessment of Samsung

Source: Samsung, Sustainable Management Report (http://samsungtomorrow.com). Accessed on Oct. 20, 2015. Fully modified by the author.

Samsung has also made the global efforts to upgrade its level of green certificates worldwide, resulting in 3,285 green management certificates in the world such as UL in the United States and CSA in Canada. Samsung has promoted the 3R system; reuse, recycle, and reduce since in 1998. It established the Asan Recycling Center and other seven local centers, where all the returned or discarded products turn into reusable resources by the recycling process. It handles not only Samsung products, but other brands as well because it helps the eco-friendly economies of scale even in the green of IT process. The recycling process consists of pre-selection process, breaking down process, and classifying and collecting process. The recycling centers produced 12,000 tons of steel, 200 tons of copper, 400 tons of aluminum, and 4,400 tons of plastics in the year 2013. Now, you cannot find any discarded items of electronics product in the streets of Korea due to the proactive efforts of Samsung in the recycling field [16].

The reason for the popularity of the Samsung Galaxy mobile phone may come from the core competence of the green of IT technology. For example, Galaxy Young 2 version of the phone is made of bio-plastic, consisting of 60 per cent general plastic, 20 per cent recycled plastic, and 20 per cent bio resin. Bio resin is extracted from the corn oil, and thus it makes the combined materials biodegradable. This new combined material decreased 10 per cent of its production costs and carbon emission levels, which is equivalent to planting 40,000 trees per 10 million of sold phones. Moreover, the earphone jack of the Galaxy Young 2 is made of 20 per cent bio-nylon, combined with the Castor oil, Nylon and gasoline-based general plastic, resulting another 10 per cent of lower costs with much less carbon emission. The third competence of the Galaxy Young 2 comes

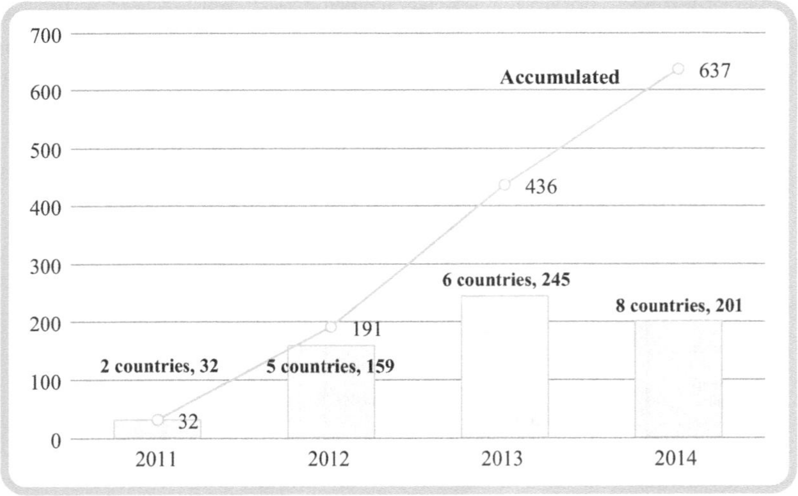

Figure 5.3 Green IT certificates worldwide by Samsung

Source: Samsung, Sustainable Management Report (http://samsungtomorrow.com). Accessed on Oct. 20, 2015.

from the battery cover, painted with the coating paint combined with sugar cane, rape blossoms seed oil. This green of IT innovation resulted in 2.5 tons of gasoline decrease and 7.6 tons of carbon emission decrease per year. As shown in the case of mobile phones, Samsung achieved outstanding certificates on the green of IT technologies as shown in the figure, including Carbon Trust in the United Kingdom every year, and took the top position in the green of IT field in the world with its patents and certificates [16].

The most important tasks for green of IT in Samsung are handled in the Environmental Evaluation Lab (EEL). Since 2004, this lab has evaluated all the product process under the guideline of "Restriction of the use of Hazardous Substances (RoHS)" enacted in European Union in 2006. RoHS regulates the emission of six hazardous substances such as cadmium, mercury, and lead. The lab insists on the strict evaluation for all the production process, and their ingredients with the belief that environmental issues are not the subject of negotiation, but the necessary survival kit for the global company.

Based on all these efforts, Samsung made 45 per cent of decrease in the GHGs per unit sales from 7.44 in 2008 to 3.85 in 2012. GHGs per unit sales is measured by the total amount of GHG emissions by the company over its sales volume (ton CO_2/million dollars). Therefore, it can compare the green of IT performance across the companies in objectively relative scale, regardless of its sales volume and the period. Samsung made an effort to reduce almost one half the emission level for its one-unit dollar of products within 3 years. It is equivalent to 4.4 million tons of GHG emission decrease or 52,812km^2 of land planted with trees to compensate the same amount of GHG emission. It has been ranked the top in its global green mark and certificates worldwide for six consecutive years from 2006, with 2,887 green certified product models as of June 2012. Samsung also has promoted diverse eco-friendly social responsibilities. It participated in the Amazon anti-deforest campaign in Brazil, in planting trees and river purification campaign in southeast Asian countries, and in special education support for the eco-friendly local education system in Slovakia. Altogether, Samsung invested 3.3 billion US dollars for 3 years from 2009 to 2012 for green of IT management [17].

From the benchmarking case of green of IT strategies by Samsung, we can learn how to initiate and operate the green of IT governance at the company level. First, Samsung clearly shared its new vision of "Creative New Value through Eco-Innovation" since its introduction in 2009. Especially, Samsung viewed green of IT not as a threat or new risks in the global market, but as a new opportunity to create value. And it understood clearly that these challenges do not come from the expansion of the traditional management system, but from the innovation of technology and innovation-oriented management. Therefore, the vision sharing with the strong leadership of the company is really important to promote the green of IT. Samsung also wanted to prove their vision is not just possible, but also feasible with financial and other quantifiable performance. The vision of creating value has been realized over time. The second factor for the green of IT governance in Samsung may come from the monitoring and evaluation system all across the inside and outside of the company about the appropriate green of IT implementation. It invested a huge amount of money to promote the green of IT, with the belief that it will certainly bring the outstanding performance. They made great efforts to certify its green of IT projects in diverse ways, such as the biggest number of the certificates worldwide, and cost reduction for the clear comparison before and after the new challenges of green of IT. It is crucial not just require people to be involved in the green growth, but to show them the direction is really workable by the quantified performance and achievements. Samsung successfully confirmed their investment in the green of IT is really valuable with many visible and invisible (but quantifiable) values.

The third factor for the green of IT governance in Samsung may come from the professional team support as the network manager of all the collaboration networks. Because of the complicated and complex process of the green of IT implementation and its resulting effect on the organization, it is really difficult for the company, which takes its objective of profit maximization in short term, to promote the long-term invisible process of green of IT without the strong commitment of the strategic task force team to the top-level control in organization-wide monitoring, evaluating, and reporting the comparative performance over time. Samsung has the EEL for the strategic planning and implementation of the green of IT, and thus it became possible to maintain the foreseeable optimal control toward the vision. Especially, this lab has supported by all the members of the stakeholder of Samsung, and thus it could facilitate, collaborate, and provide all the necessary services to the stakeholders such as employees, consumers, and local society for the green of IT governance.

Most of all, Samsung has a very open, innovating, and somewhat competitive organizational structure, and thus all workers in each department showed the proactive fever to participate in this new paradigm of green of IT. Moreover, they became proud of themselves as the leader of the global trend. This organizational readiness became the fertile platform for the successful governance of the green of IT.

5. Concluding remarks

Like Green Wave, the Internet revolution changed our everyday lives in the world, and now the understanding and utilizing Internet-related know-how is not just optional, but necessary as a survival kit in this interdependent ubiquitous society. Just think we cannot imagine our life without the Internet connection or smartphones in our hands. Due to this rapid technological development as well as the innovative business approaches, most of the traditional theories and practices are useless, as shown in the paradigm shift from the push-marketing based on the traditional marketing mix toward the web marketing mix. The most important emphasis on the price or product in traditional theoretic perspectives are not the same in the e-business era, because we can develop many innovative ways of making not just short run profits, but the long-run loyalties as well using web marketing mix. Now, most of theories and practices should consider the effective use of Internet in their present and future tasks, and it implies that e-business became the platform for all the theories and practices in terms of economies of networking with the smart approach by group intelligence.

By the same token, we already analyzed how the sustainable development became the platform for all the existing theories and practices to transform from the competitive optimal solutions such as economies (or efficiency) and/or profit maximization to the win-win type of creating values by collaboration among all the stakeholders. If we combine these two platforms of all the theories and practices, we could reach the green IT, which is the key word in Part II. Unfortunately, green IT is not too much optimistic in its conceptual characteristics. Green IT has the two faces of Janus. It could increase the cost of the industries due to the extra burden of the energy-saving, emission-mitigating process, at least in the short term. Unfortunately, most of organizations just take only the short-term profit maximization objectives, and thus they just emphasize too much on the dark side of the green IT. On the contrary, however, the case studies of green of IT industries by Samsung and KT showed the other face of Janus, the promising side of the green IT. Many global companies such as Samsung in Korea and Google in the United States made a great success by the strong commitment to the top-level strategic project and proved that the green IT could be a great future challenge for new businesses. Nokia has more than 150 years of company history, starting as a small company in timber industry, which transformed its core businesses as the utmost trendsetter toward the global leader in electronics industry. 3M and many other companies have great company profiles of successful transformation according the new global norm and emerging paradigms such as information society and ubiquitous economy. The environment surrounding the global economy has been changing rapidly, and it is becoming faster and faster. All these changes bring the environmental risks for the industries. If we accept them with proactive planning, we will get the fortune; if we avoid this risk passively, we may lose our position forever, like Nokia which sold its core business of smartphone manufacturing to Microsoft. Therefore, the green of IT is, now, not just optional, but necessary for the future survival.

As Samsung showed, the government, as well as the private sector, should make the green IT vision more clear in detail and firmly for foreseeable optimal path control. Moreover, the intermediary as the control tower of the green IT should quantify all the process of the green IT planning and implementation, and provide the organizational readiness to take the responsibilities with more pride for all partners, because the workers and all the other stakeholders are not just helpers in the harmonized collaborative network anymore. They are ready to participate in our future together. Once a friend, forever a friend in this green IT era!

References

1 Rangan, S.; Adner, R., "Profits and Internet: Seven misconceptions", *MIT Sloan Management Review*, 2001, Summer, 44–53.

2 Rigby, D.K.; Reichheld, F.F.; Schefter, P., "Best practice: Avoid the four perils of CRM", *Harvard Business Review*, 2002, February, 101–109.
3 Bunkley, Nick, "Joseph Juran, 103, pioneer in quality control, dies", *New York Times*, March 3, 2008.
4 Choi, Y., *Global e-Business Management: Theory and Practice*. Seoul: Bomyoung Book, 2012.
5 Choi, Y., "The competitive dynamics of web marketing strategies in Korea", *e-Business Studies*, 2009, 10(4), 263–277.
6 Wikipedia, *Social Networking Service* (Accessed on 29/04/2016: https://en.wikipedia.org/wiki/Social_networking_service).
7 NOAA (National Oceanic and Atmospheric Administration), *Greenhouse Gas Benchmark Reached*, Wednesday, 06/05/2015 (Accessed on 10/01/2016: http://research.noaa.gov/News/NewsArchive/LatestNews/TabId/684/ArtMID/1768/ArticleID/11153/Greenhouse-gas-benchmark-reached-.aspx).
8 Takayuki, S., *Green IT Initiative as a Policy to Provide a Solution*, OECD Workshop on ICTs and Environmental Challenges, 2008.
9 Kim, I., *Understanding of Green IT*, Educontentshupia, Seoul, Korea, 2012.
10 U.S. EPA Energy Star Program, *EPA Report to Congress on Server and Data Center Energy Efficiency Public Law*, 2007, 109–431.
11 University of Michigan, Planet Blue, *Common Sustainable Computing Myths*, 2013.
12 U.S. Environmental Protection Agency, *Fact Sheet: Management of Electronic Waste in the United States* (Accessed on 10/01/2016: http://www3.epa.gov/epawaste/nonhaz/municipal/pubs/2012_msw_fs.pdf).
13 Murugesan, San, "Harnessing green IT: Principles and practices", *IT Pro January/February 2008 (IEEE)*, 2008, 24–33.
14 The Korea Times News, *KT, Intel to Team Up for Energy-saving Data Center*, 21/08/2012 (Accessed on January 2015: http://www.koreatimes.co.kr/www/news/nation/2012/08/182_117829.html.
15 Samsung Electronics, *Green Management Special Report 1* (Accessed on 15/08/2016: http://samsungtomorrow.com/%EC%82%BC%EC%84%B1%EC%A0%84%EC%9E%90-%EB%85%B9%EC%83%89%EA%B2%BD%EC%98%81-%ED%8A%B9%EC%A7%91_%E2%91%A0-%EC%B9%9C%ED%99%98%EA%B2%BD-%EC%A0%95%EC%B1%85-%ED%95%9C-%EA%B8%B8-%EA%B2%B0%EC%8B%A4%EC%9D%84).
16 Samsung Electronics, *Green Management Special Report 2* (Accessed on 15/08/2016: http://samsungtomorrow.com/%ec%82%bc%ec%84%b1%ec%a0%84%ec%9e%90-%eb%85%b9%ec%83%89%ea%b2%bd%ec%98%81-%ed%8a%b9%ec%a7%91_%e2%91%a1-%eb%b2%84%eb%a0%a4%ec%a7%84-%ea%b0%80%ec%a0%84-%ec%83%88-%ec%83%9d%eb%aa%85%ec%9d%84-%ec%96%bb).
17 Samsung Electronics' *Green Initiatives: Three Years after the Lunching* (Accessed on 15/08/2016: http://samsungtomorrow.com/3452).

Part III

Green by IT applications and e-business

Overview

The widespread global use of information and communication technology (IT or ICT) has promoted the idea of ubiquitous society in diverse ways. Anytime and anywhere, we can communicate with a specific person through many platforms of Internet access, and even operate electric utilities of all sorts from a distance. This "4 any" scenario of the ubiquitous society has changed many aspects of our lives. Dreams could come true for everyone, especially in the field of smart or green IT, because of these remarkable innovations that prompt a ubiquitous social revolution. IT has become a powerful platform for sustainable development in all industries and for all economic agents' activities. When this ubiquitous society confronts the urgent demands of sustainable development, "green by IT policies and strategies" create eco-friendly, carbon-zero sustainable governance. In this part of the book, we shall address the sustainable revolution by IT from the perspective of "green by IT." This perspective implies that IT applications and software innovation could create new energy-efficient, environmentally friendly forms of life in diverse ways. On the green by IT perspective, we shall discuss activities ranging from government transformation via the e-Government 3.0 paradigm to the most representative technological fields of smart revolution with the theme of sustainable development. With the new smart revolution, we can see everywhere the dramatic transformation of our lives in innovative ways. Seamless automatic sensors and self-controlled artificial intelligence will result in a smart utopia for a zero carbon, sustainable society achieved through innovations such as the smart city, smart car, smart grid, and even smart factory. All these smart revolutions are based on the green by IT concept for the future. Now, based on this smart revolution trend, the main questions of these chapters are as follows: how can public and private sectors promote their businesses and activities in more environmentally friendly ways, with the support of IT applications? What kind of environmental challenges arise from these IT applications? How can companies create value, instead of maximizing profits, from a "green by IT" perspective? What are the key factors of successful green IT? We are ready to answer these questions in the following chapters about green by IT applications as part of a survival kit for the future.

6 Green platforms for IT applications and e-business

1. e-Government 3.0 and smart cities with green by IT

1.1 Paradigm shift to green IT policies

Green IT cannot be the ultimate goal or final mission of the country, but progress in this field provides a very important milestone to assess whether the nation is moving in the right direction for the optimal control of green growth. Most countries begin with a higher emphasis on greenhouse gas (GHG) reduction, such as the carbon dioxide emission trading systems in the European Union and Korea; over time, however, these carbon mitigation policies should be supported by strong green IT platforms to monitor, measure, and control all the direct and indirect activities of social and economic agents from a green or sustainable perspective. Although the Korean government pronounced a policy paradigm of green growth in 2010, this policy is still at the stage of the greening of IT industries, with greater focus on hardware-oriented green wave innovations, as we learned in previous chapters. Now is the right time for governments of the world to lead all private sector industries and individuals to innovate their economic activities in greener ways through the use of the new wave of IT applications, which approach is the core of the green by IT philosophy. This political vision of creating a platform to lead the whole national economy towards green growth became the background of Government 3.0, with much more emphasis on smart city projects in Asian countries.

Like the United States, United Kingdom, and Japan, most advanced countries have shifted their focus from a hardware-oriented green IT industry revolution toward the more diverse, indirect applications of the green by IT approach. All countries in the world advocate green growth, at least as a political slogan. However, to transform the traditional legacy system into green growth, driven by the green by IT revolution, is not easy. Nonetheless, as long as all economic entities from the government to the private sector agree on the green wave, they will need to understand in more detail the diverse range of IT software and web applications that are being developed. Since this challenging transformation of our society through the green wave of sustainable development will not be easy or effective at least until the initial stage of the green by IT revolution has been achieved, all governments in the world take the role of pioneers with the implementation of diverse green by IT innovations in the public service as well as in the administrative works of the government through a form of advanced e-government (or Government 3.0).

Thus, these e-government projects may provide a diverse, yet clear vision for the overall private sector to follow this smart revolution, because most of green IT applications and e-businesses could arise from the various pilot projects of e-government such as smart grids, smart transportation, and smart cities. Starting from these government-led pilot projects, the private sector can make continuous efforts to enhance these new services and other green IT initiatives. The role of governments in the promotion of these pilot projects in green IT is thus crucial in providing a kind of revolutionary platform to position green IT on the frontiers of the future challenges in new business strategies, new technology, and new economic and social structures. This innovative role of government should not be based on traditional show-off schemes, as has occurred in most Asian countries, but on the sustainable performance of such projects even after the pilot phase. This is why we should focus on good governance and the creation of workable mechanisms for sustainable performance in the design of e-government pilot projects.

To emphasize this kind of proactive role of e-government in terms of governance, Table 6.1 shows the historical trends of e-government. The core competence of e-government is in efficiency, led by government agencies such as public companies. For example, in the e-Government 1.0 era, you could ask for the certificate of a national citizen on the Internet, but you needed to go to the designated government office to collect the printed version. This was troublesome, because even after using the Internet applications, citizens had to visit government offices directly for the results. Therefore, e-Government 2.0 enhanced its core competence with bilateral ready-made systems within the public service. If you require a public service, then you may apply for it using ready-made menus and obtain the results right away from the Internet. This provides huge efficiency improvements in the national economy due to

Table 6.1 Paradigm shift for the sustainable e-government

	e-Government 1.0	*e-Government 2.0*	*e-Government 3.0*
Leading agent	Government	Public in general	Individual people
Core competence	Efficiency	Democracy	Open, democracy
Relational approach	Govt. Led	Limited participation	Open, proactive participation
Public services	One way	Ready-made two way	Customized two way
Service Channel	Direct visit for results	Results by Internet	Any access possible (mobile, wife, etc.)

the paperless public service automation process. Taking this one step further, e-Government 3.0 provides any individual economic entity with an open, proactive participation platform to create value from customized public services. For example, an individual could open a web business and manage a network that allows the public to reserve cabin rooms in the national forest. This agent will search all the available cabin rooms in the national forest owned by the government and negotiate with these government offices to reserve these cabins on behalf of its web-business customers. Now, under the e-Government 3.0 paradigm, all public services could be potential sources of business and, thus, government officials should have a good grasp of private service management know-how to support this creative economy, led by public–private partnerships (PPPs). We shall handle all these governance issues raised by the green by IT revolution, providing details step-by-step in the following sections about the most representative trends in Asian countries.

1.2 e-Government 3.0

Owing to the explosive diffusion of smartphones, users can very easily fabricate commercial applications ("apps") for the Internet, resulting in values and profits such as advertising commissions and membership fees from app users. This kind of value-creating Internet utilization is called Web 3.0. The original worldwide web, Web 1.0, was based on the simple passive use of the Internet for information search and sharing. By virtue of easy access to the web, users could experience the power of information. In the Web 1.0 era, Internet use became extremely popular, because information itself was the power and the effective currency driving the initial stage of web diffusion. Soon, Internet users became *prosumers*. Such consumers were not satisfied with passive one-way web surfing for information. Instead, they participated in the production of group intelligence, and these user-driven web activities created another boom in Internet popularity. Using the economies of networks, users can obtain group intelligence; and this group intelligence allowed Internet users to be smart enough to obtain *knowledge*, instead of simple, passive information. This new trend of Internet use is called Web 2.0. A representative global example of Web 2.0 can be found in the YouTube music video of "Gangnam Style". This video, made by the Korean singer Psy, rocketed in popularity and made Psy a hero of the Web 2.0 era. Soon, users began to think that creating their own content on the Internet could bring great success, even in terms of new businesses. The popularity of some Internet content and apps resulted in the Web 3.0 era. Web 3.0 is based on more proactive participation that "creates" value on the web. Now, many web users can create their own app businesses with just a few clicks. These created web contents will result in higher profits and/or better values for other Web 3.0 users.

Now, the Web 3.0 era has created opportunities even for government officials to allow users to participate in diverse public services and related state businesses, such as the weather forecast service using the government database; and this kind of PPP has created a new era of e-government. E-government – also known as electronic government, Internet government, digital government, online government, connected government, or sometimes Government 3.0 – is defined as the set of service-oriented mechanisms of government activities based on the Internet, including diverse digital content and access tools for delivering government information and services to citizens, including private sector companies, thus boosting new business in the private sector. E-government consists of the digital interactions between citizens and their government (C2G); between central government and government agencies (G2G); between government and citizens (G2C); between government and state employees (G2E); and between government and businesses (G2B). E-government aims to promote and improve the contributions of diverse stakeholders to national and community development, and deepen the governance process, and especially to enhance the harmonized sustainable performance of public services with the participating partners' cooperation.

Since all countries are now based on interdependent economic structures, and e-government can bring mutual benefits to both the public and private sectors, the United Nations conducts a biannual e-government survey, which includes a section titled "e-Government Readiness," for all its member countries. This survey provides a comparative ranking of the world's countries according to two primary indicators concerning the state of e-government readiness and the extent of e-participation. The advantage of e-government lies in its ability to offer an increased portfolio of public services to citizens in an efficient and cost-effective manner. E-government is a good guarantee of government transparency. Government transparency is vital, because it allows the public to be informed about predictable policies for the future. E-government can also create new business opportunities for the private sector to utilize all the possible information about public services, such as weather forecasts and green growth-related project information. As shown in Table 6.1, e-Government 1.0, or simply traditional government, is defined as the official system for informing the public about government policies. Compared with e-Government 1.0, e-Government 2.0 refers to government policies that aim to harness collaborative technologies to create an open-source computing platform in which government, citizens, and innovative companies can all improve transparency and efficiency. The government procurement web sites are representative of e-Government 2.0 projects. Government should show all procurement opportunities on its public web sites and all members of the private sector that have interest in fulfilling these tenders should register their price quotations in equitable and effective ways. E-Government 2.0 provided transparent bilateral communication and cooperation with the private sector as shown in these procurement projects.

In her inaugural address of 2013, Korean president Park Geun-hye defined the "creative economy" as the convergence of science and technology with industry, the fusion of culture with industry, and the blossoming of creativity at the very borders that were once barriers. This process goes beyond the rudimentary expansion of existing markets to create new markets and new jobs by building on the bedrock of convergence. At the very heart of a creative economy lie science, technology, and the IT industry, promoted by a proactive government aiming toward cooperative PPPs. This creative PPP framework is called (e-)Government 3.0. To diffuse sustainable development policies into society and allow the private sector to participate in the creative economy, the Korean government has promoted the e-government policy paradigm. As shown in Table 6.1, e-Government 1.0 is based on government-led information delivery. People can request public services by Internet, but may have to pick up the results by actual visits to government offices. e-Government 2.0 is an enhanced version with limited participation from the public, which may now obtain its service results directly from the Internet. However, open information and/or government web services are limited and thus the public sometimes cannot get what they really want. As the creative economy founded on the Internet implies, e-Government 3.0 is based on customized and proactive bilateral web services using diverse access points such as smartphones, and the mobile or Wi-Fi Internet of Things (IoT). The private sector can access a much wider range of government data sources and, using these data, can even create profit-making businesses. The private sector can sell updated weather information-based lotteries or rain check insurance. Further, the private sector can ask the public to engage in cooperative activities such as big data mining for smart car development. This kind of proactive participation concerning open information generating is the key to sustainable development, because the PPPs can harmonize the participants' needs to meet challenges in the future.

The conceptual characteristics of e-Government 3.0 may be summarized as having three dimensions, which together promote the sustainable ubiquitous society. First, it is based on *transparent government*. In principle, all government data should be open to the public and the private sector to satisfy their right to know. Open and transparent government implies that the private sector could utilize public data for its own purposes as well. Moreover, transparent government promotes the PPP regime in diverse public activities. The Korean government introduced this approach to all metropolitan areas, along with creative PPP centers to help young people to develop new ventures as creative entrepreneurs using public data sources. Second, e-Government 3.0 is based on *efficient government*. To increase its efficiency, all government departments need to "break down walls" between departments and agents, to result in more effective communication and cooperation in meeting interdepartmental challenges. Removing obstacles to communication among government offices could induce a wider range of cooperation on using big data mining to create more scientific and predictable public policies. Third, e-Government 3.0 should be based on a model of *service-oriented government*. The government should not just wait passively for the needs of the public to be expressed, and then evaluate them, and finally implement policies to meet some of these needs of the private sector. Instead, government officials should provide customized and integrated one-stop services across all related departments. In particular, this wide range of proactive one-stop services is the key to small- and micro-business startups, and to people who have very limited access and/or lack of capacity to connect to core information. This strategy could create new private businesses. Therefore, openness, mutual communication, co-sharing, and cooperation are the key words in harmonizing the diverse interests around public services.

e-Government 3.0 is a new style of government innovation for the creative economy. Its role in achieving sustainable governance in the public sector has been emphasized. The traditional paradigm of public service is based on effectiveness. From a social science perspective, effectiveness relates to ***getting the right things done***. If the government wants to help the traditional street markets, it may establish a policy goal such as modernizing 3 million markets for a maximum of 30 million dollars. If it spends exactly the same amount on 3.3 million street markets, it shows 110 per cent policy effectiveness. Even if this kind of quantitative approach is easy and shows its effectiveness, it does not guarantee the successful operation of the street markets. Most street markets could have an enhanced outlook with at least some public support. However, such policies do not guarantee this, nor do they guide better performance and/or more sales for the traditional peddlers in the street markets. In order to boost their sales volumes, the government should develop more performance-oriented, and/or field (market-) oriented strategies such as providing coupons for the traditional markets to poor people. This kind of performance-oriented policy is based not on the effectiveness paradigm of the public policy, but on the principle of governance – a workable mechanism for sustainable performance. This sustainable governance should be a core competence of e-Government 3.0.

With the support of e-Government 3.0, Air Korea is one of the most sustainable business models. For the successful hosting of the World Cup 2002, the Korean government installed an air pollution management system near all the soccer grounds nationwide, and thus expanded its measurement points in congested areas such as bus terminals, highway rest areas, and subway platforms nationwide. When Koreans began to worry about air pollution due to serious PM2.5 smog from China, the environmental management authority, as the third party of the PPP system, created real-time web sites for Air Korea. Insurance companies and some marketing companies have utilized this web site's information for their new business ventures.

2. Smart city project

The most representative e-Government 3.0 examples can be found in the many smart city projects worldwide. Many governments have promoted pilot projects related to sustainable green by IT challenges. A smart city is defined as a local community embedded with highly interconnected ICT to enhance the quality and performance of diverse city services, reduce costs and resource consumption, and improve contact between citizens and government. Diverse technological, economic, and environmental innovations have generated sustainability-related issues in smart cities, including those to do with climate change, economic restructuring, and narrowing the social digital divide, as well as moving to online retail and virtual entertainment, healthcare for aging populations, and various pressures on PPP activities. Major strategies and achievements related to smart cities are listed in the Intelligent Community Forum awards from 1999 to 2010, granted to the cities of Suwon, the Gangnam District of Seoul, and Seoul itself in Korea; Stockholm in Sweden; Waterloo and Calgary in Canada; Taipei in Taiwan; Mitaka in Japan; Glasgow in the United Kingdom; New York City and Georgia in the United States; and Singapore. All these smart cities were recognized for their efforts in developing broadband networks and e-services that sustain innovative ecosystems, growth, and inclusion.

These smart cities could be characterized as having three specific features. First, they use IT to make more efficient use of physical infrastructure (roads, built environment, and other physical assets) through artificial intelligence and data analytics that support strong and healthy economic, social, and cultural development. Second, smart cities engage effectively with local people in local governance and decision making by using open innovation processes and e-participation, which improves the collective intelligence of the city's institutions through sustainable governance, with emphasis placed on citizen participation. Third, citizens in the smart city can learn, adapt, innovate, and thereby respond more effectively and promptly to changing circumstances by improving group intelligence through sharing individual experiences. Smart cities are based on ubiquitous IT technologies. Innovative IT applications are widely utilized in promoting cloud-based services, the IoT, real-world user interfaces, use of smartphones and smart meters, networks of sensors and RFID chips, and interconnectivity that is more accurate by being based on the semantic web; these applications open new ways to automatic and/or collective action and collaborative problem solving. Online collaborative sensor and data management creates platforms for services that allow sensor owners to register and connect their devices to feed data into an online database for storage and allow developers to connect to the database and build their own applications based on these data.

Sometimes, the smart city is used interchangeably with the concept of the eco-city, because one of the most important goals of the smart city is that of zero carbon emissions, or at least the near-zero carbon city or a self-sufficient energy sector in the city. An eco-city is built on the principles of living within the means of a sustainable environmental system. The ultimate goal of many eco-cities is to eliminate all carbon waste, to produce energy entirely through renewable sources, and to incorporate the environment into the city; however, eco-cities also have the intentions of stimulating economic growth, reducing poverty, organizing cities to have higher yet sound population densities, and therefore promoting higher efficiency and improved health.

Seoul is the world's 14th largest city and 4th largest metropolitan area, with over 25.6 million people as of 2015. It is considered a leading global city, resulting from an economic boom referred to as *the Miracle on the Han River*, which transformed it into the world's fourth largest metropolitan economy, with a GDP of US$845.9 billion. Unfortunately, owing to its rapidly growing economy, its citizens' lives have been worsening, as in other metropolitan areas in the world. As Korea is well known for its strong competitiveness in IT industries, the Korean government wants to develop the smart city project, not in Seoul at the initial stage, because it is too large to be implemented from the beginning, but as a pilot project in Songdo, the western suburbs of Seoul. The total area of Songdo is 53.4 km^2 (5,340 ha), and it is expected to have a local population of 252,500 by 2020 (currently it is 55,000). Songdo hosts the World Bank Korean office as well as the GCF headquarters. Songdo smart city project is based on four visionary principles.

First, it aims to have an enhanced and reliable city infrastructure using 24 hours/7 days a week of uninterrupted smart services, as well as reliable high-speed network services. The second vision is based on energy saving, eco-friendly networks, using diverse energy resources and the seamless connection between IT and physical services (IoT). Third, the Songdo smart city is based on efficient operation with fewer human-managed service features and more centralized operations and management systems. Fourth, it aims to enhance the quality of life through information provision based on diverse platforms, and improve the safety of residents and visitors, operators, and the management system itself, in and around the common areas and residential neighborhoods.

Specifically, the Songdo development plan could be summarized as having four directions of development as shown in Figure 6.1. First, it will develop a cluster consisting of industrial, academic, and R&D organizations. Second, the area will be promoted as a hub for multinational companies in Pacific Asia. Third, it will host a complex of high-tech, knowledge-based industries. Fourth, it will develop an international business center, including a convention center, exhibition center, etc. To overcome the diverse bottlenecks and difficulties of the smart city development, Incheon U-City Company was created as a PPP to create a sustainable

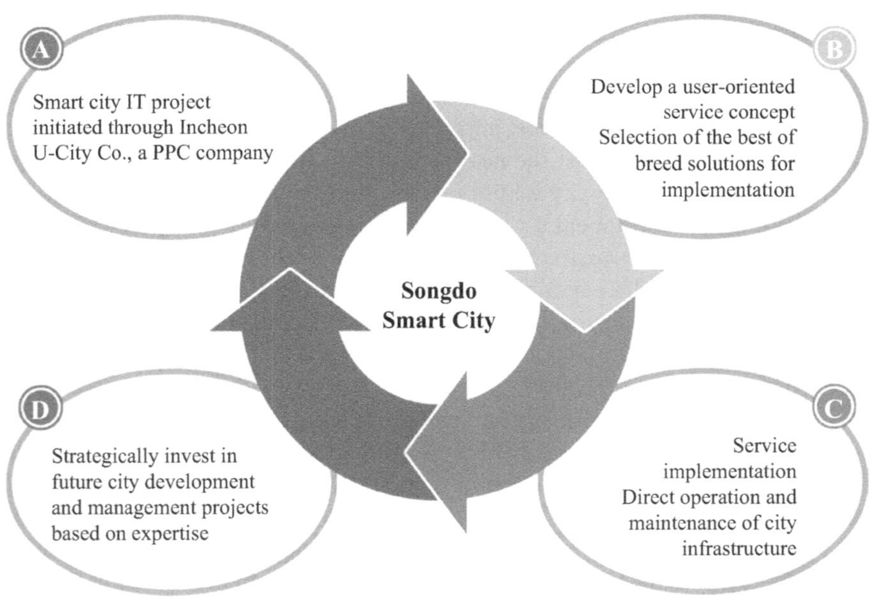

Figure 6.1 Engagement model for Songdo smart city

business model structure and design stable city infrastructure operations. Shareholders of this smart city PPP are KT as a major telecommunication company, Cisco as a network infrastructure hub developer, Incheon City as the policy supporter, and local small and medium businesses of Incheon as content developers. The major mission of the company is to implement and manage the Incheon smart city and its buildings, based on the collaboration shown in Figure 6.1.

As one of the most ambitious smart city projects worldwide, the Korean government declared its smart city project to boost its home industries, with an aim of winning 30 per cent of the global smart grid market in the future. As a pilot project, it will spend 37 billion won (33 million US dollars) to test smart-grid systems from eight local consortiums, including KEPCO. The project, which will be carried out on Jeju Island, will include a "smart transportation" system aimed at providing power and communications for electric vehicles, as well as a "smart renewable" component to integrate solar and wind energy. The system will also include two-way communications between the utility and customers to improve energy efficiency. Since Jeju Island is an isolated place with plenty of renewable resources such as solar and wind, it is the best place in Korea for an energy self-sufficient smart city. For this bilateral new energy regime to be utilized with smart grids, KEPCO is planning to build two 10-megawatt substation transformers and four power distribution lines near an area that includes 3,000 households, commercial districts, and power-generating facilities to test smart-grid technologies on real electricity networks.

Despite the benefits of sustainability and efficiency of the smart or eco-city, actual implementation can be difficult to attain, because of the conflict with existing infrastructure in terms of both the physical city layout and existing local bureaucracy. These visible and invisible barriers are often insurmountable obstacles to large-scale sustainable development; thus a stepwise approach from the micro unit may be preferable. The high cost of the technological integration necessary for eco-city development is another major challenge, as many cities either cannot afford, or are not willing to take on, these extra costs. In any case, in most smart cities the most important core competence lies in the smart grid for uninterrupted two-way electric power supply. The next section will discuss further this core feature of the smart grid, as being the most representative green by IT industry.

Terminology: Internet of Things

The ***Internet of Things (IoT)*** is the IT-based ecosystem of physical objects or "things" embedded within electronics, software, sensors, and its networked connectivity, which enables these objects to exchange data and communicate with each other to facilitate automated actions. The IoT allows objects to be monitored and controlled remotely across the existing network infrastructure, creating opportunities for more direct integration between the physical world and computer-based systems, and resulting in improved efficiency, accuracy, and overall economic value. When IoT is augmented with sensors and actuators, the technology becomes an instance of the more general class of cyber-physical systems, which also encompasses technologies such as smart grids, smart homes, intelligent transportation, and smart cities. Each "thing" is uniquely identifiable through its embedded computing system, but is able to interoperate within the existing Internet infrastructure. Experts estimate that the IoT will consist of almost 50 billion objects by 2020

Source: Wikipedia (https://en.wikipedia.org/wiki/Internet_of_Things), accessed on Apr. 15, 2016.

7 Green applications in industries

1. The smart grid and green by IT

The electricity industry has an internal, yet very critical difficulty in its operations, because electricity is a kind of spot product; it is almost impossible to store electricity and thus there is always a certain amount of oversupplied electricity, a waste of precious resources with unnecessary carbon emissions, because it is almost impossible to match the sudden change in market demand with spot-supplied electricity. This peak-matching problem creates serious challenges for the green revolution, and the smart grid could provide a route to this perfect market equilibrium using bilateral feedback between the demand and supply of the electricity in the market with the possible participation of the private sector as *prosumer*.

The smart grid is the key component of the smart city, as well as of energy and environmental (E&E) economics. A smart grid is an electrical grid that manages operations by automatically harmonizing the supply and demand of electricity using intelligent IT networks. Smart grids include a variety of operational and energy measures, including smart meters, smart appliances, renewable energy resources, and energy-efficient resources. Electronic power conditioning and control of the production and distribution of electricity are also important aspects of the smart grid. If there are shortages of electricity due to an unexpected increase in demand, then the prosumer may generate its electricity using its own resources, such as electricity storage facilities and renewable energies such as solar or wind energy. If there is too much overproduced electricity by the public company at night time, then it may ask to sell this overproduced electricity to prosumers, and prosumers would store this relatively cheap electricity in their own storage facilities. This kind of bilateral feedback within the electricity market should eliminate all the oversupply issues as well as the carbon emission issues, and overall all the consumers should enjoy a more reasonable price of electricity at last. That is the background of the smart-grid project.

In recent years, the electric grids of most countries have become very large, mature, and highly interconnected networks, with thousands of centralized power-generating stations delivering electric power to major load centers via high-capacity power lines, which then branch and divide to provide power to smaller industrial and domestic users over the entire supply area. This kind of traditional electric grid results from strong economies of scale: large coal-, gas- and oil-fired power stations in the 1 GW (1000 MW) to 5 GW or higher GW range are still found to be cost effective, because of efficiency-boosting features that come into play only when the stations become very large. Moreover, the electricity industry itself, as an infrastructure provider, needs huge initial investment for its nationwide electric power distribution grid structure.

Power stations should be located strategically to be close to fossil fuel reserves such as mines or sea ports for the supply of imports. Siting hydroelectric dams in mountain areas have also strongly influenced the structure of the emerging grid. Nuclear power plants were located based on the availability of cooling water. Finally, fossil fuel-fired power stations were initially very polluting and were located as far as economically possible from population centers, once electricity distribution networks permitted this. These days, the electricity grid reaches the overwhelming majority of the population of developed countries, except for those where outlying regional areas remain "off-grid". Metering electricity consumption is necessary on a per-user basis to allow appropriate billing according to the highly variable level of user consumption. Unfortunately, the supply and demand of electricity is difficult to balance at all times, because electricity is an immediately consumable product. In general, it cannot be stored easily and demand is unpredictable, depending largely on weather conditions. Therefore, to balance electricity's supply and demand, there have been diverse efforts such as dual rate systems for consumers; some flexible operations use buffer power stations for emergency situations only. However, there are always uncertainties at peak demand times, and thus there is still a need to have redundant facilities for emergency use. All these issues have made the price of electricity much higher than its real production costs. Moreover, it is very difficult to establish the bilateral communication necessary to avoid sudden increases in electrical demand at peak times.

As the Internet expands rapidly, opportunities to take advantage of improvements in electronic communication technology to resolve these limitations and costs of the electrical grid have become much more feasible. Technological limitations on metering no longer force peak-power prices to be averaged and passed on to all consumers equally. In parallel, growing concerns over environmental damage from fossil-fired power stations have led to a desire to use large amounts of renewable energy. Dominant renewable resources such as wind power and solar power are highly variable, and so the need for more sophisticated control systems became apparent to facilitate the connection of such sources to the diverse, yet very much more complex grid. The rapidly falling costs of the innovative renewable energy alternatives have created a major change from the centralized grid topology to a highly decentralized—yet highly controllable—new grid system, with power being both generated and consumed very efficiently within the synchronized, and thus harmonized, bilateral grid system. This Internet-based revolution on the electric grid is called the *smart grid*. The most important common element in smart grid development is the application of concurrent engineering with digital processing and bilateral communications to the traditional power grid; this makes data flow simultaneous with consumption, while the instantaneous flexibility allows the flow of electricity to be managed based on the centralized information design of the smart grid.

Traditional grids were designed for a one-way flow of electricity for integrated economies of scale, but if a local sub-network generates more power than it is consuming, the reverse flow can raise safety and reliability issues. A smart grid aims to manage these situations. To reduce demand during the high-cost peak usage periods, detecting and metering technologies inform smart devices in the home and business when energy demand is high and track how much electricity is used, and thus determine the resulting price changes simultaneously [1]. This could signal the user to consume electricity in a smarter way. The smart grid also gives utility companies the ability to reduce consumption by communicating to devices directly in order to prevent system overloads. To motivate users to cut back on use and achieve what is called "peak curtailment" or peak leveling, the prices of electricity are increased during high-demand periods and decreased during low-demand periods. Consumers and businesses will tend to consume less during high-demand periods, especially if it is possible for consumers to be made aware of the high price of electricity at peak periods. This could mean making trade-offs such as cycling on/off air conditioners or running dishwashers at 9 p.m. instead of 5 p.m. When businesses and consumers see a direct economic benefit of using energy at off-peak times, they will certainly include the energy cost of operations into their consumer devices and building decisions and hence become more energy efficient. If the benefits are sufficient, then consumers will change their position from being consumers to being producers, using diverse sources of renewable energy, such as solar and wind energy, to resell to the electricity-generating company in real time.

The smart grid allows for systematic communication between suppliers for their energy price and consumers for their willingness to pay, and permits both to be more flexible and sophisticated in their operational strategies. Only critical loads will need to pay the peak energy prices, and prosumers will be able to be more strategic in choosing when they produce/use energy. Generators with greater flexibility will be able to sell energy strategically for maximum profit, whereas inflexible generators such as base-load steam turbines and wind turbines will operate on a varying tariff based on the level of demand and the status of the other generators currently operating. The total effect is a signal that rewards energy efficiency and energy consumption that is sensitive to the time-varying limitations of supply. At the domestic level, appliances with a degree of energy storage or thermal mass, such as refrigerators, heat banks, and heat pumps, will be placed to sell power to the market and/or seek to minimize energy cost by adapting demand to the lower-cost energy support periods. This is an extension of the dual-tariff energy pricing currently in use.

The smart grid is the key green technology, because the improved flexibility of the smart grid permits greater penetration of highly variable renewable energy sources, such as solar power and wind power by prosumers, even without the addition of energy storage; this kind of sustainable participation by prosumers will promote their active participation in the electricity industry's innovations. Current network infrastructure is not built to allow for multiple distributed feed-in points and, typically, even if some feed-in is allowed at the local distribution level, the transmission-level infrastructure cannot accommodate it. Rapid fluctuations in distributed generation, such as those due to cloudy or windy weather, present significant challenges to power engineers, who need to ensure stable power levels through varying the output of the more controllable generators, such as gas turbines and hydroelectric generators. For this reason, smart-grid technology is a necessary condition for very large amounts of renewable electricity to be available on the grid.

Diverse smart-grid technologies are already used in electricity generation and bilateral telecommunications. Among all these innovative technologies, four key areas can be emphasized for optimal management of the smart grid.

First, integrated communication technologies are core components for smart-grid initiation. There are no standard technologies yet, because they have been developed in an incremental mode and are not fully integrated or standardized. In most cases, for example, data are being collected via modem rather than via direct network connections. Even so, integrated bilateral communications such as supervisory control and data acquisition management systems will allow for real-time control, information, and data exchange to optimize system credibility, asset utilization, and safety.

Second, like all the other smart projects, the self-sensing and measurement instruments of technology form core components in evaluating congestion and grid stability, monitoring equipment and preventing energy theft, and controlling strategic support. Some of the most typical technologies include advanced microprocessor meters and meter-reading tools, remote-area monitoring systems, dynamic line rating, time-of-use and real-time pricing equipment, advanced switches and cables, backscatter radio technology, and digital protective relays.

The third area of core components comprises improved interfaces and decision support systems. Information systems with improved interfaces can manage complexity so that network operators and system managers use tools to operate a grid effectively and efficiently with an increasing number of variables. Decision support technologies include visualization techniques that reduce complicated data into easily understood visual formats, software systems that provide multiple options when system operating actions are required, and simulators for operational training and accurate forecasting.

Fourth, smart power generation systems with advanced components are necessary for the bilateral grid. Smart power generation is a concept of matching electricity production with demand by using multiple matching generators that can start, stop, and operate automatically at selected loads, each independently of the others, thus making their input appropriate to the additional load and peak-power generation required. Load balancing between supply and demand of electricity is critical for a stable and dependable supply of electricity. Short-term deviations in the balance lead to frequency variations, while a prolonged mismatch results in blackouts. Operators of power transmission systems are charged with the balancing task of matching the power output of all the generators to the load of their electrical grid. The load-balancing task has become much more challenging as progressively recurrent and variable generators, such as wind turbines and solar cells, are added to the grid, forcing other producers to adapt their output much more often than it has been required in the past. Smart grids are now evolving from mega integration across countries by super grid, to the prosumer-based microgrid.

2. Super grids and microgrids

2.1 Super-grid projects

A super grid is a wide-area electricity-sharing smart grid that makes it possible to trade high volumes of electricity across countries at great distances. It is also sometimes referred to as *megagrid*. The idea of a super grid designed to take advantage of renewable sources located distantly has been continuously improved over time. In the United States in the 1950s, a proposal was made to transfer hydroelectric power from dams to be constructed in the Pacific Northwest to consumers in Southern California. After a long period of trial and error, this project was completed in 1970 as a close collaboration between General Electric of the United States and ASEA of Sweden. With numerous upgrades of the converter stations in the intervening decades, the system now has a capacity of 3.1 GW and is known as the Pacific DC Intertie. Over time, the scales of energy and distance have become much more expanded than it could be even imagined. Europe began merging its grids during the 1950s, and its largest integrated grid is the synchronous grid of Continental Europe, which serves 24 countries. Currently, most countries in the world promote the super grid through regional cooperation projects, as shown in Figure 7.1. Except for Northeast Asia, almost all countries are participating in these transnational super-grid development projects. Among these projects, three international super-grid projects are well known. Nord-EU Super grid is a new regeneration energy project in west Europe. It utilizes a wind power generation technology on the North European Sea, to produce 25 GW in the initial stage, then 500 GW in its final stage, to be shared by the northern European countries such as the United Kingdom, Finland, Belgium, and Germany.

By contrast, Sud Eu-Maghreb is a desert utilization project. Its goal is that if even 1 per cent of the solar energy on the Sahara Desert is made available, all the Mediterranean countries' electricity demands will be fulfilled. Combining these two super-grid projects has resulted in the European super grid as a super- or mega-sized grid. A possible future super grid might eventually interconnect the many European countries and the regions around Europe's borders – including North Africa, Kazakhstan, and Turkey – with a high-voltage direct current (HVDC) power grid. The background of these super-grid projects is based on the following motivations. First, a super grid could lower the cost of power in all participating countries by allowing the whole region to share the most efficient power plants. Second, an EU super grid would pool load variability and power station unreliability, reduce the margin of inefficient spinning reserves that have

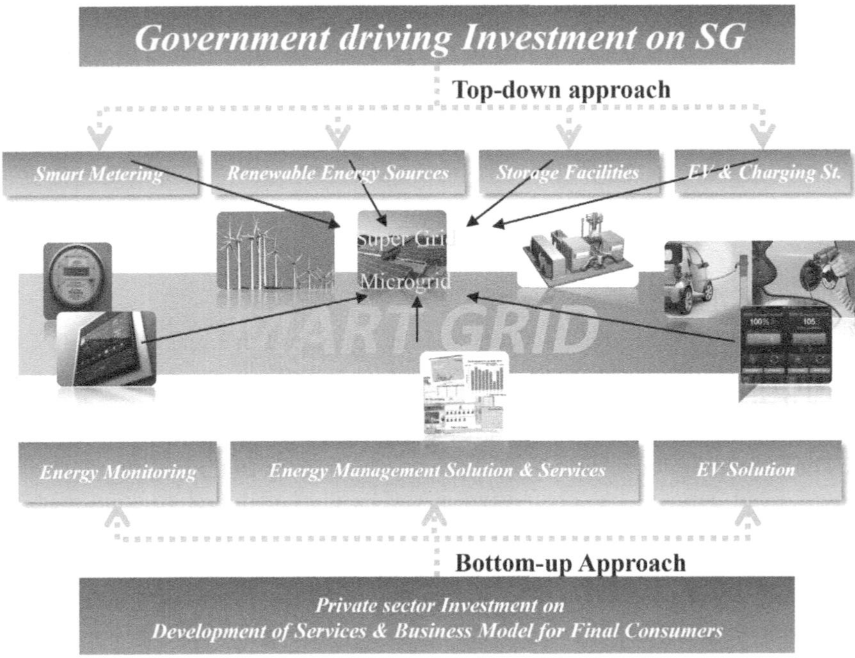

Figure 7.1 Comparison of super grid and microgrid

to be supplied, and thus result in much more stable electricity among the member countries. Third, it would allow for wider use of renewable energy. As explained in the two trunk super-grid projects, wind energy could be much more effectively utilized as it is always windy somewhere in this vast area. For example, the weather tends to be windy in the summer in North Africa and in the winter in Europe. Moreover, the Sahara Desert will add much more solar energy potential for all the participating countries. With the additional investment, every member country could enjoy this clean energy boost, and the economies of networking will result in much speedier and more efficient technological development and dissemination. This megagrid would allow wider sharing of the total European hydro-power resources, which constitute about 6 weeks of full-load European output. Moreover, this integrated water management could bring about collaborative development among the member countries. Instead of water conflict, a megagrid that integrated water resources could lead to a harmonious solution for all countries involved. In this concept of the super grid, a number of other specific schemes have been proposed to create super grids of varying extents within Europe. Even if the European super grid is still evolving, developments could begin in any part of this grand picture, and other dimensions could be connected with each other in the future. This step-by-step approach could provide the most feasible solution to overcome all the obstacles systematically.

The Grand Inga super grid project is based on the proposed hydroelectric Grand Inga Dam at Inga Falls on the Congo River. The planned dam will probably be the largest in the world, with an expected generating capacity of 39 GW (52,000,000 hp). If the Grand Inga project is completed, it will be the largest hydroelectric power-generating facility on Earth. It will fulfill all African electricity demands simultaneously. Even if the project is still at the stage of feasibility study, it could provide a great opportunity for African countries to harmonize their ambitious future goals together.

Unfortunately, the northeast Asian countries are not involved in any big super-grid projects yet. However, Korean president Park proclaimed the Eurasia Initiative in October 2013 to develop and promote regional cooperation, and Chinese leader Xi Jinping published the New Silk Road project to cooperate in the region's development in September 2013. Around the same time, Russian president Vladimir Putin also emphasized his nation's new eastern policy in September 2012 and the Eastern Vector Policy in 2014. Japanese leader Abe Shinzo, who experienced the nuclear power plant shut down in 2011, vigorously promoted renewable energy in the region with a strong Japan playing a role. In Japan, the CEO of Yahoo Masayoshi Son raised a strong voice in favor of creating an Asian super grid that includes China, Korea, Japan, Russia, and Mongolia.

There are several trial research studies being undertaken, and the initial stage of feasibility analyses in these countries could initiate the Asian super grid, but due to delicate historical issues as well as the competitive relations among countries, this task is much more difficult to achieve. However, these northeast Asian countries are the most dynamically growing countries in the world, and thus, they change their profiles every year with respect to ever-increasing carbon emissions. A super grid could be a serious issue as the prime survival kit for energy saving and environmentally friendly development in the region. Since 1990, carbon emissions in China have increased by 373 per cent, and in Korea, they have increased by 258 per cent in only 22 years.

Fortunately, there are several potential possibilities for countries in the region to develop new renewable energies, including wind in Mongolia, gas in central Asia, and high technology in Japan and Korea. Owing to the unique cultural background of the region, it may be better for the Asian super grid to be initiated not by private sector companies such as Yahoo, but in a top-down approach that has the agreement of political leaders. Therefore, the first step toward an Asian super grid should be based on a governmental memorandum of understanding (MOU) that initiates the cooperative research necessary to establish the feasibility of the super grid; based on the MOU, the representative team from each member country should then conduct a joint feasibility study concerning suggestions on the PPP's formation and role. When the member countries have finalized negotiations for the formal contract on major issues such as capacity, size, connection points, etc., then governmental steering committees would empower private partners to launch a pilot project to demonstrate the project. For this purpose, we shall further discuss the microgrid as an extreme case of a bottom-up approach to harmonizing with the super grid.

2.2 Microgrid and picogrid projects

Traditionally, the structure of fossil fuel electric power generation is based on locally concentrated, supply-oriented mass production and consumption due to the economies of scale and huge amount of infrastructure investment initially required. However, renewable energy and the concept of the smart grid created a new frontier for a widely distributed, decentralized, sharing economy. Even the smart grid used by traditional power generation companies could still be based on a mass production scheme with large-scale capacity like the super grid, and thus the super-grid type of smart grid is still a supply-oriented structure, although one that lacks prosumer engagement. To engage final customers (end users) in the energy industry in various ways, the microgrid could ultimately be the best option. Microgrids are modern, localized, small-scale grids, in contrast to the traditional, centralized electricity grid (i.e., the macrogrid). A microgrid can disconnect from the centralized grid and operate autonomously, strengthen grid resilience, and help mitigate mismatching problems between demand and supply of the electricity in local areas. Generation and loading typically occur within low-voltage grids, often using diesel generators that are installed by the communities they serve. Microgrids increasingly employ a mixture of differently distributed energy resources, such as solar hybrid power systems, which reduce the amount of emitted carbon significantly. Microgrid power generation resources can include stationary batteries, fuel cells, solar, wind, or other energy sources. The multiple dispersed generation sources and ability to isolate the microgrid from the larger network provide highly reliable electric power. For example,

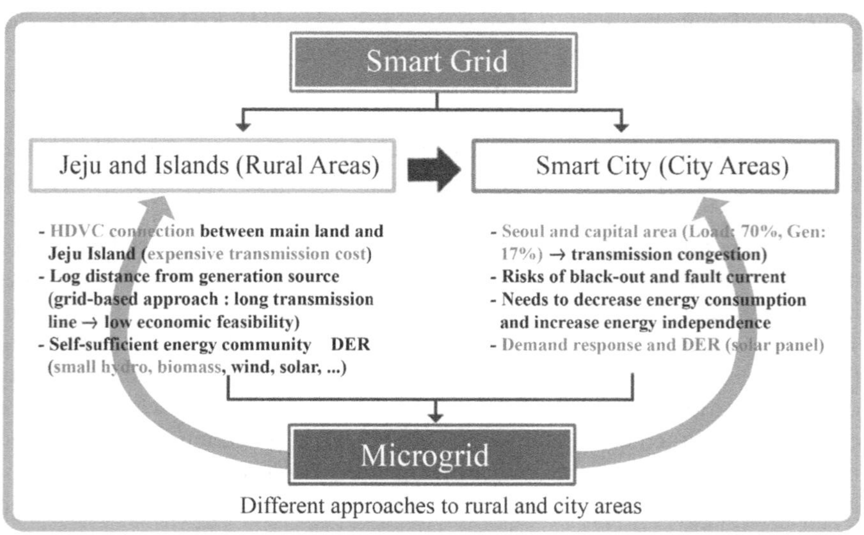

Figure 7.2 Microgrid strategy of Korea

Source: Dong-Joo Kang, *Microgrid as New Solution for Climate Change and Energy Security,* 2015 International Conference on Climate Finance and Industry

produced heat from generation sources such as micro turbines could be used for local process heating or space heating, allowing a flexible trade-off between the needs for heat and electric power.

Due to overly energy-intensive production facilities, undesirable carbon emissions are produced as externalities of the traditional electricity power generation industry; however, eco-friendly efficiency gains no longer come from increasing generating capacity, but from smaller units located closer to sites of demand. This is the background to the microgrid. As shown in Figure 7.1, the super grid or ordinary smart grid is based on a top-down approach with the government taking the initiative, while the microgrid is based on a bottom-up approach with voluntary participation by smart prosumers. In a soft economy,[1] every business is moving from hardware to software and from software to service industry. Moreover, service businesses have been evolving into customer-oriented community businesses such as social commerce. When social networks meet the smart grid, a community of people could become interested in environmentally friendly energy issues as active prosumers.

Especially when an alternative energy source can generate electricity at a level cost equivalent (LCOE) that is less than or equal to the end consumer's retail price, the grid parity occurs. Reaching grid parity is considered to be the point at which an energy source becomes a contender for widespread development without subsidies or government support. Since the 2010s, grid parity for solar and wind has become a reality in a growing number of markets, including Australia, several European countries, and some states in the United States.

Unfortunately, this is not true in most developing countries. Korea ranked 10th in the world for its energy-guzzling industry structure with 10.78 quadrillion BTU in energy consumption in 2013, with most of that energy coming from fossil fuels. As shown in Figure 7.3, the proportion of fossil fuels is 87 per cent, and this consumed about 15 per cent of GDP.

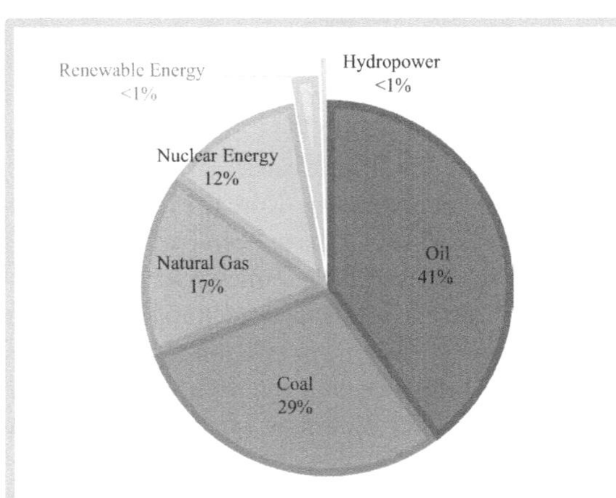

Figure 7.3 Energy mix in Korea in 2013
Source: KPX, KEMCO, OECD/IEA, U.S.EIA

Like other developing countries, Korea desperately needs to make much greater efforts to see that renewable energies such as wind power, solar power, micro-hydro power, and sea power accomplish the goal of achieving 20 per cent of needed energy from renewable sources by 2050. Therefore, the micro-smart grid could and should be the key enabler. In Korea, micro-grid-based smart grid strategies are founded on the bidirectional mode shown in Figure 7.4. Jeju Island, the southern island of Korea, has been selected as the first pilot project for a wider range of smart grids because, even though the island has a large area of 1,848 km^2 with 0.6 million residents, it is connected with the mainland by a very expensive HVDC; this great distance from the generation source indicates low economic feasibility. Therefore, the Korean government took the initiative for Jeju Island to be a self-sufficient energy community with near-zero carbon emissions by using a microgrid project. Based on this pilot project, further microgrid projects could diffuse through diverse smart city projects, especially in Seoul and its suburban areas, such as Songdo of Incheon and Kimpo city of Kyeonggido, to solve the transmission congestion and the risks of unexpected blackouts or fluctuating currents.

The smart grid and smart city project in Jeju Island is based on the eight-dimensional sub-business fields shown in Figure 7.4. From a demand management perspective, the project has been developing electricity resale modules, demand response modules, and market transactions involving demand side generation resources. From a smart transportation perspective with electric vehicle (EV) charging and services, the project has been developing fast/slow vehicle-to-grid (V2G) EV-charging services and vehicle to operator-based vehicle paging, and providing service modules, mobile EV-charging service modules, and virtual power plants. From a value-added-services perspective, the project has been developing smart home service modules, EV-rent service modules, and renewable energy output stabilization and power quality improvement modules.

Based on the successful operation of the pilot project in Jeju Island, the Korean government has now selected eight smart city candidates in which to apply these business models nationwide (see Figure 7.4). Individual cities have differentiated their identities and domains for diverse smart grid projects according to local conditions. Many leading companies in Korea, such as KT and SK Telecom, Samsung, LG, Hyundai, and POSCO, have been participating in these smart city and smart grid projects within the PPP framework. Of course, there are many obstacles and difficulties related to financial, technological, and regulatory risks. However, we could learn not only from the pilot projects in Korea, but from many smart city projects worldwide, that the smart city and smart grid approach is no longer "mission impossible," especially when we consider the critical importance of sustainability.

Picogrids are defined as micro-microgrids creating self-sufficient energy mechanisms in a house or building, and the term is thus sometimes used interchangeably with the low-carbon or carbon-zero house. The picogrid aims to use electricity sources inside a house or building to meet its own energy demands,

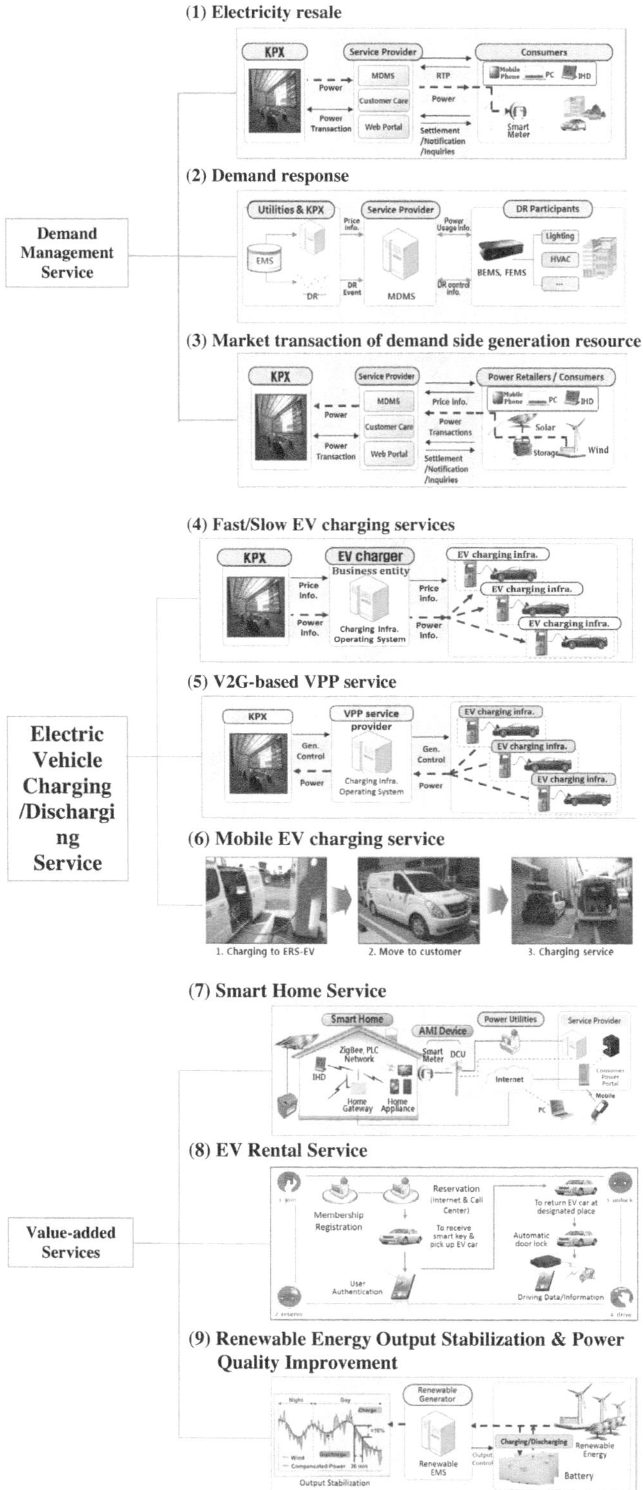

Figure 7.4 Business models in Jeju Island smart grid project

Source: Dong-Joo Kang, *Microgrid as New Solution for Climate Change and Energy Security*, 2015 International Conference on Climate Finance and Industry

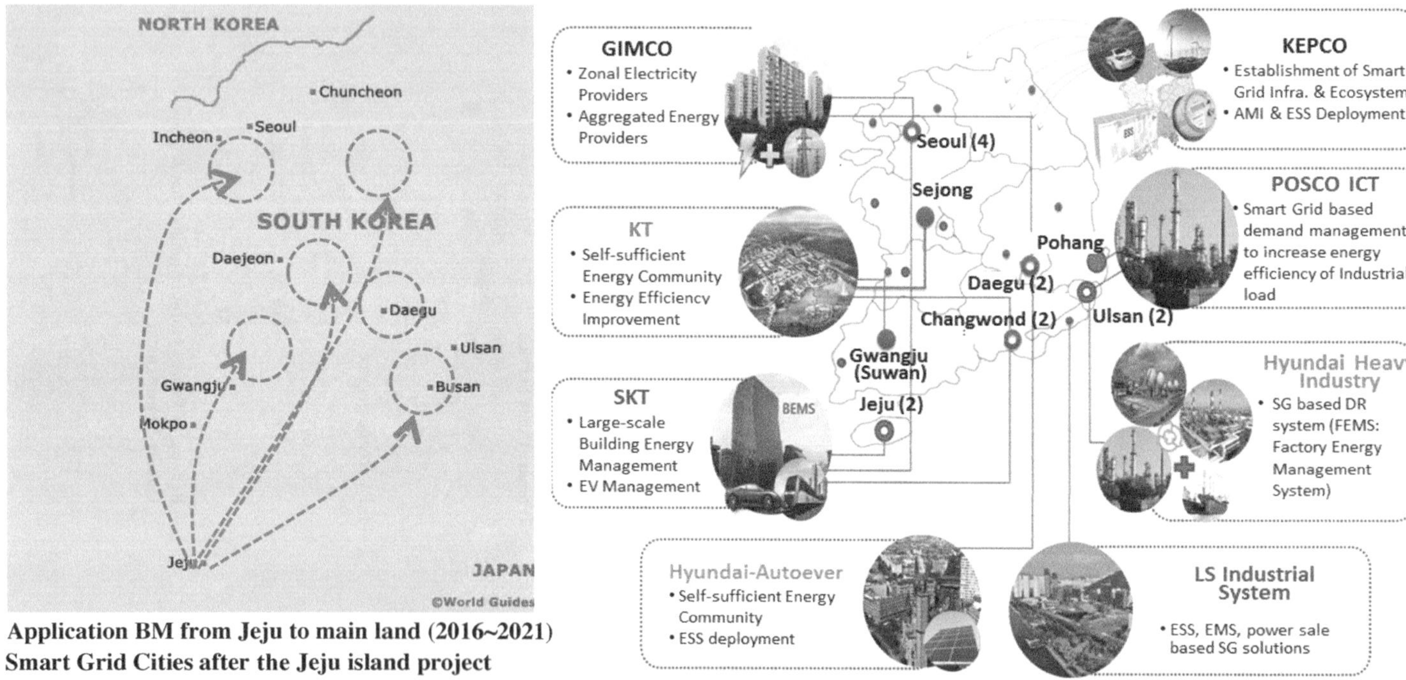

Figure 7.5 Diffusion of smart city and smart grid projects in Korea

Source: Dong-Joo Kang, *Microgrid as New Solution for Climate Change and Energy Security*, 2015 International Conference on Climate Finance and Industry Proceedings.

rather than outside, via diverse renewable energies such as solar and wind energy. Buildings alone are responsible for 38 per cent of all human GHG emissions (20 per cent residential, 18 per cent commercial) [2], and thus buildings and houses should utilize the most cost-effective opportunities for GHG reductions, using diverse, innovative means to generate electricity such as geothermal energy, solar and wind energy, etc. Many picogrid proposals are based on geothermal energy, which is thermal energy generated and stored below the surface of Earth. Thermal energy is the energy produced by temperature differences in matter, and geothermal energy uses the continuous conduction of thermal energy in the form of heat from the core to the surface of Earth. In general, this process provides hot water that can be used to produce electricity via small turbine engines for house use only. However, it can sometimes also be used for commercial purposes with huge megawatt-size facilities.

Picogrids can in principle utilize all the available renewable energies for their self-sufficient energy needs. This implies that such grids should monitor all the possible demands for electricity over time, and impose self-control on the stable matching of consumption with power generation with the support of IT applications such as building energy management systems and carbon dioxide capture and storage (CCS) devices. To maintain the balance between its own demand and self-produced electricity supply, electricity storage tools are essential for the picogrid. At the same time, the picogrid approach is based on diverse innovative efforts to mitigate the loss of energy through roofs, walls, windows, and all the other boundaries of the house and its facilities. Picogrids are in their initial stage of development globally, but due to strong support from the Chinese government, we can easily see solar-panel covered houses in almost all the small, remote towns of China. The Chinese government provided strong incentives through subsidies for these remote areas to install solar panels to cover at least to some extent their basic energy demands.

All these efforts from smart grid to super grid to picogrid in Korea have been supported directly and/or indirectly by Korea Electric Power Corporation (KEPCO), the largest public company for electricity power generation. KEPCO was founded with the objective to facilitate the development of electric power supply in Korea, meet the country's power supply needs, and contribute to the national economy in accordance with the Korea Electric Power Corporation Act. Over the last 116 years, KEPCO has achieved a history of light by serving as the only supplier of electric power in the nation. KEPCO has opened a new era as a smart energy creator to stretch itself beyond Korea to global markets. KEPCO was ranked first in the world in the electricity supply sector by the World Bank in 2014. In 2015, it reduced additional emissions of greenhouse gases by 403,000 tons compared with the goal for 2014, and thus it achieved the first place in the Carbon Disclosure Project (CDP) energy sector ratings in Korea. Due to this sustainable management, it recertified the Carbon Trust Standard (CTS), a global certificate for carbon management. KEPCO is certainly a global leader in eco-friendly smart energy creation [3]. To lead the Northeast Super Grid for the government-led Eurasia Initiative Implementation, KEPCO developed a business model and made an execution plan as shown in Figure 7.6.

KEPCO also proactively participated in the demonstration project for the smart grid and spread its business into diverse areas. As the government aims to establish the world's first nationally based smart grid by 2030, KEPCO has successfully completed the Jeju Smart Grid Demonstration Project (2009–2013) and has been selected as a prospective participant in the expansion of the SG Deployment Project to be carried out over 2016–2018. With the aim of efficiently operating the electricity grid, reducing CO_2 emissions, and fostering new growth engines, the company is actively developing related infrastructure such as advanced metering infrastructure, smart grid stations, energy storage systems (ESSs), facilities for charging electric vehicles, and microgrids. Based on these core technologies, KEPCO will create the basis for building region-based smart grids by 2020 and pioneer the overseas market for smart grid technology and systems by establishing a nationally based smart grid by 2030 [4]. In 2013, KEPCO established the world's first smart-grid station. This system efficiently monitors and controls renewable energy sources, as well as the electrical storage,

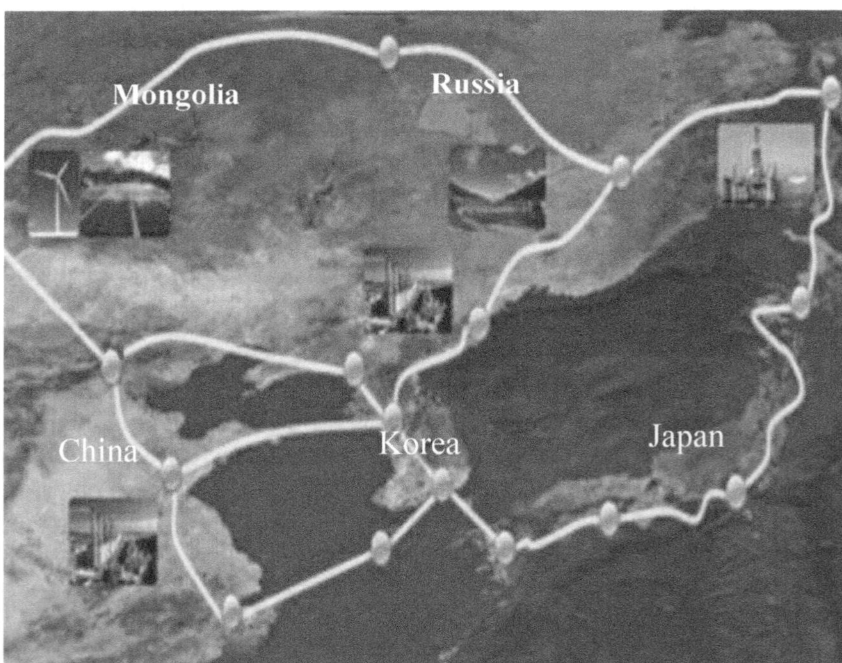

Figure 7.6 Future business model for Northeast Asia Super Grid

Source: 2015 KEPCO Sustainability Report, (http://home.kepco.co.kr/kepco/EN/D/C/KEDCPP004.do?boardCd=BRD_000014&menuCd=EN04010601), accessed Aug. 26, 2016.

metering, and EV-charging devices in buildings on a real-time basis. Recognized for its innovation and technological extensibility, KEPCO's smart-grid station was granted an Honorable Mention in the 2nd International Smart Grid Action Network (ISGAN) Awards, an international smart-grid technology contest held in Mexico in June 2015. Smart-grid stations that were installed in 29 KEPCO branch offices in 2014 not only reduced energy use and GHG emissions, but also contributed to the growth of SMEs [5].

KEPCO established a microgrid system, substituting diesel generators in remote and isolated regions with renewable energy and utilizing ESSs in Gapado of Jeju Island and Gasado in Jeonnam province. On completing construction, the company developed the business model for a "Carbon-Zero" and "Energy-Independent Island", which will produce energy with low-carbon emissions and reduce energy supply expenses. In 2014, based on this development, KEPCO signed an agreement for joint establishment of a microgrid with the company *PowerStream* for the first time in Canada and North America and will also build microgrids in Ulleungdo and Deokjeokdo in Incheon. As a part of the greenhouse gas target management system in 2014, KEPCO was tasked with reducing GHG emissions by 40 per cent compared with the base period (2007–2009) and secured the required amount of early reductions. This amount of reduction can be utilized by supplementing certified emission reductions (CERs), which may be insufficient after implementing the Emission Trading System (ETS) from 2015. As KEPCO was designated as a company with assigned certified emission reductions from 2015, the company was allocated free emission credits for each year in the first period of the plan from 2015 to 2017. The cost for implementing the ETS for this first period is estimated at KRW 19.5 billion [5].

With the ambitious mission to become a global energy network manager, KEPCO had an agreement to acquire the world's largest high concentration solar photovoltaic power generation facility for about $30 million from US private equity firm Carlyle Group LP in 2016. With this big deal in the United States, KEPCO could make headway in the US renewable energy market. KEPCO has been running a total of 37 projects across 22 countries, mostly emerging economies. It has been eyeing renewable energy markets in advanced countries to diversify and bolster its business portfolio. KEPCO also initiated the Smart Grid Stations project with the Dubai Electricity & Water Authority Green Garage in Dubai in 2016. This project aims to create an electric power network that uses ICT intelligently to maximize the efficiency of the energy produced.

KEPCO has conducted challenging and proactive activities to ensure efficiency in its facilities, expand the supply of renewable energy, and make energy conservation a way of life in order to reduce energy and water use. Despite the construction of new buildings, such as its new headquarters, and increased personnel, the amount of energy use increased by only 1.4 per cent compared to 2011, and KEPCO decreased its water use by 25 per cent [5].

3. Green supply chain management and green transport

3.1 Green supply chain management

As explained earlier, we live in a soft economy with interdependent economic structures. There is no single manufacturer in the world that exists without any support from other companies. In this interdependent economy, most companies are implicitly or explicitly related by supply chain management (SCM). Here, a supply chain is a network consisting of all parties involved in creating and delivering a product to consumers. A supply chain therefore includes suppliers, manufacturers, distributors, wholesalers, retailers, and even customers and related government (or its agents), as all these parties are, directly or indirectly, involved in producing and distributing products or services to end customers from both upstream and downstream locations through physical materials, information, and finance flows in the collaborative network. As SCM practices become mature, leading companies and their supply chain partners, under visible or invisible pressure from government and the surrounding society, are moved to collaborate to minimize environmental problems and risks, to reduce waste, excessive energy use, and pollution, and to improve community goodwill. This is sometimes called green SCM, but in general, almost all SCM is green SCM in principle, due to the diverse pressures from inside and outside of these collaborative networks. As many more partners become involved in a single unified SCM, there is a growing need to integrate environmentally sound choices into the process.

As an enhanced form of SCM, *green supply chain management (GSCM)* can be defined as integrating efforts that address environmental challenges into supply chain management. All stages of the product life cycle can be targeted: product design, material sourcing and selection, manufacturing methods, delivery of the final product, and disposal of the product after its useful life, which, for example, can be done in eco-friendlier ways, such as recycling. In general, SCM emphasizes concurrent engineering (CE) to maximize its profits in the short term; this approach is designed for the leader company to deliver one-way process optimization, while GSCM has a totally different mission: to create and distribute long-term values among the partners. To successfully manage GSCM, CE is a necessary working methodology based on the parallelization or synchronization of tasks (i.e., performing tasks concurrently). This refers to an approach used in product development and manufacturing in which design engineering, manufacturing engineering, and other such functions are integrated to reduce the time required to bring a new product to the market. Since the 1990s, CE was also adapted for use in the information and content automation field, providing a basis for organization and management of projects outside the physical product development sector for which it was originally designed; thus, CE became the core structural determinant of SCM. CE brings a series of challenges, such as a need for early design reviews. CE further depends on efficient communication between engineers and teams, as well as software compatibility and transparency in the design process. There are many successful business cases that use CE, such as the "fast fashion" houses of Zara, Uniqlo, H&M, and Mango. Fast fashion is a contemporary term used by fashion retailers that try to capture current fashion trends as quickly as possible. Fast fashion clothing collections are based on the most recent fashion trends in the current market. CE seeks an optimal control path in the supply chain that allows for these trends to be designed and manufactured quickly and inexpensively to allow the mainstream consumer to buy current clothing styles at a lower price.

Unfortunately, however, CE does not guarantee sustainable performance, because it maximizes benefits only for the leader company, and thus there is no guarantee that other member companies in the SCM will continue to produce the same parts and materials. When the trend changes, the leading company should change all its partners to reflect the new trend in parts and materials. Because of these decisions concerning short-term profit maximization, it is very difficult for those other than leading companies in the SCM to participate in the innovation of new items. To maintain the group members' sustainable performance, the paradigm must shift from a zero-sum game with a short-term focus, toward a win-win game involving partners' long-term loyalties. Therefore, one of the core requirements of successful GSCM is collaboration. The practice of collaboration, such as sharing distribution methods to reduce waste by, for example, ensuring that half-empty vehicles do not get sent out and that deliveries to the same address are carried on the same truck, is not yet popular, because many member companies working in a collaborative network fear the loss of commercial control by working with others. Investment in alternative modes of transportation, that is, green transportation or sustainable logistics, can play an important role in helping companies reduce the costs and environmental impacts of their deliveries.

To manage this GSCM network, IT technologies involving CE are vital for sustainable performance. By utilizing CE in green by IT technologies, sustainable management strategies can be maximized throughout the environmentally friendly advanced supply chain, beginning with the concept of environmentally conscious development, then continuing through all phases of production, and finally customer distribution, creating greater energy savings and lower emissions of greenhouse gases. Sustainable strategies here focus on efforts to increase sustainability by materials suppliers, product manufacturers, and retailers.

One of the best ways IT applications can be used to enhance sustainability in the GSCM is through the concept of the carbon footprint. A carbon footprint is historically defined as the total set of greenhouse gas emissions caused by an organization or a group of organizations for a specific economic output, expressed as CO_2e (equivalent carbon dioxide). Greenhouse gases can be emitted throughout each product's life cycle, from research and development to manufacturing, distribution, consumption or use, and finally, disposal. The carbon footprint of a specific product can be measured by undertaking a GHG emissions assessment or similar calculation method denoted as "carbon accounting", with the support of various sensing, monitoring, and measuring IT technologies. Once the size of a carbon footprint is known, a strategy can be devised to reduce it, for example, by technological developments, better process and product management, different, greener procurement, carbon capture, altered consumption strategies, carbon offsetting, and other such measures. The most popular way to reduce the carbon footprint of humans is to reduce, reuse, and recycle (the "3Rs"). In manufacturing, this can be done by recycling packing materials and by creating reusable items such as recyclable containers rather than disposable ones. All these efforts could and should be handled by the application of green IT technologies, and customized information networking among the participating members of GSCM should result in the GSCM's sustainable performance. Since SCM is based on collaborative networks among the partners, a leader company, as the network manager of GSCM, plays a vital role in influencing the total environmental impact of any partners involved in supply chain activities; it thus contributes to sustainability for the whole society. These efforts in enhancing sustainability are undertaken to decrease the impact of the supply chain on future generations.

3.2 Green transport and smart cars

To reduce the size of carbon footprints, one of the most important green by IT applications may be green transport. The transport industry provides important cooperative network services to other industries. The industry has also witnessed rapid development, especially in Northeast Asia. China and Korea have introduced express railways with speeds of more than 300 km per hour nationwide; this new renaissance of the railroads has supported the explosive growth of Internet shopping and e-business in these countries. Unfortunately, the transport industry is one of the world's biggest emitters of carbon dioxide, accounting for about 61 per cent of global oil consumption, 28 per cent of energy consumption, and 22 per cent of carbon emissions in 2012 [6]. According to the China Statistical Yearbook 2013, China's transport industry accounted for 14 per cent of energy consumption and 10 per cent of total carbon emissions in 2012. Therefore, reducing carbon emissions in the transport industry is crucial for sustainable development in developing countries. Because environmental issues have become increasingly serious in China and Korea, their governments have launched several policy initiatives aimed at mitigating excessive energy consumption and carbon emissions in the transport industry.

These efforts are attempts to implement green transport policies. Sustainable or green transport is defined as the broad range of eco-friendly transport mechanisms (not just systems!), sustainable in the sense that they reduce social, environmental, and climate impacts, and their sources of energy can be procured indefinitely on a global basis. The European Union Council of Ministers of Transport defines a sustainable transportation system as having three dimensions. First, it should allow for basic access and for the development needs of individuals, companies, and society to be met safely and in a manner consistent with human and ecosystem health; it should also promote equity within and between successive generations. Second, green or sustainable transport should be affordable, operate fairly and efficiently, offer a choice of transport mode, and support a competitive economy as well as promote balanced regional development. Third, green transport should limit emissions and waste within the planet's ability to absorb these, use renewable resources at or below their rates of generation, and use non-renewable resources at or below the rates of development of renewable substitutes, while minimizing the generation of noise and the impacts on the use of land.

Components for green transport mechanisms include the eco-friendly vehicles used for road, water, or air transport; sources of energy such as renewable energy or bio-energy; and the infrastructure used to build the transport system, such as roads, railways, airways, waterways, canals, and terminals. One of the most dynamic challenges in green transportation is the strategic development of smart car projects worldwide. There are diverse dimensions to the conceptual characteristics of smart cars. The concept includes eco-cars, autonomous cars, and IT-driven human-interface cars, etc. Most of all, the eco-car concept aims to advance the level of vehicle technologies capable of reducing energy consumption, especially that of fossil fuels energy, as well as GHG emissions, while demonstrating competitive performance with a range of technological options. The technologies for eco-friendly smart cars include full-function electric, hybrid, plug-in hybrid, and fuel cell hybrid vehicles with advanced-technology powertrains, lightweight materials, and aerodynamic improvements. If an eco-car is equipped with autonomous driving, its concept evolves into the autonomous cars such as Google cars.

One of the most outstanding smart car projects, in the range of autonomous cars, is Google's self-driving cars, developed by Google X as part of its project to develop green IT-based future-generation cars. An autonomous car (driverless, self-driving, or robot car) is a vehicle that is capable of sensing its surrounding environment on the road and navigating without human intervention. Autonomous cars can detect rapidly changing environmental conditions using a range of technologies such as radar, GPSs, odometers, and computer vision. Advanced control systems manage sensory information to recognize appropriate navigation paths, as well as obstacles and relevant traffic signals. In May 2014, Google presented a new concept for their driverless car that had neither a steering wheel nor pedals, and they unveiled a fully functioning prototype at the end of 2014, which they planned to test on San Francisco Bay area roads beginning in 2015. Google plans to make these cars available to the public in 2020 [7]. Google's robotic cars are based on automatic sensing and self-control equipment, such as LIDAR systems, a surveying technology used to measure distance by illuminating a target with a laser light. The range finder of the laser device is mounted on the top of the Google cars. This laser allows the vehicle to generate a detailed 3D map of its environment. The car then takes these generated maps and combines them with high-resolution maps of the landscape, producing different types of data models that allow the car to drive itself [8]. Even if there were serious accidents on the road during tests of these Google cars, there has been a fever of optimism for the commercialization of this smart car concept in the near future, and thus many competitors worldwide have jumped in to develop similar autonomous smart cars.

Until recently, the major paradigm of China's policies has been based mainly on quantity- and supply-oriented economic development. Despite its success in the early stages, this type of supply-oriented policy has not worked well since 2003, leading to serious oversupply problems across the Chinese economy. Although some parts of the newly installed transport infrastructure have strengthened the economy, empirical results show that it has crowded out private investment in innovation as well as transport firms' efforts to catch up with benchmark technologies. Choi (2015) refers to this type of government intervention as "consultocracy", a kind of moral hazard coming from bureaucracy, and suggests that it results only in unsustainable and short-term showing-off effects [9]. Therefore, green transport policies in Asian countries should be based on voluntary participation by the transport industry to strengthen catch-up effects for eco-friendly challenges and to increase the feasibility of transport policies.

4. Green computing and business solutions

To promote sustainable development policies as well as sustainable business management strategies, green computing or IT sustainability is another central field of research and practice where the mission is to use energy and resources efficiently and effectively with minimal or no impact on the environment. The goals of green computing are multiple: it should reduce the use of hazardous materials, maximize energy efficiency during a product's lifetime, promote the recyclability or biodegradability of defunct products and factory waste, and use smart information-oriented facilities and software. Green computing is important for all classes of systems and organization, ranging from small legacy systems to large-scale automated manufacturing systems. Many corporate IT departments, as well as the e-government department, have promoted green computing initiatives to increase energy efficiency and to reduce the environmentally undesirable impacts of their IT operations.

Many governmental agencies have also continued to implement standards and regulations that encourage green computing, including direct methods such as environmental tax and the carbon emission trading system, as well as using indirect approaches such as e-government public service networks. Many countries impose heavy taxes on the use of oil and other carbon-intensive energies, while subsidies for renewable energies promote the public's perceptions of green growth. Many countries put deposits on bottled products, resulting in these bottles being recycled more effectively.

In the private sector, there are several green IT initiatives that we could not explore fully, because most of these projects are in their initial or pilot project stages. Climate Savers Computing Initiative (CSCI) is a global organization dedicated to reducing the electrical power consumption of PCs in their active and dormant states. The CSCI evaluates green products from its member organizations and provides information for reducing PC power consumption. There are several similar organizations globally and at the local level. The Green Grid is a global consortium dedicated to advancing energy efficiency in data centers and business computing ecosystems. It was founded in February 2007 by several key companies in the industry such as AMD, Dell, HP, IBM, Intel, Microsoft, and Sun Microsystems. Currently, with hundreds of members worldwide, including end users and government organizations, Green Grid emphasizes improving the efficiency of data center infrastructure.

There are diverse software and deployment optimization solutions among the green by IT strategies. One of these solutions is the virtualization of information systems. Computer virtualization refers to the abstraction of computer resources, such as the process of running two or more logical computer systems on one set of physical hardware. With virtualization, a system administrator could combine several physical systems into virtual machines on one single, powerful system, thereby unplugging the original hardware and reducing power and cooling consumption. Virtualization can assist in distributing work so that servers are either busy or put in a low-power sleep state. Several commercial companies and open-source projects now offer software packages to enable a transition to virtual computing. One of the virtualization applications using green by IT could be teleconferencing. Teleconferencing technologies are often implemented in green computing initiatives. The advantages of such virtual meetings could be multilayered: increased worker satisfaction, reduction of GHG emissions related to travel, and increased profit margins as a result of lower overhead costs for office space, heat, and lighting. Therefore, the savings could be significant.

Microsoft has provided limited PC power management features in its Window software since Windows 95. These initially provided for standby (suspend-to-RAM) and a low-power monitor state. This kind of power supply management has been developed and diffused by diverse software companies as well as the information management departments of various organizations, as one of the core green by IT strategies. Likewise, to boost the public conception of green by IT, there are diverse green IT educational systems as well as certificate programs. All these educational supports increase the perception that green IT applications in our daily lives lead toward more energy saving, reduce waste, and involve better, that is, eco-friendly ways of working.

Note

1 In general economic use, a *soft economy* is an economy that is in recession or is declining. Thus, in this book, the concept of "soft economy" needs clarification. A more common term might be information economy, or knowledge economy. As explained earlier, our society is based on the networking of the business activities, and thus intangible management power of the networking is much more important. Even manufacturing industry relies increasingly on software and the information or knowledge economy. Therefore, to emphasize the role of soft power in network management, this book is using a different concept of soft economy.

8 Future challenges for IT-led green growth

1. Internet of Things (IoT)

Omnipresence or *ubiquity* originates from the Latin word for the property of being present everywhere. Ubiquitous society in terms of computing networks is based on an advanced computing concept in which computer applications may appear anytime and anyplace, to anything, and in any way; thus it is sometimes called the "4 any" system society. In contrast to desktop computing, ubiquitous computing can occur using any device (freedom of access: in any way), in any location and time (unlimited in time and space: anytime and anyplace), and in any form or style of activity (freedom of action: anything). This concept implies not only the sharing of information, but also utilization of the information to initiate definite actions. For example, we could turn on the air conditioner by mobile phone (anything) before we enter the house. A user interacts with the computer and/or computer-interconnected electrical items, which can exist in many different forms, including laptop computers, smartphones, refrigerators, lights, smart cars, air conditioning systems, and many more electrical and electronic devices. We can even manipulate some electrical utensils through the interconnectivity of other Wi-Fi terminals. The underlying technologies to support ubiquitous computing include the Internet, advanced middleware, operating systems, mobile codes, auto sensors, microprocessors, new input/output devices and user interfaces, networks, mobile protocols, location and positioning software, and new materials.

As mentioned earlier, the Internet of Things (IoT) is one of the most important tools for green growth in this ubiquitous society. As ubiquitous society is based on the *4 any system* of any place and any time (no limits in time and space), anything (no limits on activities), and any way (no limit of access method), any ubiquitously connected system could be the key prompter of the IoT, in the sense that the IoT interconnects with human-to-human (H2H), human-to-machine (H2M), and even machine-to-machine (M2M) interfaces for diverse information sharing and simultaneous multi-tasking jobs. In general, the IoT is expected to offer diverse, yet enhanced connectivity for devices, systems, and service contents that goes beyond H2M or M2M connections and covers a variety of protocols, domains, and applications. In the interconnection of these embedded devices, the user is expected to execute automatic multi-tasking in nearly all fields of activity, while also enabling advanced applications like smart grids, and smart use of facilities in ubiquitous areas such as smart cities. In the future, the IoT will be one of the most vital platforms for the sustainable performance of a smart city, and for green growth policies and business strategies, because it will be the contact point as well as the gateway to the world of ubiquitous society.

A person's ability to interact with objects could be altered remotely based on instantaneous needs coming from the surrounding situations, in accordance with predetermined and/or real-time end-user agreements for these remote services. According to Gartner, there will be nearly 26 billion devices on the IoT by 2020 [6]. Using these IoT applications, we can imagine all the activities of humanity to be controlled as shown in futuristic science fiction movies such as *The Matrix*. We can monitor our children at school and in the street, and take any necessary actions right away when they are in danger, using the IoT's interconnected smart devices. By using IoT tools, a smart company could exert invisible control over environmental problems, as we shall see later in discussing the smart factory.

Green by IT with the environmental applications of the IoT typically uses diverse, yet customized sensors to assist in environmental protection by monitoring air or water quality and atmospheric or soil conditions, even including the habitats and movement of wildlife. Development of resource-flexible devices connected to the Internet also means that other applications like earthquake or tsunami early-warning systems can be used by emergency services to provide more effective protection. IoT devices in this type of application typically span a large geographic area and can also be wireless. The argument has been made that the diverse uses of the IoT will revolutionize the fields of wireless sensing and control.

The integration of sensing and actuation systems connected to the Internet is also likely to optimize energy consumption. IoT devices will eventually be integrated into all forms of energy-consuming devices (including switches, power outlets, bulbs, televisions, etc.) and be able to communicate with the utility supply company in order to balance power generation and energy usage effectively. Such devices would also offer the opportunity for users to control their devices remotely, or manage them centrally via a cloud-based interface, and enable advanced functions like scheduling (e.g., remotely powering heating systems, controlling ovens, changing lighting conditions on or off). In fact, a few systems that allow remote control of electric outlets are already available in the market.

In addition to home-based energy management, the IoT is especially relevant to the smart grid, as it provides systems to gather and act on energy and power-related information in an automated fashion with the goal of improving the efficiency, reliability, economy, and sustainability of producing and distributing electricity. Using sensor and monitoring IoT devices connected to the Internet backbone, electric utilities can not only collect data from end-user connections, but also manage other automated devices such as transformers and the power supply.

In the future, if artificial intelligence is integrated with the IoT, then the Internet of Things could involve a non-deterministic and open network mechanism in which auto-organized or intelligent entities, such as web services, and virtual objects like avatars in the movies, will be interoperable and able to act independently to pursue either their own or shared objectives, according to much more complicated contextual conditions, circumstances, or environments. The object's ability to behave autonomously through collecting and reasoning with contextual information, detecting changes in the environment, for example, faults affecting sensors, and introducing suitable mitigation measures, constitutes a major research trend, and one that is clearly needed to provide credibility to IoT technology.

The IoT is a key component for the smart grid, smart city, and many other "smart" applications of green IT. Using the IoT, it becomes much more effective to sensor, measure, and monitor diverse imprudent activities in order to correct inefficiency and increase eco-friendly effectiveness in the facilities and objects connected with the IoT. For green growth, the IoT could bring diverse opportunities to bear in creating new jobs, new businesses, and new ways of life with better quality. However, even if there are many technologists and researchers advocating the IoT as a step toward a better world, scholars and social observers raise strong objections to the threats emerging from this ubiquitous computing revolution. With the vastly numerous interconnections, the privacy threats of forming a "big brother" society are enormous, as is the potential for social control and political manipulation. Individuals are monitored 24 hours a day in this IoT world, and thus, there are strong concerns about privacy, autonomy, and indirect control. Therefore, there should be very careful scrutiny of the application of IoT devices in the autonomous implementation of their respective activities, with deep consideration of the ethical issues and appropriate constraints.

Moreover, concerns have been raised that the IoT's rapid development does not involve appropriate consideration of the profound security challenges involved. For example, smart cars equipped with IoT-based automobiles parts such as brakes, engine, locks, and dashboards could be vulnerable to attackers who have access to the onboard network or other access to the IoT. The disadvantages and threats coming from the seamless connectivity by IoT become quite upsetting when we consider the challenge of artificial intelligence outlined below.

2. Artificial intelligence

If the IoT provides the contact point with the interdependent society, artificial intelligence (AI) provides the control tower, like a CPU in a computer, for the diverse activities in ubiquitous society. Here, AI is the intelligence empowered by machines or software to perceive its environment and take optimal actions to increase its chances of success autonomously, with or without any inputs from outside. At the initial stage, AI is used to describe a machine that can be made to precisely simulate human actions. The term is sometimes interchangeably used with the academic field of study concerning how to create cloud computing systems and software applications that are capable of intelligent behavior. The former definition is intended to emphasize the soft mechanism of the automatic troubleshooting machine, while the latter focuses on research into the

AI-embedded infrastructure or machine. AI has been the subject of rose-tinted speculations about the future, where it acts as a panacea to solve all the society's problems, while at the same time, it has been regarded as a suspect guide to a doomed future. Despite these extreme views, AI has become an essential part of the technology industry, providing the heavy lifting for many of the most challenging problems in computer science.

As sustainable development faces very diverse, yet overly complex challenges, it requires multi-dimensional approaches, each of which is based on the use of particular tools that can accomplish particular applications. The background of AI research was to find a harmonized general equilibrium for all these conflicting approaches within society. The core issues of AI research include reasoning, knowledge formatting by logic, planning, learning, natural language processing (communication), perception, and the ability to move and manipulate objects. Therefore, AI research is an interdisciplinary field of study involving computer science, mathematics, psychology, linguistics, philosophy, and neuroscience, as well as other specialized fields such as artificial psychology.

Recently, an AI computer named "AlphaGo", a kind of AI developed by Google DeepMind to play the board game Go, competed and won against the world chess champion and the baduk (Go) champions. In October 2015, it became the first computer Go program to beat a professional human Go player. In March 2016, the computer beat Lee Sedol, the Go world champion, in a five-game match. The world was shocked by this news, because for the first time in history, a computer Go program had beaten a ninth-level Go professional without handicaps. AlphaGo's AI used a combination of machine learning and tree search techniques, combined with extensive training, from both human and computer play. It employs a Monte Carlo tree search, guided by a ***value network*** and a ***policy network***, both of which are implemented using deep neural network technology [10]. AlphaGo's search algorithm is much more human-like than those used in previous approaches. When it played the Go program with Sedol Lee, AlphaGo looked ahead by playing out the remainder of the game in its "imagination" many times over – a technique known as a Monte Carlo tree search. Unlike previous Monte Carlo programs, however, AlphaGo uses deep neural networks to guide its search. During each simulated game, the policy network suggests intelligent moves to play, while the value network astutely evaluates the position that is reached. Finally, AlphaGo chooses the move that is most successful in simulation [10]. It also evaluates all the possible challenges using the computer's information as well as the moves of the previous player, and finds the best solution. This reinforced learning gives the AlphaGo type of AI ever accelerating performance skills. This kind of AI can detect the basic details of the roots of invisible or intangible challenges by itself and identify so-called *butterfly effects* with fuzzy solutions. This kind of AI could certainly handle the complex issues of sustainable development more effectively.

There are diverse AIs performing very well in certain professional fields of activity, such as detecting and evaluating cancer in medical firms, substituting for human personnel in hotel and restaurant reception desks, detecting fires or toxic emergencies in buildings, driving smart cars automatically, and being used in diverse toy and gaming industries. Some AI devices perform simple activities, while others are engaged in extremely complex and diverse response activities. One thing is clear, however: AI devices have themselves accelerated their enhancing functions over time, due to their intrinsic nature. Some people have already begun to worry about a dismal future in a computer-driven society run by AI robots over which there is no control or appropriate management by humans. Therefore, we need to solve the following issues before we promote AI machines and software.

First, general AI is not possible. A machine cannot solve any problem that a human being can solve using intelligence, because humans may use history and emotional insights to think of much more innovative solutions, and the machine cannot, in general, predict all of these possible issues. There could and should be firm limits on AI accomplishments concerning unexpected challenges. That happened in a way in the fourth round of Go play by AlphaGo with Lee Sedol. As Mr. Lee put his Go counter onto an unexpected site, AlphaGo could not move its defensive player appropriately, and thus the AI lost one game because of Lee's unexpected play within Go in 2016.

Second, intelligent machines could be dangerous, if the developer does not provide *appropriate* decisions. Even so, it is not possible for AI machines to behave ethically on their own, so they must be programmed and used ethically. This ethical issue is critical for an AI, because it always chooses its own algorithms, which sometimes conflict with each other. For example, whom should a smart driverless car choose to protect in case of a car accident? Should a car protect the driver? Or, should a car protect children in the street? Research into machine ethics is key to alleviating concerns with autonomous systems. It could be argued that the notion of autonomous machines without such a dimension is at the root of all fears concerning machine intelligence. There are many ethical issues in the execution of certain activities by AI, and thus ethical principles should be carefully considered at all stages during AI development.

Third, note that an AI cannot have a mind, consciousness, or mental states in exactly the same sense that human beings do. A machine cannot be sentient, and thus does not deserve certain rights. Because it does not have feelings, a disaster could result if the machine was deliberately programmed to cause harm to humans. Thus, there are always high risks involved in AI. This is even more true as AI becomes more complex and advanced in its activities.

Nonetheless, specialized AI applications in robotics and other forms of automated systems will ultimately free workers from dirty, difficult, and dangerous (3Ds) jobs and exceed the capability of workers to perform most routine and repetitive jobs. At the same time, unfortunately, the wide use of AI-related robots will decrease the demand for human labor, resulting in significant unemployment as machines begin to replace people. Therefore, the cautious use of AI should confine it to specific and limited uses only; it is preferable that AI requires supporting staff to control and manage its procedural performance.

Considering all these challenges, AI should be developed with systematic control mechanisms for all possible occasions, including those involving ethical issues and emotional communications. Moreover, regulations concerning the use of AI should be comprehensively provided.

3. Smart factory

The smart factory is the next generation of manufacturing factories that is built on the principles of the Internet of Things and Big Data. All necessary information related to operations is shared among applications, and all pieces of equipment and machinery in the factory exchange information with each other through attached sensors, allowing smart systems to resolve problems preemptively before products become defective and malfunctions occur within facilities. Transformation to the smart factory is one of the great challenges in the whole area of business, resulting in "industry 4.0" or the fourth industrial revolution. The first industrial revolution utilized mechanization in the production process with water and steam power from the 1850s, while it evolved into the second industrial revolution of mass production with the help of electric power. The third revolution followed the digital revolution and the use of electronics and IT to automate production further from the early 1970s, and finally resulted in machine to machine (M2M) data interchange and interconnected autonomous activities by cyber-physical systems, the Internet of Things, and cloud computing. The smart factory does not only enhance automation and productivity in the production process, but implements diverse sustainable performance regimes for green growth. These stages are easy to demonstrate in the business case of POSCO, the largest steel manufacturing company in Korea, in examining the fourth industrial revolution of the smart factory.

POSCO was established with the colonial compensation funds from the Japanese government after World War II. In the 1960s, there were not enough funds for the Korean government to develop its economy, especially in social platform industries such as steel manufacturing; thus, the Korean government asked the Japanese government to compensate for their colonial economic plunder of over 36 years. Through a kind of compensation fund from the Japanese government, the Korean government constructed POSCO along the southeast seaside of Korea. Due to this inaugural background, POSCO has had a unique and sustainable mission from the beginning, as shown in Figure 8.1. As shown in the figure, POSCO was founded to provide steelmaking for "*the nation.*" Ever since then, it has led the growth of the Korean economy and the development of its industry. One of the factors that defines POSCO as being distinct from other companies is its inclusive approach to shared growth through cooperation with small and mid-sized companies, which remains a major axis of its management activities. Continued low global growth and the prolonged economic downturn are expected to impede any quick solution to the tough economic conditions. However, POSCO's mutual growth activities are being implemented as part of a push to *create shared value* in order to help small and mid-sized companies

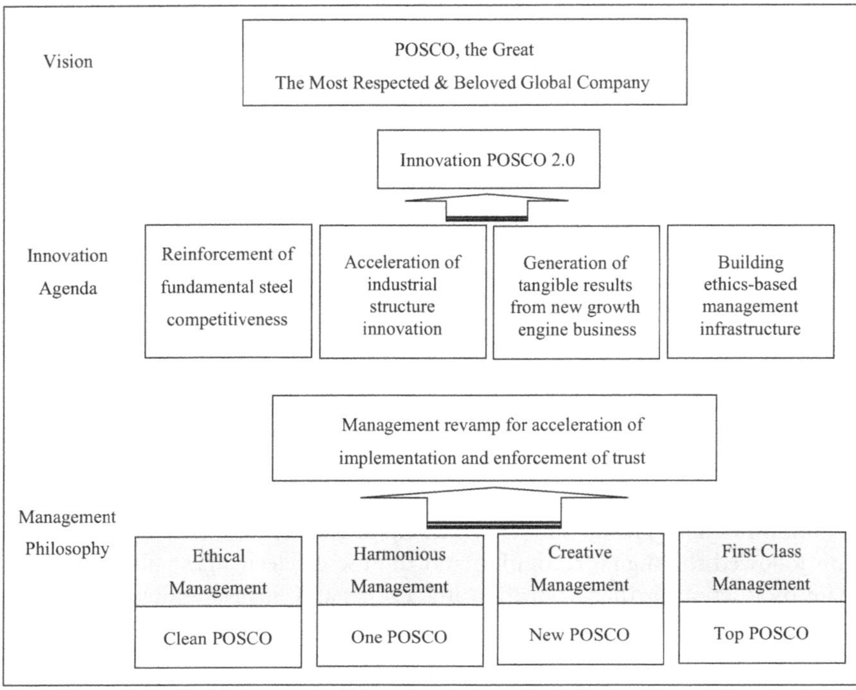

Figure 8.1 Vision and strategy of POSCO

Source: POSCO Sustainability Report 2015, (http://www.posco.co.kr/homepage/docs/eng5/dn/sustain/customer/2015_POSCO_Report_EN.pdf), accessed Aug. 26, 2016.

practically to enhance their competitiveness and the surrounding environment for future generations [9]. POSCO is steadily improving its corporate governance structure based on a corporate governance charter that clarifies the vision and principles of POSCO's governance for the sustainable management and green growth of Korea.

POSCO initiated its Quick Six Sigma (QSS+) program, a set of highly stringent quality control routines in the production process, in 2006. After its successful enhanced efforts, POSCO won the "Best Steel Manufacturer in the World" title, as designated by the world business magazine *Fortune*, for seven consecutive years. During these 10 years of smart factory development, more than 8,000 innovations were made toward sustainable green growth, such as decreases in toxic air pollution, hazardous waste, and diverse greenhouse gas emissions; spontaneous troubleshooting solutions for sudden production facility shutdowns; and increases in the successful operation rate, up to 95 per cent from 70 per cent in 2006.

For example, in the production process, thick steel plate is huge and heavy and emerges continuously from the high-temperature furnace, making it difficult to monitor all the sides of the plate, especially the bottom; therefore, POSCO used laser auto sensors from the floor to the bottom of the thick plate. Since monitoring the process from beneath the thick plate is very hot and not easy to capture in detail, it was a very difficult and dangerous job. However, using smart controls, the system used big data of its own to analyze all the possible bad spots in the thick plate in the production process and so managed its quality smoothly and efficiently. Likewise, there have been diverse improvements on the working environment with mostly invisible troubleshooting devices and software. POSCO eliminated a huge amount of possible waste in the production process, such as the steel debris cut from the final stage. Substances generated in the course of steelmaking are called byproducts. POSCO pursues various activities to make effective use of byproducts that contain various elements and to minimize waste output. The total volume of byproducts produced at Pohang and Gwangyang Works in 2014 was 24.11 million tons. Among these byproducts, 49 per cent was blast furnace slag, 28 per cent was steelmaking slag, 15 per cent was dust and sludge, and 8 per cent was other byproducts. Among the byproducts produced, 98.4 per cent is reused as resources. In particular, all blast furnace slag and steelmaking slag is used as cement material, aggregate substitutes, and raw material for silicate fertilizers. POSCO aimed not to retain any waste at the end of production process and not to do any harm to the environment, that is water, air, and soil [11].

Based on these goals, POSCO upgraded its efforts to the smart factory. On July 10, 2016, POSCO decided to develop its own smart factory technology by launching the joint POSCO Group TF to implement innovative ways of working based on data by applying converged ICT and secure "superlative" cost and quality competitiveness that the second largest company cannot match. Once the smart factory is completely upgraded, stable operating conditions can be maintained and facility lifespan can be extended, as measures will be taken to enable the facilities to isolate potential problems before they actually occur by diagnosing and predicting conditions in real time with facility management using the IoT and analyzing the collected data thoroughly. The quality management system will also be dramatically improved. The system is changing from merely responding to problems by finding causes when they occur, to a preemptive system that responds to defective products by isolating causes of defects in advance.

This system increased the quality of used water in the steel production process, and this reused water could be used even for drinking, thus contributing to a clean, energy-saving, eco-friendly, and very efficient smart factory in Korea. POSCO also contributed to the car manufacturing companies in Korea such as Hyundai by providing lighter, yet much more eco-friendly and durable steel, due to this smart factory project. Moreover, this process has emphasized the importance of organizational culture and manpower education, including the contribution of a huge amount of educational funds for its own Pohang University of Science and Technology, one of the top universities in Korea.

By the virtue of the smart factory, many businesses could cut hidden costs of the production process, increase the resilience of the factory environment against unexpected potential blackouts in production management, and increase energy-saving and lower carbon-emitting production control performance. Including the smart factory, the fourth industrial revolution could be conceptualized through a combination of the following factors:

- the transition to renewable energy sources (RESs) such as using the biomass energy coming out of the production process;
- conversion of existing passive buildings (both industrial and residential) into positive ones for the production of energy by equipping them with solar thick plates, mini wind turbines, and heat pumps on the factory (or residential house) roof;
- the development and introduction of energy-saving technologies and resources (both in industrial production and in residential housing) by the complete utilization of residual waste as a reusable resource, and the use of autonomous power control systems to prevent losses of electricity, steam, water, and heat;
- transformation of the entire automobile (passenger and freight) industry and all public transport to electric or at least hybrid vehicles based on hydrogen or bio-energy, as well as the development of new types of fuel-efficient transport, such as airships, underground express subways, etc.;
- decentralized manufacturing by the transition from the industrial complex to local and even residential production by remote cyber-office and tele-manufacturing, with the support of innovation technologies such as 3D printers and sharing economic assets, etc.;
- the transition from metals to composite materials, especially carbon-based nanomaterials, as well as the replacement of metals by durable, less energy-intensive, and less GHG-emitting technologies;
- expansion of agriculture into the city center by means of agricultural factories or building technologies such as vertical farms.

All these efforts imply that the smart factory is no longer simply a business-oriented manufacturing site. Instead, such factories will enhance the life quality of all the employees and their families to promote the self-sufficient ecosystem with the 3R (recycle, reuse, reform) approach and innovative ways of assembling the diverse business functions inside and outside the factory.

4. Sustainable governance and metamediaries

To overcome future challenges in the soft economy under global warming and climate change, the most important mission is to innovate across all the legacy systems, based on the two pillars of sustainability and IT or e-business, for improved sustainable performance. These platforms should be based on the win-win game type of collaboration with multilateral governance. Even if the regulatory system and its policies are well provided within the legacy system, a specific economic agent that wants only to maximize its own profits will lose the loyalties derived from diverse reciprocal teamwork activities with employees, consumers, local society, and the central government etc., resulting in the irreversible, undesirable byproducts such as dirty water, toxic air, antipathy from consumers, demonstrations by workers, terrible quality of parts and modules from the outsourcing helper companies, and so on. We have already experienced two world wars during the first half of the twentieth century, because of this kind of zero-sum game in international colonialism.

Economically, the two world wars were based on the maximization of the home countries' national welfare, which comes from the excessive supplies produced by industrialization. Unfortunately, some countries such as Germany, Russia during World War 1, and Japan in World War II, achieved industrialization much later than other advanced countries, and thus did not have colonies to which they could sell these oversupplied outputs from industrialization. Therefore, these countries had to invade other countries as colonies, because they needed new markets to absorb their oversupplied products. On the way to terminate these two world wars, all countries in the world pledged reciprocity in international trade, and this new paradigm, the Bretton Woods Agreement, became the basis of the Pax Americana during the 1960s. *If you make me a hero, I will make you a hero, too!* Based on this bilateral beneficial trading under the free trade Bretton Woods system, all governments could develop their economies together, resulting in high-rocketing economic growth for the whole world together. This proactively open trading regime is thus called the Pax Americana, a peaceful and prosperous global economic regime, because this regime is based on the altruistic support by the United States, with its dollar value guaranteed for international trade by the International Monetary Fund, and its market opened without many tariffs or other non-tariff barriers by General Agreement on Tariffs and Trade (GATT).

By a similar token, at the end of the twentieth century, all countries in the world experienced serious challenges resulting from global warming. If they merely retain the traditional paradigm of maximizing national welfare for each individual country, they may face a doomed future, as we experienced in the early twentieth century era of colonialism. This is the right time for these nations to cooperate with altruistic governance in their economic development, as well as in the sustainable management of their everyday business operations. Otherwise, nobody can be a hero in the paradigm of competitively maximizing profits and efficiency. Unfortunately, this altruism is not easy to attain, nor is it effective for successful performance.

There are many conflicts involved in evaluating and accepting the serious challenges of global warming among diverse interest groups including countries, companies, and individuals. It is not easy for a company and/or an economic entity such as a consumer to handle these challenges, because it is very complicated to identify appropriate inputs and undesirable outputs. There are diverse approaches in the literature to finding the appropriate means of measuring, monitoring, and alleviating these challenges in sustainability. There are many guidelines to measure, monitor, and assess all these efforts and their performances in green IT. One of the most important guidelines for green IT can be found in the efforts of the International Organization for Standardization (ISO). The ISO

50001 standard was published in 2011 to provide a kind of platform for all organizations in the public and private sectors to manage their energy flows systematically with a set of energy management protocols for the guidance of IT use. Based on this requirement, all economic entities could manage their overall energy flow to decrease their energy intensity through lowering energy consumption and increasing energy efficiency, while the ISO standard guides the mitigation of all GHG emissions, resulting in the greening of all the structural and procedural operations of these organizations.

Most of all, however, the system as well as the policies are not as important in themselves for promoting a sustainable society, because the issues require totally different approaches from the usual rules of the zero-sum game for daily life in the legacy system. Because there are too many complex issues to harmonize all the interests in the interdependent society, and cooperation among businesses to create shared values in innovative ways is often too weak for partners to maintain their trust, the role of intermediation has become much more important, especially in the private sector.

As mentioned earlier, the public–private partnership could be one of the best intermediaries, if the spirit of reciprocity for all is shared. Unfortunately, this is not the case in many projects, because for its part, the government always wants to be visible and effective in the short run by *consultocracy*, while the private sector wants to exploit these blind money contributions from the government as their free lunch. Thus, to enhance the governance of the intermediary, we need to provide a cultural revolution toward the challenges. All the members of the PPP or other intermediaries should have a "*you* attitude", and at the same time, the stakeholder businesses should innovate in ways that create shared values. Instead of just involving simple intermediaries, we need a stronger intermediation role, as implemented by network managers such as Nike and Apple. We call this kind of energetic, proactive network managers "metamediaries", because they take all possible measures to allow interest groups to participate more aggressively; this involves higher obligations, as well as a deeper commitment to values [12]. There are lots of helpers in sustainable development, but most of those involved are not partners. We need the network manager, not as a helper, but as the "partner of partners".

To promote good governance of the collaborative network, most Asian companies emphasize innovation or creative economics in the transformation of their businesses. There is no guarantee, even for the most successful performance of Samsung with its Galaxy smartphones and semiconductor products, because today's success cannot continue tomorrow unless the company innovates its products, business, and even services. In the 1980s, Samsung had a slogan saying, "You should change everything except your wife and children." This slogan implied that you should not be satisfied with almost anything in your life, at home or in the workplace, in this risky environment. After considering contingent scenarios based on the worst risks and threats in the global market, Samsung indeed changed almost everything from its major product to its business organization and even its organizational culture. The company did not just emphasize this slogan, but made a feasible plan for all its employees to propose any innovative ideas and compete in all their performances with their colleagues. Due to these revolutionary innovations, the company displayed successful performance in the 2010s.

Therefore, all businesses should utilize green IT for the transformation of their operations. This could be much harder than the reengineering of production procedures and/or quality control in the legacy system, because such a move needs to change everything from the beginning. Fortunately, we all have the common goal of green IT, which requires lower energy intensity, more energy savings, more comfort, and more added value for members of all interest groups. Business leaders should not consider these green IT projects as additional costs, but as the best possible investment for the future, as shown in the Samsung case above.

The successful operation and resulting performance of green IT depends heavily on the role of the network manager in the collaborative networks. If these managers are too pessimistic and passive with their innovations and/or the participation of other partners, then this network will not operate well. Therefore, the role of a metamediary as a proactive network manager, should be much concisely and systematically specified and its performance monitored not from its own perspective, but considering interests of all the stakeholders.

We now live amid the turmoil of the smart revolution. We can see innovations appearing every day in our ways of life through smart developments. The Internet game Pokémon became extremely popular globally through its new version with augmented reality. This is so much more powerful than simple virtual reality. You can feel everything in the game seen on the screen, as well as in the real place on the field. With your game screen, you can find "monsters" surrounding you everywhere. Very few people anticipated this kind of augmented reality game, but it brought a new era of augmented reality for diverse purposes in our daily life. The most important point is not to restrict yourself, your business, or your policy; otherwise, you will lose leadership in this turmoil of the smart revolution. Bill Gates of Microsoft said, "Go online, or get out of business." This is the right time for us to participate in this smart revolution in the direction of green IT as the essential platform to open the future of human history.

5. Concluding remarks

All issues that have to do with sustainability, as well as IT-related topics, have one thing in common: they need to be handled through an appropriate harmonization of all possible interest groups such as government, outsourcing companies, consumers as prosumers, regional society, and the environment, for the next generation. This approach is quite different from the traditional legacy system and its related theories based on competitive efficiency and/or profit maximization. Since all global economies are approaching the saturation point of their industrial revolution, it is quite possible for most of the advanced countries, including the Northeast Asian countries such as China, Korea, and Japan, to approach the limit of input-oriented quantitative economic development. Given their rapidly aging populations, it is very difficult for these societies to source further inputs such as more labor and capital to continue their growth. Rather, the quantitatively growing economies have been met with sluggish growth rates, with fewer jobs and more unemployed people.

Now, these Asian countries should certainly change their main emphasis from more investment in inputs for the legacy system, toward the new way of qualitative innovation for the next stage of their economic development. If quality control systems and highly efficient production organization cannot bring more jobs and guarantee growth, these economies should transform their quantity-oriented production systems and focus on quality-based innovation. If there is no room for further production process innovation, it is better to change everything, not just inside of the business, but the business entity itself. Just remember that the most successful global companies with long histories have certainly transformed their businesses several times over the decades. There was great success in the camera industry in 1990s, but it was threatened by the instant snapshots provided by smartphones, and thus all the camera industries have had to change in order to survive. This is true even at the level of national economic restructuring. For this purpose, the green growth approach explained throughout this book emphasizes strongly that even if there are numerous risky factors and threats, green growth is still the only promising direction to take to face the future challenges in most countries, including developing countries such as China. If governments and leading companies hesitate to initiate these challenging moves toward green IT, they could face terrible problems, such as the digital divide in society and the bipolarization of the economy. Green growth is the only answer for all these future challenges, because it is based on sustainable development within the time and space limits of human history.

To promote green IT, the most important issue is to keep an open mind to collaborate while facing the unexpected, uncertain tasks for the future. This philosophy implies that governments should open the way more aggressively for these new businesses, new technologies, and new ways of social development. It is noteworthy that China is nominally a socialist country, but with the very flexible mechanism for capitalistic performance, while Korea is a democratic country with perhaps the worst governance, with a rigid negative system for capitalism. Sometimes, Korea exhibits a more passive, prohibitive conservatism than its partner, socialist China. For example, in China, Alibaba introduced a new fintech business to support its online shopping web site, Alibaba.com. Alipay was a great success, because most online shoppers are ready to put their money into this Alipay account. The reason is that Alipay gives more interest than the commercial bank, and thus it is beneficial for consumers to deposit into Alipay. If the consumers have their money in an online Alipay account, then it is much easier and more convenient for them to use these deposits to buy something from the online Alibaba shopping web site. Financial technology, also known as fintech, is a newly emerging industry composed of venture companies that use technology to make financial services more efficient. Financial technology companies are generally startups trying to disintermediate incumbent financial systems and challenge traditional corporations that are less reliant on software.

Unfortunately, this is not the case in Korea. There have been several new online ventures initiated by businesses in the Korean market, including Samsungpay, but they have had to struggle with excessive regulations and a pessimistic attitude from the government. They cannot easily offer new business approaches, such as that of Alipay giving more interest the consumer deposits, because these practices are *illegal* in Korea. Basically, there nothing is illegal in China before the government says no. However, all new ways of doing business and all new services are illegal before the government allows them in Korea. This extreme paradigm of a regulatory regime could be a terrible obstacle in moving toward an autonomous, advanced society. In the United States, it may appear that you can drive as fast as possible; it seems there are no police cars on the road. But this kind of autonomy requires you to take your own responsibility, because if you are caught speeding only once, you will face a huge penalty. This kind of openness or proactive negative policy regime with autonomous self-control on the part of the private sector is one of the key governance factors for green IT.

In order for the fintech industry, one of the emerging new frontiers in the financial service market in the world, to be successful, there should be three key success factors provided. Like in other new businesses, these are technology, business strategy, finance, and policies. Although Korea and Japan provide good environmental policies for the technology, business strategy and financial support for new fintech industry are missing, unfortunately. Unfortunately, the policy makes a bottleneck. Since there are huge demands on this emerging fintech businesses, XNtree, a PPP company from the United Kingdom that provides support to the fintech venture startups, has entered the Korean market. XNtree is placed in the new financial center as a link between the public promotion policies and the private investors looking for the promising new fintech industries. In the United Kingdom, the government does not lead, intervene, or even help the new fintech market. Rather, it participates in the new market as a strong supporter with full responsibility of "one-stop services on the administrative regulations".

Unfortunately, this is not in the case in Korea and Japan, because they want to lead any new frontier with too much intervention and sometimes long leadership. Fintech has begun with the payment services such as a mobile wallet, but soon it upgraded its functions to provide financial data analysis to the user. One of the United States fintech companies provides a new financial service for users to find the lowest, and the most reliable loan based on the user patterns on the Internet and its resulting credit analysis. Currently, fintech is evolving into a future platform for every new financial service. For these reasons, there should be a good policy environment provided as follows.

First, the regulation on the new technology and/or business should be at its minimum under the negative regulation system. Unfortunately, most of Asian government officials do not allow new businesses unless there are some preceding, reliable cases, and this kind of consultocracy prohibits any new business activities. Even if these governments cannot at the moment change their policy regimes from the positive system toward negative system, they should provide at least some "regulation-free zone for these new businesses", as shown in XNtree in the United

Kingdom. Second, the public bug data such as financial information on the public banking system should be open. In most cases, these data are prohibited due to privacy protection or are too expensive for a new business to use it. Third, there should be new creative financial service models for a venture to get the support by the public. For this purpose, they should easily and effectively be accessible for the one-stop services on their new services in terms of their feasibility and promotional support. Otherwise, most of new small ventures could be absorbed into the big companies in these Asian countries. In Korea, many new businesses could not find the successful roadmap, and thus they begin with the big leading companies in the market for the possible support, but soon, these big companies got all the information and just kicked out their small partners. Of course, the governments should provide transparent, predictable roadmaps for any new businesses, not as the regulator, but as the promotor, at least in the initial stage.

Another challenge in northeast Asian countries comes from the creative economic culture of the region. Recently, the augmented reality game applications are so hot worldwide, especially in some Asian countries such as Japan, Korea, China, and Taiwan. Pokémon Go is a hybrid game combining offline and online through the augmented reality (AR) technology. Based on the Google Maps on a mobile phone, the game user will search and hunt the game characters in the street. Due to the national security issues, it is difficult to use Google Maps in Korea. Nonetheless, the northeastern province of Sokcho city is open for Google Maps because it is located very close to Japan, and thus it is possible for the Internet user to use the Google Maps in the city. All the Pokémon Go gamers gathered in this unique spot of Sokcho city to hunt the game characters. There has been an unexpected booming in this region due to this AR game. Similarly, Xinbeitou is located at the northern area of Taipei, Taiwan, and this area was famous for its outdoor hot spring and related activities. But not anymore! Due to the great popularity of Pokémon Go game, tens of thousands of people gather in this area not to visit the hot spas, but to hunt game characters. As seen in Figure 8.2, all kinds of people, regardless of their age, sex, and educational level, are flocking around the Xinbeitou public library and public open hot spa to hunt game characters with their mobile phones. It is a truly interesting and exotic scene for non-gamers.

AR technology is different than virtual reality. The former brings virtual experiences into our everyday lives as real, while the latter lets the virtual reality users feel the unreal, virtual things with the support of digital devices. Already, the Pokémon Go usage time overtook the Facebook and even in Korea, where Pokémon Go is almost useless due to its national security restrictions against North Korea, reached the number of 0.8 million users during the first 3 months. The potential future market seems huge, promising more than 100 billion dollars, and its range of applications is enormous, including the green growth area. It will provide the IT users with more energy-saving opportunities in business and households as well. It will also decrease the possible GHG emissions due to the real, but not diverse, experience in the new businesses and new services using AR technologies.

Figure 8.2 Pokémon Go game hunters in Xinbeitou, Taiwan

Another major emphasis for green IT should come from voluntary collaboration on these green challenges. If one of your partners is pessimistic, then that partner will ruin all the possible outcomes. Maybe, the partner will say that you should knock on the wood before you cross the stream for good luck, and this indeed might be true. However, if the partners just knock on the wood over and over again without any trial and error, they will never get across the river! Let them participate in more proactive ways if you want to manage your collaborative network to be perfectly workable for performance. It is vital in this new paradigm of green IT for all the partners in the network to contribute more proactively, not routinely, but with innovative passion. Wal-Mart, a global discount store, has the slogan, "Everyday low prices", which implies that all their outsourcing partners in the world should innovate to bring their products in at lower prices every day; otherwise they will be replaced with others. This may be good governance in the traditional legacy system, but it is not good for green IT, which requires voluntary participation. The author of this book has participated in an international symposium since 2009, the Sustainable Asia Conference, and its slogan is "Once a friend, forever a friend!" You should treat your associates as partners, not as helpers, for the successful operation of the green IT philosophy. POSCO, one of the best companies in the field of sustainable management in Korea, has improved its value-sharing system with workers inside the company and small and medium outsourcing partners outside. If your proposal is acceptable, POSCO gives you some portion of newly added performance for your innovation. Of course, there are no penalties in case of failure or the malfunction of your new idea. This gives all the partners open opportunities to innovate in their everyday working performance; overall, this approach guarantees that POSCO will maintain its top position in the world, even in these sluggish times of global economic recession.

Unfortunately, green IT has the two faces of Janus. It could increase the costs of industry due to the extra burden of the energy-saving, emission-mitigating processes, at least in the short term. Unfortunately, most organizations are concerned only with short-term profit maximization objectives, and thus they merely emphasize the dark side of green IT. In contrast, case studies of green IT industries by Samsung and KT show the other face of Janus—its promising side—and make a great success of this approach by showing strong commitment at the strategic top levels of the project, which proves that green IT can provide great future opportunities for new businesses. 3M, Proctor & Gamble, and many other companies also have great company profiles demonstrating successful transformation to the new global norms and emerging paradigms such as the information society and the ubiquitous economy.

Nokia, which has more than 100 years of company history, started as a small company in the timber industry, then transformed its core businesses as the ultimate trendsetter in the electronics industry. However, it may be worth noting that Nokia has since been bought by Google and has virtually disappeared as an autonomous company. This was widely regarded as a consequence of a failure to innovate. Even the most successful companies and governments should transform their major missions drastically, yet with much prudential management on the smart revolution, as Google did. Google started as a web-search company, but has now become a technology giant, leading the future smart revolution with smart cars and the artificial intelligence of AlphaGo. As shown in the Go (Baduck) battle with Korean Go champion Lee Sedol, the proliferation of artificial intelligences, such as AlphaGo with its self-learning system, could result in unforeseeable disasters for humankind if we are not well prepared for this new trend in self-sufficient mechanisms. Likewise, green IT may sometimes result in worse effects due to its unexpected and undesirable byproducts. The digital divide could be one of these kinds of bipolar outcomes. Moreover, the smart car may kill several children in the street to protect a driver in an emergency. To harmonize all of society's interests, we need to take much more care in considering the complex mechanisms of sustainable development. Thus, ethical altruism and efforts to harmonize a performance-oriented philosophy should be carefully embedded in all the policies and business strategies involved in creating a green IT future.

Even if green IT leads to unexpected outcomes, we cannot just wait for the best solution for all parties to appear, because the environment surrounding the global economy has been changing rapidly. All these changes bring about environmental risks for industry. If one accepts these risks while planning proactively, one may obtain a fortune; but if one passively avoids these risks and merely criticizes the undesirable possibilities, one will certainly lose the competitive edge soon, and this loss of opportunity may be irreversible. Therefore, green IT should not just be an option at the present time, but a necessary core competence for future survival. Further, we should not just wait for everyone to take this direction, because if one does not plan today, the evaluation time may not be there tomorrow. Do dream if you can, and as soon as possible. Do not be afraid that there is no forerunner, because we do know that sustainable development with green IT is the right direction for the marathon of humankind to take. Not knowing the direction means never winning the marathon, even if one is faster than anyone else. To become a winner, one must focus on moving in the right direction to achieve the goal, and then all that is needed is enthusiasm in cooperating with the surrounding networks. This kind of proactive leadership in the northeast Asian countries could be found at the COP21 meeting at Paris.

Since the Paris Climate Agreement in December 2015, Korean government has made its best efforts to take promotion policies to brace for a low-carbon economy. The policies aim to develop new energy businesses, with the aim of not only fighting climate change, but also nurturing the new growth engine for the future. One of the outstanding projects is green energy towns project, which is aimed at turning undesirable and energy-intensive facilities into eco-friendly ones that generate green energy using renewable sources, thereby integrating two conflicting issues of environment and energy in a harmonized way. So far, the Korean government has created a total of 19 green energy towns nationwide and will diffuse these movements into the green ocean for the business sectors. In preparation for this paradigm shift to a low-carbon economy, Korea stands at a critical moment, when the government should not intervene in the market with too regulation-oriented leadership and let the business partners take this new opportunity. Only through such nudge efforts by Korean government can Korea succeed in pioneering the emerging new energy industry.

To provide new impetus to the country's economic growth, Korean government revealed a detailed next-generation growth engine projects with nine fields of industries in July 2016, as shown in Figure 8.3. The core impetus of this national strategic plan is that the Korean government will invest with the private partners a combined 36.6 billion US dollars into new energy businesses by 2020, including renewable energy, electric vehicles (EVs), energy storage systems (ESS), and smart grids. The plan aims not only to fight climate change, but also to nurture a new export industry as shown in Germany. The revolutionary German green growth policies provided a model for how the climate crisis can be turned into an opportunity. The renewable energy sector has been transformed into one of Germany's fastest-growing export industries, becoming the Europe's largest economy export with more than 65 per cent of the solar power generated in the country and nearly 70 per cent of the wind power. These green growth industries also became one of the country's biggest job creators, with tens of thousands of new jobs in this field. Whether these green growth challenges turn out to be an opportunity or a burden to Korea will depend on a transparent policy direction and reliable action plans [13].

As the Korean government and Samsung have shown, the government as well as the private sector should make the green IT vision clearer and firmly oversee control of its optimal development path. Moreover, the metamediary, as the control tower of green IT, should quantify all the processes involved in green IT planning and implementation, and provide the organizational readiness to take on its responsibilities with pride in all partners, because the workers and all other stakeholders are no longer just helpers in the harmonized collaborative network.

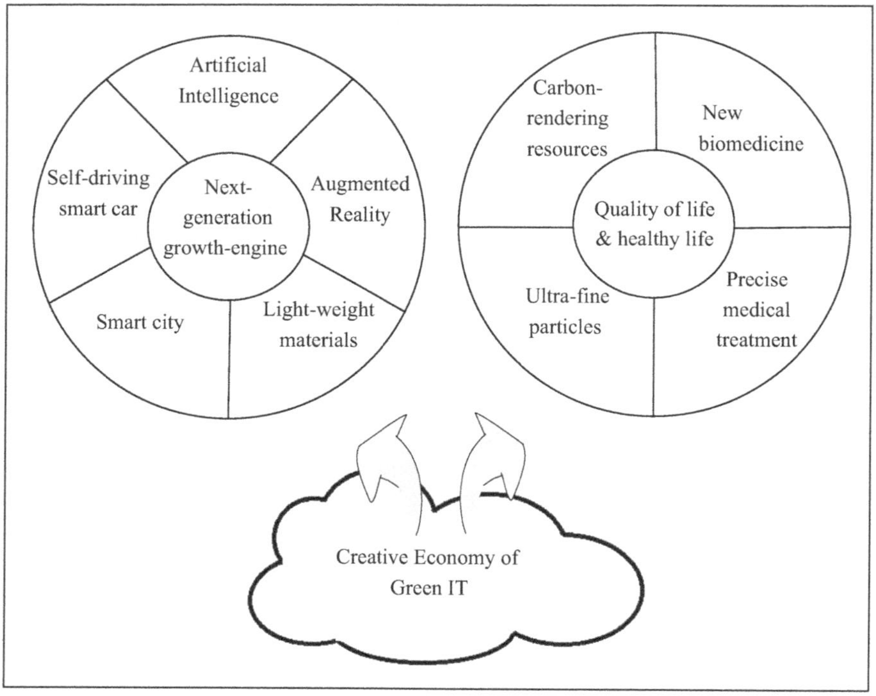

Figure 8.3 National Future Challenge Projects of Korea

All of us should be partners in promoting sustainable development, because sustainability issues are not just for individuals or companies, but for all of society's economic agents.

References

1 Research Publish Journals, *Smart Grid* (Accessed on 15/04/2016: http://www.researchpublish.com/download.php).
2 U.S. EPA. *Inventory of U.S. Greenhouse Gases Emissions and Sinks: 1990–2006*, 2008, p. ES8.
3 *Sustainability Management Highlight of KEPCO 2015* (Accessed on 26/08/2016: http://home.kepco.co.kr/kepco/EN/D/htmlView/ENDAHP00101.do?menuCd=EN040101).
4 Kim, Hyun-cheol, *Smart Grid Becoming KEPCOs Core Biz*, Korea Times, 24/02/2010 (Accessed on 26/08/2016: http://www.koreatimes.co.kr/www/news/tech/2010/02/133_61398.html).
5 *2015 KEPCO Sustainability Report* (Accessed on 26/08/2016: http://home.kepco.co.kr/kepco/EN/D/C/KEDCPP004.do?boardCd=BRD_000014&menuCd=EN04010601).

6 Gartner. *Gartner Says the Internet of Things Installed Base Will Grow to 26 Billion Units by 2020*, 12/12/2013 (Accessed on 10/03/2016: http://www.gartner.com/newsroom/id/2636073).
7 Liz Gannes. *Google Introduces New Self Driving Car at the Code Conference – Re/code*. Re/code (Accessed on 15/08/2016: http://www.recode.net/2014/5/27/11627262/googles-new-self-driving-car-ditches-the-steering-wheel).
8 *How Google's Self-driving Car Works – IEEE Spectrum*. Spectrum.ieee.org (Accessed on 15/08/2016: http://spectrum.ieee.org/automaton/robotics/artificial-intelligence/how-google-self-driving-car-works).
9 Choi, Yongrok, "The role of intermediation on the international aid for the governance of technical training program", *Technological Forecasting & Social Change*, 2015, 96, 32–39.
10 *Research Blog: AlphaGo: Mastering the Ancient Game of Go with Machine Learning*. Google Research Blog, 27 January 2016 (Accessed on 15/08/2016: http://googleresearch.blogspot.kr/2016/01/alphago-mastering-ancient-game-of-go.html).
11 *POSCO Sustainability Report 2015* (Accessed on 26/08/2016: http://www.posco.co.kr/homepage/docs/eng5/dn/sustain/customer/2015_POSCO_Report_EN.pdf).
12 Accessed on 15/08/2016: http://www.posco.co.kr/homepage/docs/eng5/jsp/sustain/environ/environment_02_03.jsp.
13 Choi, Y.N.; Zhang, C. Bone, "Sustainable policies and strategies in Asia: Challenges for green growth", *Technology Forecasting & Social Change*, 2016, 112, 134–137, http://dx.doi.org/10.1016/j.techfore.2016.05.021.

Index

For Product Safety Concerns and Information please contact our EU representative GPSR@taylorandfrancis.com Taylor & Francis Verlag GmbH, Kaufingerstraße 24, 80331 München, Germany